Library of Congress Cataloging-in-Publication Data

ISBN: 979-8-89530-696-3

Published by Nova Science Publishers, Inc. † New York

Julie Taylor Lowe
Editor

Inflation

Background, Causes and Current Policies

snova
New York

Economic Issues, Problems and Perspectives Series

Healthcare: Costs, Competition and Transparency
Liam Moore (Editor)
ISBN: 979-8-89530-633-8
eBook ISBN: 979-8-89530-648-2

Financial Sector Development and Pandemics in an Era of Sustainable Development Goals
Paul Adjei Kwakwa, PhD (Editor)
ISBN: 979-8-89530-548-5
eBook ISBN: 979-8-89530-617-8

Original Research Matters in Marketing, Innovations and Beyond
Sergey E. Barykin, Doctor of Economic Sciences (Editor)
eBook ISBN: 979-8-89530-576-8

Finance of Renewable Energy in a Sustainable World
Faruk Dayi, PhD (Editor)
ISBN: 979-8-89530-541-6
eBook ISBN: 979-8-89530-593-5

Economic Integration: Strategies, Challenges and Global Implications
Alina Hyz, PhD and
Panagiotis E. Kaldis, PhD (Editors)
ISBN: 979-8-89530-338-2
eBook ISBN: 979-8-89530-404-4

The New Geography in the Global Automotive Industry
Marcelo José do Carmo, PhD,
Mário Sacomano Neto, PhD,
Júlio César Donadone, PhD,
Aditya Kuthar and Shreya Gupta
ISBN: 979-8-89530-029-9
eBook ISBN: 979-8-89530-077-0

More information about this series can be found at
https://novapublishers.com/product-category/series/economic-issues-problems-and-perspectives/

Economic Issues, Problems and Perspectives

snova
New York

Contents

Preface

Inflation is defined as a general increase in the price of goods and services across the economy, or, in other words, a general decrease in the value of money. As inflation occurs, individuals can purchase fewer goods and services with the same amount of money. Measures of inflation are used to adjust monetary figures to keep purchasing power constant over time, allowing for more accurate comparisons across disparate time periods. In general, inflation can be costly to the economy because it tends to interfere with pricing mechanisms in the economy, resulting in individuals and businesses making suboptimal spending, saving, and investment decisions. This book begins by explaining what inflation is and how it is measured. It then discusses the costs of inflation Finally, the book analyzes the causes and implications of the current situation.

Chapter 1

Introduction to U.S. Economy: Inflation*

Lida R. Weinstock

What Is Inflation?

Inflation is defined as a general increase in the price of goods and services across the economy, or, in other words, a general decrease in the value of money. Conversely, deflation is a general decrease in the price of goods and services across the economy, or a general increase in the value of money.

As inflation occurs, individuals can purchase fewer goods and services with the same amount of money. For this reason, an individual would need about $326 in 2021 to purchase the same amount of goods and services as $100 would have purchased in 1980. Measures of inflation are used to adjust money figures to keep purchasing power constant over time, allowing for more accurate comparisons across disparate time periods. Monetary figures that have been adjusted for inflation are referred to as *real*, and non- inflation-adjusted figures are referred to as *nominal*.

Measuring Inflation

The rate of inflation can be measured by observing changes in the average price of a consistent set of goods and services, often referred to as a market basket. Inflation is generally measured using a price index, such as the Consumer Price Index (CPI). A price index is constructed by dividing the price

---

* This is an edited, reformatted and augmented version of Congressional Research Service Publication No. IF10477, updated January 5, 2023.

In: Inflation: Background, Causes and Current Policies
Editor: Julie Taylor Lowe
ISBN: 979-8-89530-696-3

of a market basket in a given year by the price of the same basket of goods in a base year. The rate of inflation is then measured by calculating the percentage change in the price index across different periods. For example, the CPI was about 277 in October 2021 and about 298 in October 2022, which amounts to an inflation rate of about 7.8% over this 12-month period.

Alternative Measures of Inflation

Alternative price indices will use different goods within their market baskets and are generally used for different purposes. For example, the CPI includes consumer goods and services typically purchased by households, which is often used to adjust household incomes for inflation over time. By contrast, the gross domestic product (GDP) deflator, which is generally used to adjust GDP for inflation over time, measures inflation for all of the final goods and services produced in the United States. There are a number of additional measures of inflation, including the Producer Price Index, Employment Cost Index, Personal Consumption Expenditures Index, and Import/Export Price Index. Different inflation measures are calculated differently. For example, the CPI uses a (mostly) fixed basket of goods and services, whereas the GDP deflator allows the composition of its market basket to change with spending patterns from period to period.

Additionally, within a specific price index, researchers often make separate calculations for so-called *headline inflation* and *core inflation*, as seen in *Figure 1*. Headline inflation includes the full set of goods and services within the basket of goods, whereas core inflation excludes energy and food prices from the basket of goods. Core inflation is often used by researchers in place of headline inflation due to the volatile nature of the price of food and energy.

Headline inflation can provide a more accurate sense of the price changes actually faced by individuals.

Complications in Measuring Inflation

The fundamental concept behind inflation is to measure changes in the price of the same goods and services over time. In reality, this is nearly impossible for two reasons. First, the quality of goods and services change over time. As such, some portion of increasing prices over time is due to improvements in quality rather than inflation. Second, new products are introduced into the marketplace over time that are fundamentally different than any previously available products and are only slowly incorporated into price indices with fixed baskets. Statistical agencies try to adjust data to account for these factors, because, if these complications are not correctly accounted for, measured inflation would be inaccurate and most likely overstated.

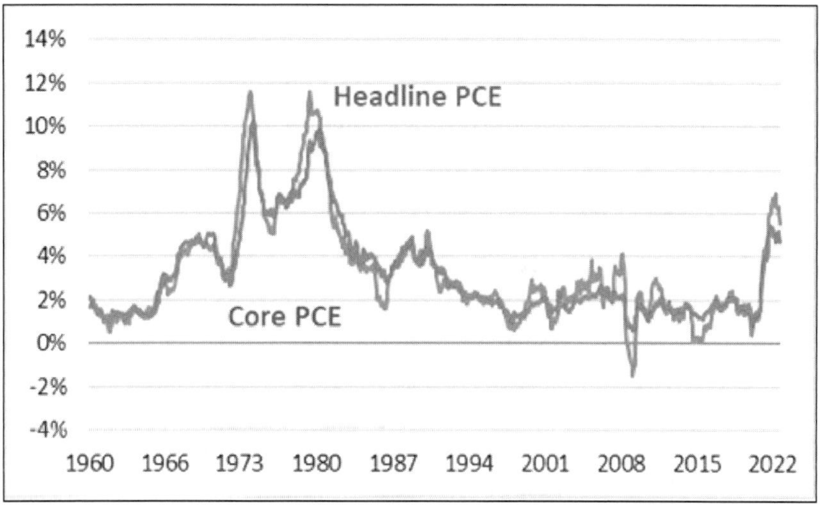

Source: Bureau of Economic Analysis.

Notes: Annual percentage change as measured by Personal Consumption Expenditures Index.

Figure 1. Annual Inflation Rate. January 1960 to November 2022.

Causes of Inflation

Inflation is largely the result of two different phenomena, which are often referred to as demand-pull and cost-push inflation. Demand-pull inflation occurs when demand for goods and services within the economy exceeds the economy's capacity to produce goods and services. As demand exceeds supply within the economy — "too much money chasing too few goods"— there is upward pressure placed on prices, resulting in rising inflation.

Cost-push inflation occurs when the price of input goods and services increases. The classic example of cost-push inflation is the result of an oil shock, which sharply decreases the supply of oil and other petroleum products.

The decrease in oil supplies increases the price of oil and petroleum products. Petroleum products are an input good for a significant portion of goods and services across the economy, and as the price of this important input good increases, so does the price of the final goods and services, resulting in inflation. Cost-push inflation results in only a temporary increase in inflation unless accommodated by monetary policy.

Changes in inflation expectations can also cause changes in actual inflation. Individuals form expectations around the future rate of inflation and incorporate those expectations when setting prices at the firm level or when bargaining for wages as a worker. For example, if the general consensus is that prices will increase 2% in the next year, businesses will want to increase prices by at least 2%, and workers will want at least a 2% raise.

Inflation's Impact on the Economy

Inflation tends to interfere with pricing mechanisms in the economy, resulting in individuals and businesses making less than optimal spending, saving, and investment decisions. Additionally, in the presence of inflation, economic actors often engage in actions to protect themselves from the negative impacts of inflation, diverting resources from other more productive activities.

Ultimately, these inefficient decisions reduce incomes, economic growth, and living standards. For this reason, it is generally accepted that inflation should be kept low to minimize these distortions in the economy. Some would argue that an inflation rate of zero is optimal. However, a target of zero inflation makes a period of accidental deflation more likely, and deflation is thought to be even more costly than inflation, as it can be associated with recessionary conditions. In an effort to balance these two risks, policymakers, including the Federal Reserve, often target a positive but low inflation rate, generally around 2%, which reduces inefficiencies within the economy while protecting against deflation.

The Federal Reserve and Inflation

The Federal Reserve has been charged with promoting stable prices by statute since the late 1970s, largely as a result of the volatile and exceptionally high inflation experienced in the years preceding the law, as shown in Figure 1.

Beginning in 2012, the Federal Reserve began explicitly targeting a long-run inflation rate of 2%. In 2020, the Federal Reserve amended this strategy slightly to target an average rate of 2%. The Federal Reserve generally uses its ability to impact short-term interest rates to combat demand-pull and cost-push inflation in an effort to decrease the volatility of inflation and keep inflation close to its target rate.

Beginning in the 1980s, the rate of core inflation, which excludes energy and food prices, started to decrease, as did the volatility seen in the measure. Beginning in the late 1990s, the inflation rate remained relatively close to 2%, and large swings in inflation mostly disappeared. The moderation of inflation largely seen between the 1970s and the current high inflation has largely been attributed to the actions undertaken by the Federal Reserve as part of its mandate to promote stable prices.

In the time between the financial crisis and the COVID-19 pandemic, inflation ran below 2% fairly consistently, despite an 11-year economic expansion that ended in 2020 and several notable periods of quantitative easing by the Federal Reserve. However, inflation started rising in March 2021 and has been high since then. In response to this high inflation, the Federal Reserve has raised the federal funds rate consistently beginning in March 2022, tapered asset purchases, and begun shrinking the balance sheet. The Fed has indicated that it will continue tightening monetary policy until inflation comes down. For more information about inflation since COVID-19, see CRS Report R47273, Inflation in the U.S. Economy: Causes and Policy Options, by Marc Labonte and Lida R. Weinstock.

Adjusting for Inflation

Comparing figures in real terms is often beneficial to observe actual changes in purchasing power over time rather than changes in the number of dollars.

Real Figure = Nominal Figure x (CPI Target Year / CPI Base Year)

Source: CRS.

Figure 2. How to Adjust for Inflation.

To adjust nominal figures for inflation, multiply the nominal figure by the ratio of the price index value in the target year to the price index value in the base year, as shown in Figure 2. For example, median household income in 1990 (the base year) was $29,943 in nominal terms. To determine the equivalent income in terms of purchasing power for 2019 (the target year) using CPI, multiply $29,943 by the ratio of CPI in 2019 (256) to the CPI in 1990 (131), which comes out to about $58,515.

As discussed previously, there are a number of different price indices, and within those indices more specific deflators are available to make inflation adjustments. It is important to use the most relevant index for the subject being researched. For example, when looking at corporate revenues in the United States, it would be advisable to use the Producer Price Index, which uses a market basket consisting of the price of goods and services sold by domestic producers, as opposed to the CPI, which is designed to reflect the goods and services purchased by the typical household.

Resources

The Bureau of Labor Statistics and the Bureau of Economic Analysis both create various price indices, which are available at http://www.bls.gov/bls/inflation.htm and https://www.bea.gov/data/prices-inflation, respectively.

(Note: This in Focus was originally authored by Jeffrey Stupak, former CRS Analyst in Macroeconomic Policy.)

Chapter 2

Inflation in the U.S. Economy: Causes and Policy Options*

Marc Labonte
and Lida R. Weinstock

Summary

The Federal Reserve (Fed) defines stable prices to be inflation (the general rise in the price of goods and services) of 2% annually. After decades of low inflation, inflation has been above the Fed's 2% target since March 2021. Since February 2022, inflation (measured as the 12-month change in the Personal Consumption Expenditures index) has exceeded 6%, its highest level in decades. For inflation to be problematic from a policy perspective, the increase has to be sustained, persistent, and sizeable. Inflation in 2022 meets all three of these criteria.

COVID-19 caused unprecedented disruptions to both the demand side (spending) and the supply side (output) of the economy. High inflation originated in some of the supply disruptions to specific markets. Faced with production shortages, prices rose. By late 2021, inflation ceased to be limited to specific disrupted markets and became widespread across virtually all goods and services. Inflation can be thought of as a mismatch between overall supply and demand. Supply was still constrained relative to its pre-pandemic path because of ongoing supply disruptions, which were then further exacerbated in 2022 by the war in Ukraine. In this context, demand would also need to be constrained to avoid an acceleration in inflation. Instead, demand made a relatively rapid recovery after the brief recession thanks in part to unprecedented fiscal

---

* This is an edited, reformatted and augmented version of Congressional Research Service Publication No. R47273, dated October 6, 2022.

In: Inflation: Background, Causes and Current Policies
Editor: Julie Taylor Lowe
ISBN: 979-8-89530-696-3

and monetary stimulus. These imbalances are also evident in the labor market, where employers are unable to fill openings and the labor force participation rate remains below its pre-pandemic level.

Policymakers assumed that the initial increase in inflation in 2021 was transitory and decided to leave monetary and fiscal stimulus in place to guard against the economic recovery becoming derailed by the ongoing threat of the pandemic. In hindsight, inflation proved to be a bigger threat than a weak recovery was, but decades of sustained low inflation—at times, undesirably low inflation—may have led policymakers to underestimate the threat of high inflation. The Fed did not stop purchasing assets or start raising interest rates above zero until March 2022. Fiscal stimulus was designed to be temporary, but the American Rescue Plan Act of 2021 (ARPA, P.L. 117-2), increased the budget deficit by about $530 billion in FY2022. By the time stimulus began to be withdrawn, inflation was higher, more widespread, and more deeply embedded. To date, inflationary pressures have neither subsided on their own nor proven responsive to the tightening of policy that has taken place so far. The wait-and-see approach to tightening means that fiscal and monetary policy continue to be stimulative overall despite the significant withdrawal of stimulus that has occurred in 2022.

Some commentators have argued for addressing inflation by tackling its cause. In other words, supply-driven inflation should be controlled via supply-side solutions, and demand-driven inflation should be controlled via monetary or fiscal tightening. However, as inflation is caused by an imbalance in supply and demand, any solution that brings the two back into equilibrium would be successful, regardless of underlying cause. Demand-side tightening has the advantage of being potentially faster and having a more substantial impact than supply-side solutions, perhaps making it more attractive to those who seek to reduce inflation quickly. For example, the Fed can raise interest rates instantly, although their economic impact takes longer to be fully felt. Supply-side solutions take longer to be implemented and rely on individuals and businesses responding to incentives, making their effect more unpredictable and operating at the margins. In the current case, supply-side solutions are also hindered by the fact that many current supply problems, such as global supply chain disruptions and reductions in commodities output, are located outside of the United States. Some supply disruptions should eventually resolve themselves, relieving one source of inflationary pressures. The risk of waiting for supply to increase without trying to lower demand is that by the time that happens, expectations of high inflation will have become entrenched, making high inflation more difficult to reduce.

The last time inflation was this high was during the "Great Inflation" from the mid-1960s to the early 1980s, when a series of supply shocks, changes in inflation expectations, and a failure to sufficiently tighten monetary policy ultimately resulted in double-digit inflation. A number of policy initiatives over that period proved unsuccessful at reducing inflation, including price controls and credit controls. Inflation fell only after a long and deep recession in which the Fed raised interest rates as high as 19%. The 117th Congress has debated legislative options to reduce inflation, such as the budget reconciliation measure commonly called the Inflation Reduction Act of 2022 (P.L. 117-169), and Congress has also debated whether earlier legislation, such as ARPA, has contributed to high inflation.

Introduction

The COVID-19 pandemic has led to many unexpected and unprecedented economic developments.[1] One such development is higher price inflation than the United States has experienced in recent decades. The consensus view among economists is that inflation warrants a policy response only if it is high, widespread across goods and services, and sustained—exactly how high and for how long is open to debate. At this point, however, few disagree that inflation in 2022 meets all three of these criteria.

According to several measures, including the Consumer Price Index (CPI) and the Personal Consumption Expenditures (PCE) Index, prices have risen more rapidly than usual on a monthly basis each month since February 2021.[2] For 2021 as a whole, PCE inflation was 4.2%. Since February 2022, PCE inflation (measured as the 12-month change) has exceeded 6%. The last time PCE inflation ran that high was in the early 1980s at the end of the "Great Inflation."[3] Since peaking in the summer of 2022, inflation has fallen a little primarily because of falling energy prices. Excluding energy prices, other price increases show little sign of deceleration.

High inflation raises multiple policy issues for Congress. First, higher prices automatically increase spending on many mandatory government programs and reduce the spending capacity of other government programs at a given spending level. Second, high inflation is unpopular with the general

---

[1] See CRS Report R47115, U.S. Economic Recovery in the Wake of COVID-19: Successes and Challenges, by Marc Labonte and Lida R. Weinstock.

[2] CPI inflation is the more commonly cited measure in the media, whereas PCE inflation is the Federal Reserve's preferred measure. PCE inflation is typically somewhat lower than CPI inflation but nonetheless has also been high of late. See Bureau of Economic Analysis (BEA), Personal Consumption Expenditures Price Index, at https://www.bea.gov/data/personal-consumption-expenditures-price-index.

[3] See the section below entitled "Great Inflation."

public because it erodes purchasing power and creates inequities for those who cannot protect themselves against it. Third, rising inflation might be a signal of an overheating economy. Some economists fear that an overheating economy may result in a recession.[4] Finally, Congress has oversight responsibilities for the Federal Reserve, and Congress has mandated that the Fed achieve price stability.[5] Since March 2021, inflation has been higher than the 2% threshold that the Fed has chosen as its definition of price stability (when measured over the previous 12 months). The 117th Congress has examined legislative options to reduce inflation, enacting the budget reconciliation measure commonly called the Inflation Reduction Act of 2022 (P.L. 117- 169), and debated whether other legislation, such as the American Rescue Plan Act of 2021 (ARPA, P.L. 117-2), has contributed to high inflation.

This report begins by explaining what inflation is and how it is measured. It then discusses the costs of inflation, as well as the costs of inflation being too low. Next, it discusses the potential causes of inflation. Then it discusses the history of inflation in the United States since World War II. Finally, the report analyzes the causes and implications of the current situation and prospects for future inflation.

What Is Inflation?

Inflation refers to the general increase in the price of goods and services (not including asset prices) across the economy. As inflation occurs, individuals can purchase fewer goods and services with the same amount of money. Thus, inflation can also be thought of as a general decrease in the value of money. Measures of inflation are used to adjust monetary figures to keep purchasing power constant over time, allowing for more accurate comparisons across disparate time periods. Monetary figures that have been adjusted for inflation are referred to as *real*, and non-inflation-adjusted figures are referred to as *nominal*.

The rate of inflation can be measured by observing changes in the average price of a consistent set of goods and services, often referred to as a market "basket." Inflation is generally measured using a price index, such as the CPI

---

[4] See CRS Insight IN11963, Where Is the U.S. Economy Headed: Soft Landing, Hard Landing, or Stagflation? by Marc Labonte and Lida R. Weinstock.

[5] See CRS In Focus IF11751, Introduction to U.S. Economy: Monetary Policy, by Marc Labonte.

or PCE, which is constructed by dividing the price of a market basket in a given year by the price of the basket in a base year. *Chain weighting* considers changes in spending habits. The rate of inflation is then measured by calculating the percentage change in the price index across different periods.[6]

Different price indices use different goods and services within their market baskets and are generally used for different purposes. CPI includes consumer goods and services typically purchased by U.S. households and is often used to adjust household income over time. PCE measures inflation for all final goods and services purchased by consumers in the United States. Because of methodological differences, inflation as measured by CPI is slightly higher than as measured by PCE. PCE inflation is the Federal Reserve's preferred measure of inflation. There are a number of additional measures of inflation, which do not necessarily focus on what consumers purchase. For example, the gross domestic product (GDP) deflator, which is generally used to adjust GDP for inflation over time, measures inflation for all final goods and services produced in the United States, including those not typically purchased by consumers. Other inflation indices include the Producer Price Index, Employment Cost Index, and Import/Export Price Index. For the purposes of this report, PCE inflation will be the measure used moving forward.

Inflation is often characterized by one of two measurements: *headline* inflation or *core* inflation. Headline inflation includes the full set of goods and services within a given market basket, whereas core inflation excludes energy and food prices. Researchers often focus on core inflation due to the volatile nature of food and energy prices, which can mask the longer-term trends in headline inflation that concern policymakers and economists. However, headline inflation can provide a more accurate sense of the price changes that individuals actually face.[7]

As inflation measures the general increases in prices across the economy, a change in price of any single good or service does not equate to overall inflation. However, goods and services in a particular basket are given different weights to convey their relative importance to the overall economy. For example, food is weighted more heavily in determining overall inflation than a category of lesser importance, such as apparel.[8]

---

[6] See CRS In Focus IF10477, *Introduction to U.S. Economy: Inflation*, by Lida R. Weinstock.

[7] See CRS In Focus IF10477, *Introduction to U.S. Economy: Inflation*, by Lida R. Weinstock.

[8] Federal Reserve Bank of Cleveland, *Consumer Price Data*, https://www.clevelandfed.org/our-research/center-for- inflation-research/consumer-price-data.aspx.

Costs of Inflation

In general, inflation can be costly to the economy—especially when it is unexpected—because it tends to interfere with pricing mechanisms in the economy, resulting in individuals and businesses making suboptimal spending, saving, and investment decisions. Additionally, economic actors often engage in actions to protect themselves from the negative impacts of inflation, diverting resources from other, more productive activities.

Note that some of the costs of inflation also apply to deflation (falling prices), although they may manifest themselves in different ways. Most economists believe deflation to be even more costly to the economy than inflation is, as it is often associated with recessionary conditions, and therefore a small amount of inflation is considered to be ideal so as to make potential deflation less likely by giving the Fed room to conduct monetary policy.

This section describes several potential types of costs of inflation and the difficulty in measuring some of these costs. Many costs of inflation increase the higher or more sustained the inflation is. The discussion that follows provides a general description of potential costs, which may be felt more or less keenly depending on the particular circumstances.[9] In a case where inflation rises only temporarily and moderately, the costs described below would be expected to be modest relative to sustained and high increases.

Costs of Anticipated vs. Unanticipated Inflation

Some costs are incurred only when inflation is unanticipated, while other costs arise even when the inflation is fully anticipated. When unanticipated, price signals can become misinterpreted, and this can reduce economic efficiency. But once individuals adjust to the new higher inflation rate, accurate price signals are restored, and so this cost is only temporary. Only one-time increases in inflation are typically unexpected. Periods of sustained increasing inflation are typically anticipated because when prices rise in one month, individuals and markets may likely anticipate prices to rise in the following month. Thus, inflation is at least somewhat anticipated most of the time. Individuals can safeguard themselves against some of the effects of inflation

[9] Richard G. Anderson, *Inflation's Economic Cost: How Large? How Certain?* Federal Reserve Bank of St. Louis, July 1, 2006, https://www.stlouisfed.org/publications/regional-economist/july-2006/inflations-economic-cost-how-large- how-certain.

if they expected the inflation. For example, if inflation is expected to rise, workers can demand an increase in nominal wages, or lenders can require that the interest rate they receive be tied to the rate of inflation in some way. In reality, inflation is never entirely predictable, and, as such, individuals and businesses attempt to put safeguards in place, especially when inflation is high. Some costs occur only because of the absence of appropriate safeguards: for example, the absence of indexed contracts.

To understand the costs of anticipated inflation, imagine a hypothetical, fully indexed economy— one in which all contracts are adjusted for changes in the price level. In such an economy, inflation can impose only two real costs: (1) the less efficient arrangement of transactions that result from holding smaller money balances; and (2) "menu costs," or the necessity to change posted prices more frequently.[10] Both individuals and businesses hold money balances in cash or bank accounts because it allows them to arrange transactions in an optimal or least costly way (e.g., for business this involves paying employees, holding inventories, billing customers, maintaining working balances) and to provide security against an uncertain future. Holding wealth or assets in money form, however, incurs an opportunity cost—that is, what is given up when one action is taken as opposed to another. The opportunity cost of holding money is the nominal interest rate (equal to the real interest rate plus the inflation rate) that could be earned if the excess money were used to purchase an interest-earning asset. Thus, when the rate of inflation rises, holding money becomes more costly. Individuals and businesses then attempt to get by with smaller money balances. For businesses, this may mean billing customers more frequently. For employees, it may mean demanding to be paid more frequently. The new patterns are less efficient. They use more time or more resources to effect a given transaction. Similarly, efficiency is lost when more time and resources are used to frequently adjust prices to match inflation. This is an example of a permanent cost of inflation, which rises as inflation rises.

In an economy that is not fully indexed, inflation can lower the real value of income and the real rate of return on investments, both of which can distort incentives for individuals to work and businesses to grow their capital. For

[10] To some extent, the advent of certain technologies has decreased menu costs. The name comes from the costs to restaurants of printing new menus—which, prior to personal computing, had to be contracted out to printing services— but refers more generally to the costs to producers of changing their nominal prices. For example, employees of many businesses still need to take time to monitor prices and make and communicate price change decisions, time that could have been used more efficiently in the absence of increasing inflation.

example, some parts of the tax system are indexed for inflation, but others are not. Consider what happens to the real after-tax rate of return on business capital during inflation. For tax purposes, the depreciation of business plant and equipment is based on actual or historical costs. When inflation rises, charging depreciation based on historical cost raises the nominal profits of businesses and the basis on which corporate profits taxes are levied. As a result, the after-tax real rate of return falls, and this discourages businesses from adding to their stock of plant, equipment, and structures—a basis for future economic growth.

This is another example of a permanent cost associated with higher inflation.

Distributional Costs

Costs of inflation to individuals may not impose a burden on the overall economy because they represent a redistribution of income or wealth: What is lost by some is gained by others.

Nevertheless, these redistributions can have real effects on the individuals affected. According to the Bank of International Settlements, that redistribution is likely to be regressive from lower- income households to higher-income households, because the latter are more capable of protecting themselves against inflation.[11] The bank's logic states that relatively low-income households largely hold their savings as cash (which earns no return and thus has a value that falls by the full rate of inflation) or in bank accounts (which typically earn no or low returns unlikely to keep up with inflation), whereas relatively high-income households avail themselves of a wider array of investment options, a number of which better control for inflation or have values that typically rise along with prevailing inflation.

In addition to savers, there is some amount of real redistribution of wealth felt by lenders and borrowers when inflation increases. Inflation lessens the value of money and therefore can be seen to benefit borrowers when the terms of repayment do not account for inflation—the borrower, for all intents and purposes, will pay the lender back with money that is worth less than it was when the money was first borrowed.

---

[11] Bank for International Settlements (BIS), *Annual Economic Report*, 2021, ch. 2, https://www.bis.org/publ/arpdf/ ar2021e2.pdf.

Inflation can also have differential effects on households across the income distribution, because a typical high-income household consumes a different basket of goods from a typical low-income household. For example, food at home comprises a larger share of spending for low income households, so if food at home had a higher-than-average inflation rate, inflation would negatively affect low-income households more than it would high-income households. However, that effect will not be consistent or predictable over time because the goods that experience above-average and below-average inflation are not consistent over time.[12]

Optimal Level of Inflation

Many economists have argued that low and stable inflation is conducive to higher long-term economic growth, because it minimizes the costs of inflation and reduces the risk of costly deflationary periods.[13] How exactly to define low and stable is subject to debate. High levels of inflation are clearly not optimal. For example, economies experiencing hyperinflation (when annual inflation reaches triple or quadruple digits) have historically experienced costly disruptions to the normal functioning of their economies. However, there is little consensus among economists over whether, say, 2% or 4% inflation is preferable.[14] Likewise, there is generally agreement that stable and predictable inflation is preferable, although there is some debate on how much inflation should be allowed to vary at the margins from its target. Since 2012, the Federal Reserve has identified an average inflation rate of 2% (as measured

---

[12] For example, see Jonathan Church, *The Cost of "Basic Necessities" Has Risen Slightly More Than Inflation over the Last 30 Years*, U.S. Department of Labor, Bureau of Labor Statistics (BLS), June 2015, https://www.bls.gov/opub/btn/ volume-4/the-cost-of-basic-necessities-has-risen-slightly-more-than-inflation-over-the-last-30-years.htm; and Josh Klick and Anya Stockburger, *Experimental CPI for Lower and Higher Income Households*, BLS, March 8, 2021, pp. 1- 20, https://www.bls.gov/osmr/research-papers/2021/pdf/ec210030.pdf.

[13] Testimony of Fed chairman Ben Bernanke before the Senate Committee on Banking, Housing, and Urban Affairs, in U.S. Congress, November 15, 2005.

[14] The low level of nominal interest rates that has prevailed since the 2008 financial crisis has led some economists to argue that the Fed should target a slightly higher rate of inflation than 2% so that the Fed is less likely to hit the zero lower bound on interest rates during economic downturns. (Economists assume that higher inflation will pass through on a one-to-one basis to higher nominal interest rates over time. A higher nominal rate would give the Fed more room to reduce rates before reaching the zero lower bound.) See Laurence Ball, *The Case for a Long-Run Inflation Target of Four Percent*, International Monetary Fund, June 2014, https://www.imf.org/external/pubs/ft/wp/2014/wp1492.pdf.

by the PCE) as optimal.[15] In practice, inflation always fluctuates a little from year to year, and since the early 1980s a rise in inflation in one year has not been predictably followed by higher inflation in the next year. At this time, arguments for transitioning to a slightly higher optimal inflation rate face the added challenge of whether doing so when inflation is too high would make it more difficult to keep inflation expectations anchored and to maintain the credibility of policymakers' commitment to price stability.

What Causes Inflation?

There are several potential causes of inflation in an economy. A change in the inflation rate usually reflects an imbalance between overall supply and demand, which can be demand or supply driven or both—as is the case today. Demand-driven inflation can be caused by fiscal or monetary stimulus or originate in private spending dynamics. But in the long run generally, inflation is said to be "always and everywhere a monetary phenomenon," meaning it is driven by monetary policy. It is useful to distinguish between supply and demand causes of rising inflation, because supply-driven (or cost-push) inflation is associated with a decline in output, while demand-driven (or demand-pull) inflation is associated with a rise in output. This section discusses in greater detail a few causal categories of inflation and the role of monetary policy in controlling inflation in the short and long term.

Demand-Pull Inflation

Inflation that is caused by an increase in aggregate demand (overall spending) absent a proportional increase in aggregate supply (overall production) is known as demand-pull inflation. When aggregate demand increases by more than its trend rate, typically the productive capacity of the economy does not immediately adjust to meet higher demand, particularly if the economy is at or near full employment.[16] In response to the increased demand in the

---

[15] Board of Governors of the Federal Reserve System, "Guide to Changes in the 2020 Statement on Longer-Run Goals and Monetary Policy Strategy," in *Review of Monetary Policy Strategy, Tools, and Communications*, https://www.federalreserve.gov/monetarypolicy/guide-to-changes-in-statement-on-longer-run-goals-monetary-policy- strategy.htm.

[16] In an economy that is not near full employment, an increase in aggregate demand would be less likely to create inflation as this would imply that the economy is not working at its full

economy, producers will attempt to increase the quantity of goods and services they provide. To increase production, producers may attempt to hire more workers by increasing wages. Assuming producers are not willing to eat into profits in order to ramp up production,[17] they are likely to increase the prices of their final goods and services to compensate themselves for the increase in wages (which increases production costs), thereby creating inflation.[18] Inflation can work to lower demand and increase supply and thus can be the means to bring supply and demand back into equilibrium, particularly in an overheating economy in which demand has risen above what the economy can produce at full employment.[19]

Any number of factors could contribute to increases in aggregate demand, including the normal ebbs and flows of the business cycle, consumer and investor sentiment, the value of the dollar, and fiscal and monetary policy, among others. Expansionary fiscal policies include an increase in the budget deficit by lowering taxes or increasing government spending or transfers to individuals. Such policies work to increase overall spending in the economy by driving up consumer demand, in the case of lower taxes, or both consumer demand and government purchases in the case of increased spending. This in turn can lead to increased production and decreasing unemployment levels. The downside to achieving these benefits through expansionary fiscal policy is that it can result in demand-pull inflation in the short term, particularly if the economy is at full employment. Expansionary fiscal policy is unlikely to cause sustained inflation, as it typically involves temporary increases in spending. Such one-time increases may produce similar one-time increases in inflation but would be likely to cause persistent increases in inflation only if such policy were persistently applied. Additionally, monetary policy can potentially be used to offset the inflationary effects of such policy.

---

productive capacity. In other words, if aggregate demand is lower than aggregate supply, aggregate demand has some room to increase before outstripping aggregate supply.

[17] Of note, producers do not always respond to wage increases with one-to-one price increases. A producer's willingness to eat into profits is a product of many factors, including the state of the economy, current profit margins, consumers' responsiveness to price changes, and how competitive markets are, among others.

[18] Federal Reserve Bank of San Francisco, *What Are Some of the Factors That Contribute to a Rise in Inflation?* October 2002, https://www.frbsf.org/education/publications/doctor-econ/2002/october/inflation-factors-rise/.

[19] An economy is typically thought to overheat when actual GDP surpasses potential GDP—that is, the theoretical GDP an economy is capable of achieving under a situation of full employment.

The Role of Monetary Policy in Responding to Inflation

Economists generally believe that the long-run rate of inflation is tied to monetary policy. The Federal Reserve, which ultimately controls the supply of money, is tasked with maintaining stable prices in the economy. In other words, the Fed has a mandate to keep inflation in check. The Fed has tools to control inflation, mainly the federal funds interest rate (FFR)—the overnight rate at which banks lend to one another. Other interest rates in the economy tend to move in the same direction as the FFR, with shorter-term rates moving more closely with it and longer-term rates less so. Changes in interest rates affect overall economic activity by changing the demand for interest-sensitive spending (goods and services that are bought on credit). The main categories of interest-sensitive spending are business physical capital investment (e.g., plant and equipment), consumer durables (e.g., automobiles, appliances), and residential investment (i.e., new housing construction). All else equal, higher interest rates reduce interest-sensitive spending, and lower interest rates increase interest-sensitive spending.

Interest rates also influence the demand for exports and imports by affecting the value of the dollar. All else equal, higher interest rates increase net foreign capital inflows as U.S. assets become more attractive relative to foreign assets. To purchase U.S. assets, foreigners must first purchase U.S. dollars, pushing up the value of the dollar. When the value of the dollar rises, the price of foreign imports declines relative to U.S. import-competing goods, and U.S. exports become more expensive relative to foreign goods. As a result, net exports (exports less imports) decrease. When interest rates fall, all of these factors work in reverse and net exports increase, all else equal.

Business investment, consumer durables, residential investment, and net exports are all components of GDP. Thus, if expansionary monetary policy causes interest-sensitive spending to rise, it increases GDP in the short run. This increases employment, as more workers are hired to meet increased demand for goods and services. Most economists believe that monetary policy cannot permanently raise the level or growth rate of GDP or employment, because long-run GDP is determined by the economy's productive capacity (the size of the labor force, capital stock, technological innovation, and so on).[20] However, monetary policy can permanently change the inflation rate. If monetary policy pushes demand above what the economy can produce, then

[20] Olivier Blanchard and David R. Johnson, *Macroeconomics*, 6th ed. (Upper Saddle River, NJ: Peason Education, 2013), p. 221.

inflation should eventually rise to restore equilibrium.[21] Unless contractionary monetary policy is then used to slow economic activity, inflation is likely to remain at its new, higher level—in which case monetary policy is said to have accommodated higher inflation. When setting monetary policy, the Fed must take into account the lags between a change in policy and economic conditions. Otherwise, high inflation can become endemic, which might then require monetary policy to become contractionary enough to cause a recession to root it out. Although estimates vary, the general belief is that it can take from 18 months to several years for the effects of Fed policy changes to fully feed through to inflation and output.[22]

Cost-Push Inflation

Inflation that is caused by a decrease in aggregate supply as a result of increases in the cost of production absent a proportional decrease in aggregate demand is known as cost-push inflation. An increase in the cost of raw materials or any of the factors of production—land, labor, capital, entrepreneurship—will result in increased production costs.[23] Assuming producers' productivity is at or near its maximum, producers will not be able to maintain existing profit margins in response. Much the same as the demand-side issue, if producers cannot or will not accept lowered profits, they will raise prices.[24]

The classic example of cost-push inflation is the result of a commodity price shock, which sharply decreases the supply of a given commodity and increases its price. Certain commodities are inputs in the production process, and as the price of an important input good increases, so does the price of the final goods and services, resulting in inflation. Cost-push inflation, especially when caused by a supply shock, tends to result in only a temporary increase

---

[21] Olivier Blanchard and David R. Johnson, "The Phillips Curve, the Natural Rate of Unemployment, and Inflation," in *Macroeconomics*, p. 171.

[22] Tomas Havraneka and Marek Rusnak, *Transmission Lags of Monetary Policy: A Meta-Analysis*, International Journal of Central Banking, December 2013, p. 39, https://www.ijcb.org/journal/ijcb13q4a2.pdf. Of note, financial markets often react more quickly than other markets do.

[23] Federal Reserve Bank of St. Louis, "Factors of Production," in *The Economic Lowdown Podcast Series*, https://www.stlouisfed.org/education/economic-lowdown-podcast-series/episode-2-factors-of-production.

[24] Federal Reserve Bank of San Francisco, *What Are Some of the Factors That Contribute to a Rise in Inflation?*

in inflation unless accommodated by monetary policy. Supply disruptions are often alleviated naturally, and for inflation to be persistently high, supply shock after supply shock would need to occur.[25]

One of the reasons a commodity shock in particular is a widely cited example of something that causes cost-push inflation is that demand for many commodities is considered to be inelastic. The elasticity of demand refers to how consumers' appetite for a good changes given the price it is offered at.[26] A completely inelastic good is one that consumers would purchase at the same rate regardless of the price. For example, demand for oil and its derivative petroleum products—such as gasoline, diesel fuel, and petrochemicals—is generally fairly inelastic, because they are necessary purchases for consumers and businesses, with few substitutes readily available.

Another commonly cited example of cost-push inflation is caused by increases in the cost of labor, often referred to as wage-push inflation. An increase in the federal minimum wage, for example, could theoretically cause inflation. When producers need to pay their workers more, they may opt to pass that cost along to the consumer, reduce profits to pay the increased cost, or decrease the amount of workers they employ to keep costs down. The extent to which an increase in wages affects the price level depends largely on how many workers are affected by the wage increase and the size of the increase. In the case of the minimum wage, very few workers or very many workers could be affected, depending on the level of increase.

Expectations

Inflation expectations can add to inflationary pressures and become self-fulfilling. When individuals expect prices to rise, they generally behave according to this belief. For example, if a consumer expects prices to rise in the future, he or she may decide to spend more today, before the purchasing power of the dollar decreases. If expectations change across the economy, this can lead to increased levels of spending and therefore increased aggregate demand, which, all else equal, would result in demand-driven inflation. Likewise, workers may demand wage increases to compensate themselves for

---

[25] Dallas S. Batten, *Inflation: The Cost-Push Myth*, Federal Reserve Bank of St. Louis, June 1981, p. 21, https://files.stlouisfed.org/files/htdocs/publications/review/81/06/Inflation_Jun_Jul 1981.pdf.

[26] Federal Reserve Bank of St. Louis, *Price Elasticities of Demand*, https://research.stlouis fed.org/dashboard/9575.

future inflation, which can result in cost-push inflation, particularly if wage growth outstrips inflation. When expectations are met, this serves to further ingrain expectations that inflation will persist or even accelerate, which in turn leads to more inflation, and so on and so on. This situation is often referred to as a wage-price spiral in the case when wage and price growth continue to cause each other to increase, leaving the potential for inflation to become increasingly high and hard to reduce.[27]

Inflation expectations can be measured by surveying consumers or professional economists, or it can be gleaned from market data, such as Treasury Inflation-Protected Securities. Historical experience suggests that individuals respond to a significant increase in actual inflation by increasing their expectations of future inflation, although this may not occur instantaneously.

Another determinant of expectations is how credible individuals find the Fed's commitment to low inflation.

Inflation Trends

Earlier high inflation experiences in U.S. history may provide insights on how to address high inflation today. There are two notable types of high inflation periods to consider: the "Great Inflation" from the mid-1960s to early 1980s and some shorter-lived inflationary episodes surrounding U.S. wars.

"Great Inflation"

As shown in Figure 1, after averaging around 1% in the first half of the 1960s, inflation (as measured by the PCE) began rising to 2.5% in 1966, above 4.5% in 1970, nearly 10.5% in 1974, and above 10.5% in 1980. (CPI showed a similar but somewhat higher pattern.) Inflation then began declining rapidly, with PCE falling below 4% in 1984, and it was mostly low from then until 2021, as discussed below.

---

[27] Blanchard and Johnson, "The Phillips Curve, the Natural Rate of Unemployment, and Inflation," p. 164.

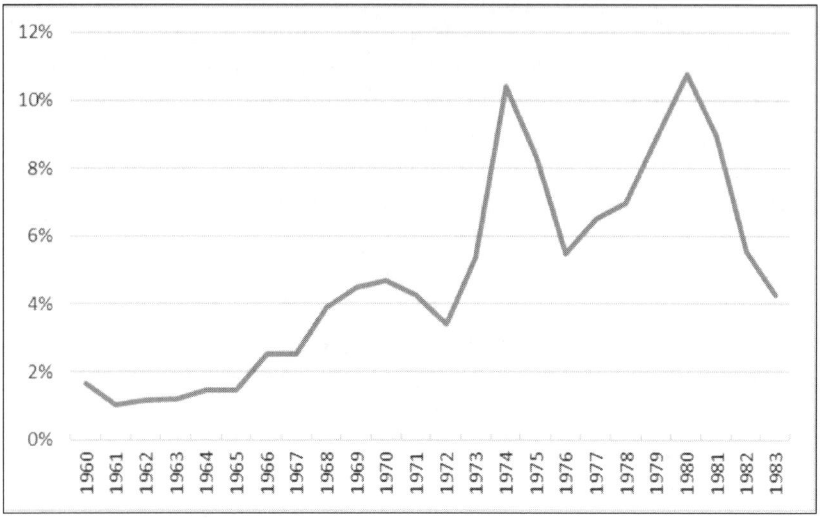

Source: CRS calculations using U.S. Department of Commerce, Bureau of Economic Analysis data.

Figure 1. Annual Inflation, 1960-1983. PCE Index.

Economists attribute this "Great Inflation" to several causes.[28] In thinking about those causes, it can be helpful to distinguish between "supply shocks" that caused short-term spikes in inflation during that period and causes of the long-term upward trend in inflation.[29] Short-term causes include the removal of wage and price controls (implemented in 1971 and completely removed in 1974),[30] the end of fixed exchange rates in 1971 and subsequent depreciation of the dollar in real terms,[31] oil price shocks in 1973-1974 and 1979, and food price shocks in the 1970s. Inflation reached a new high after each of these shocks, which would have been unlikely to occur in their absence. But each of

[28] Michael Bryan, "The Great Inflation," *Federal Reserve History*, November 2013, https://www.federalreservehistory.org/essays/great-inflation. See also Edward Nelson, "How Did It Happen? The Great Inflation of the 1970s and Lessons for Today," Board of Governors of the Federal Reserve System, June 2022, https://www.federalreserve.gov/econres/feds/the-great-inflation-of-the-1970s-and-lessons-for-today.htm.

[29] Alan S. Blinder and Jeremy B. Rudd, "The Supply-Shock Explanation of the Great Stagflation Revisited," in Michael D. Bordo and Athanasios Orphanides, eds., *The Great Inflation: The Rebirth of Modern Central Banking*, (Chicago: University of Chicago Press, June 2013), https://www.nber.org/system/files/chapters/c9160/c9160.pdf.

[30] The removal of wage and price controls allowed pent-up price increases to occur, causing inflation to rise.

[31] The depreciation of the dollar caused import prices to rise and increased demand for exports, which put upward pressure on overall inflation.

these factors would be expected to increase inflation only temporarily. A one-time increase in the price of oil in isolation, for example, would lead to a one-time increase in the inflation rate, but if oil prices then levelled off at the higher level, it would make no further contribution to inflation in later years (because inflation measures the change in prices, not the level of prices).

The long-term upward trend in inflation over the entire period is attributed to monetary policy that was persistently too "easy" (i.e., stimulative) and the unmooring of inflation expectations.[32] (Fiscal stimulus was employed sporadically over this period but not consistently enough to explain the long-term upward trend and not in the years with the largest increases in inflation.) The reason policy was too easy differed in the 1960s and 1970s. During the 1960s, policymakers attempted to exploit the Phillips Curve, a belief that lower unemployment could be achieved at the cost of higher inflation. At first, this seemed to work—unemployment fell from 4.5% in 1965 to 3.5% in 1969—but then unemployment began rising and did not return to 4.5% again for the remainder of the Great Inflation. Once inflation expectations rose,[33] higher inflation no longer yielded lower unemployment, and higher unemployment was not sufficient to bring inflation down to low levels.[34] In the 1970s, when inflation rose in response to oil shocks, the Fed faced a tradeoff between raising interest rates to mitigate the inflationary effects or "accommodating" inflation to mitigate the negative effects on growth and employment. The Fed largely chose the latter option throughout the decade. The high inflation period was brought to an end when the Fed sharply tightened monetary policy under new Fed Chair Paul Volcker in the early 1980s, bringing inflation expectations back under control but triggering a deep recession in the process. For more information on Volcker-era inflation and policies, see CRS In Focus IF12177, Back to the Future? Lessons from the "Great Inflation," by Marc Labonte and Lida R. Weinstock.

---

[32] Allan Meltzer, "Origins of the Great Inflation," Federal Reserve Bank of St. Louis Review, vol. 87, no. 2, Part 2 (March/April 2005), pp. 145-175, https://files.stlouisfed.org/files/htdocs/publications/review/05/03/part2/Meltzer.pdf.

[33] Data on inflation expectations going back to the 1960s is limited, but what is available seems to confirm this view. See Jan J. J. Groen and Menno Middeldorp, "Creating a History of U.S. Inflation Expectations," Federal Reserve Bank of New York, August 21, 2013, https://libertystreeteconomics.newyorkfed.org/2013/08/creating-a-history-of-us- inflation-expectations/.

[34] One lesson taken from this experience was that persistently keeping labor markets "too hot" would not yield any lasting benefits in terms of labor market outcomes. The experience of keeping labor markets "too hot" without any noticeable increase in inflation in the years before the pandemic (and, to a lesser extent, in the 1990s) casts doubt on whether this lesson still holds.

Because equilibrium interest rates, economic growth rates, and unemployment rates are not constant over time, it was not obvious during the Great Inflation that monetary policy was too easy. Although short-term interest rates rose at times in nominal terms, monetary policy remained easy because interest rates did not increase quickly enough to keep up with inflation, so real rates were low or even negative.[35] In hindsight, real rates compatible with the stable inflation experienced in periods before and after turned out to be too low during the Great Inflation, as will be discussed in more detail below. Further, equilibrium growth rates were falling and unemployment rates were rising, but because policymakers did not realize it quickly enough, they were still aiming to achieve what had become unachievable growth and unemployment rates. By current standards, budget deficits were also small—they exceeded 3% of GDP in only two years of the Great Inflation. Thus, the main evidence after the fact that policy was too easy is that inflation was too high, not that interest rates were lower or budget deficits were higher than in other periods.

Some commentators have compared current inflation with the Great Inflation period,[36] leading to concerns that current inflation could become entrenched if it does follow the patterns of the Great Inflation. Some parallels can be drawn between these two periods, including low unemployment and supply shocks. However, the economic context is not an exact match, and, therefore, the extent to which the economy is headed for another Great Inflation is not at all certain. For more information on the lessons of the Great Inflation and whether they might hold today, see CRS In Focus IF12177, Back to the Future? Lessons from the "Great Inflation," by Marc Labonte and Lida R. Weinstock.

Policymakers took several actions to lower inflation during the Great Inflation that are discussed in the section below entitled "Historical Policies."

Wars

Unlike the Great Inflation, in which inflation became entrenched in the economy and long lasting, there have been several periods of high inflation

---

[35] The FFR was not the Fed's policy target at the time, but rates that the Fed set directly, such as the discount rate, were also increased.

[36] For example, see Jeff Sommer, "Lessons from the '80s, When Volcker Reigned and Rates Were High," *New York Times*, August 5, 2022, https://www.nytimes.com/2022/08/05/business/inflation-investing-paul-volcker.html.

when inflation fell quickly after the causes abated, notably during wars. The shift to a wartime economy can lead to a sudden increase in the production of military equipment and a sudden reduction in the production of nonmilitary goods and services and, in some cases, temporarily high household saving as a result.[37]

The Vietnam War occurred during the Great Inflation period, covered in the previous section. This experience would seem to lend credence to the idea that wars can have long-lasting effects on inflation, but as the previous section outlines, several other factors are seen as the primary causes of high inflation at that time. Instead, the best examples of wars leading to inflationary pressures are World War II and the Korean War.

As shown in Figure 2, inflation was high during and after World War II. It was above 4% each year from 1941 to 1948, peaking at 12% in 1942 and 10% in 1947, as measured by the PCE. Prices then fell in 1949 and generally remained low until the late 1960s.[38] The one year when inflation was high in that period—almost 7% in 1951—was during the Korean War.[39] By 1952, inflation was below 2% again, where it would remain through 1956. The economy did not experience the same unmooring of inflation expectations and long-lasting wage-price spiral as the Great Inflation. This may be because a recession occurred shortly after both wars (in 1948-1949 and 1953-1954) that contributed to the decline in inflation. Nevertheless, both episodes demonstrate that a rise in inflation does not necessarily have to be persistent.

More recent wars—such as the first and second Iraq Wars and the Afghanistan War—were arguably too small in terms of military expenditures and economic impact to have a significant effect on inflation.

---

[37] Laura Nicolae, "US Daily: Pent-Up Savings and Inflation After World War 2," Goldman Sachs Research, February 25, 2021.

[38] World War I featured an even more extreme case of high inflation followed by deflation. That experience may be less relevant today, however, because monetary policy was then governed by the gold standard.

[39] Joseph E. Gagnon, "Inflation Fears and the Biden Stimulus: Look to the Korean War, Not Vietnam," Peterson Institute for International Economics, February 25, 2021, https://www.piie.com/blogs/realtime-economic-issues-watch/inflation-fears-and-biden-stimulus-look-korean-war-not-vietnam.

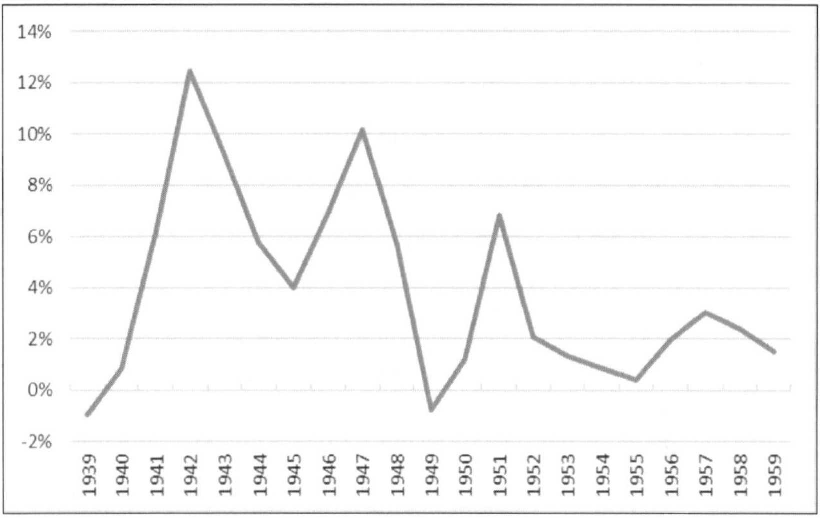

Source: CRS calculations using U.S. Department of Commerce, Bureau of Economic Analysis data.

Figure 2. Annual Inflation, 1939-1959. PCE Index.

1980s-2020

After the recessions of the early 1980s, the economy did not experience comparably high inflation again until 2021. From 1984 to 1991, it averaged about 3.5%. On an annual basis, inflation (as measured by the PCE) averaged a little under 2% from 1992 to 2020, as shown in Figure 3. (As measured by CPI, inflation has been slightly higher.) As a result, many economists and policymakers believed high inflation was no longer likely enough to present serious concern.

The highest annual inflation rate since 1992 was in 2008, when it nearly reached 3%. This was mainly driven by a 14% increase in energy prices that year. That episode also featured three consecutive months of unusually rapid price increases, similar to the present. The Fed did not react to this increase in inflation—in the midst of the deepest and longest recession since the Great Depression—by tightening monetary policy.[40] Instead, the Fed was engaged

[40] As this example illustrates, the Fed has typically been more concerned with core inflation than headline inflation. Core inflation was only 2% in 2008. Unlike the 1970s, increases in food and energy prices did not feed through to increases in core inflation in the low inflation

in a then-novel asset purchase program (popularly referred to as "quantitative easing" or QE) that caused an unprecedented increase in the monetary base, which many critics worried would lead to runaway inflation. Critics' fears were not realized. In 2009, the economy experienced slight price deflation. This example illustrates that inflation can temporarily rise even during an unusually deep recession but that a rise in inflation does not necessarily lead to sustained high inflation. In hindsight, some believe that a mistaken concern with inflation that never materialized led policymakers to tighten fiscal and monetary policy prematurely, leading to a weaker recovery and prolonged return to full employment after the Great Recession.

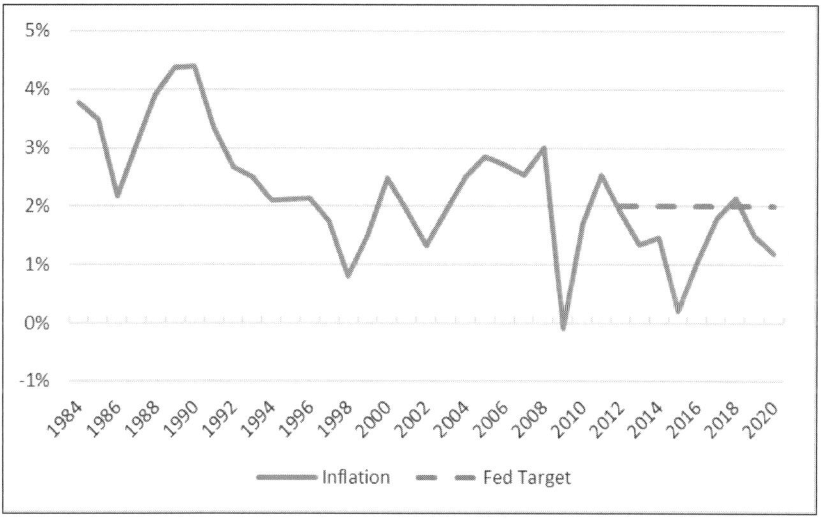

Source: CRS calculations based on U.S. Department of Commerce, Bureau of Economic Analysis data.

Notes: In 2012, the Fed instituted an inflation target of 2%, as measured by the PCE index.

Figure 3. Annual Inflation, 1984-2020. PCE Index.

Many economists believe that monetary policy was too easy during the Great Inflation, and some believe it was too tight during and after the Great Recession. Yet the FFR averaged 6.8% from 1968 to 1978 and 0.7% from 2008 to 2020. This illustrates that the interest rate consistent with stable inflation is not itself constant over time. For one thing, interest rates need to

period, because inflation expectations remained stable and energy was less important to production.

be adjusted for inflation, but even once this is taken into account, "real" interest rates were higher (0.9%) from 1968 to 1978—when monetary policy was viewed as too easy—than from 2008 to 2020 (-0.9%, meaning nominal rates were on average lower than inflation)—when policy was viewed as too tight.[41] This undercuts arguments that monetary policy has been too easy since 2021 based solely on the fact that nominal interest rates were low.[42]

Since the 2007-2009 financial crisis, the Federal Reserve, as well as many economists and policymakers, have been more concerned that inflation has been too low. Since the Fed identified its ideal longer-run goal for inflation to be 2% in 2012, inflation was below 2% each year through 2020 except for 2018, when it very slightly rose above. This persistent undershooting led the Fed to switch its focus (in terms of achieving its price stability mandate) from preventing too high inflation to preventing too low inflation. As a result, the Fed changed its monetary policy strategy in 2020 by explicitly stating that it would try to overshoot 2% inflation after periods when inflation has been below 2% in order to achieve a 2% average over time.[43]

Recent High Inflation

The first year of the pandemic saw low and even falling prices in some months due to the collapse in demand, particularly for services. With the rapid economic recovery underway, high inflation initially manifested itself in 2021 as large price increases in a handful of goods and services that were particularly disrupted by the pandemic, with most other prices remaining stable. For example, as will be discussed below, disruptions to automobile production resulted in used automobile prices rising by as much as 10% a month (or an annualized rate of 120%) in the spring of 2021.

---

[41] Adjusted using actual headline PCE.

[42] One challenge that the Fed has experienced since the Great Recession of 2007-2009 is the limits on monetary policy imposed by the "zero lower bound." The Fed has been limited in how much stimulus it can provide by lowering the FFR, because it cannot be reduced below zero. As a result, the FFR was essentially zero from December 2008 to December 2015 and from March 2020 to March 2022. Arguably, this limit on conventional monetary policy made it more difficult in the years following the Great Recession for the economy to recover and made the Fed reliant on unconventional policy to stimulate the economy.

[43] Federal Reserve, *2020 Statement on Longer-Run Goals and Monetary Policy Strategy*, August 27, 2020, https://www.federalreserve.gov/monetarypolicy/review-of-monetary-policy-strategy-tools-and-communications-statement-on-longer-run-goals-monetary-policy-strategy.htm. For more information, see CRS Insight IN11499, *The Federal Reserve's Revised Monetary Policy Strategy Statement*, by Marc Labonte.

As the months went by, inflation became higher and more widespread across a greater share of goods and services until virtually all categories were rising rapidly. One way to measure this is through the trimmed mean PCE, produced by the Federal Reserve Bank of Dallas.[44] The trimmed mean reports the inflation rate after removing outliers, meaning the goods with the highest and lowest inflation rates for the month. Although overall inflation started rising in February 2021, the trimmed mean was not unusually high until September 2021 and remains above 4% as of July 2022 (as measured by the percent change in the past 12 months). And although the trimmed mean omits goods and services with the fastest rising prices, representing 30% of the overall consumption basket, it nevertheless includes individual goods and services whose prices have risen as much as 11% at an annualized rate over the past month. Official and private forecasters expect inflation for 2022 as a whole to be lower than the 12-month changes seen in the first half of 2022 (as earlier price spikes drop out of the data) but remain well above 2%.

Higher inflation has not been limited to the United States. The International Monetary Fund reports that inflation in advanced economies increased from 0.7% in 2020 to 3.1% in 2021 and projects that it will average 5.7% in 2022.[45] Inflation has been high nearly everywhere because all of the world is experiencing many of the same root causes as the United States is. However, inflation has been higher in the United States than in most other advanced economies.

Rising Asset Prices and Inflation

Asset prices are not included in the calculation of inflation, which is meant to measure only the change in the price of goods and services. Notably, houses are considered assets, so rising house prices do not factor directly into inflation. However, "owners' equivalent rent" is a large share of consumer price inflation measures and represents the hypothetical rent that homeowners would pay if they rented their houses.[46]

Equity (stock) prices, housing prices, and prices of alternative assets (such as cryptocurrencies) all increased significantly through the end of

[44] Data and methodology available at https://www.dallasfed.org/research/pce.

[45] International Monetary Fund (IMF), *World Economic Outlook*, April 2022, https://www.imf.org/external/ datamapper/datasets/WEO.

[46] It is not based on house prices or mortgage payments, which determine what homeowners actually pay out of pocket for their housing costs. It is imputed using actual rents of similar rented properties.

2021 after initially declining at the beginning of the pandemic, with housing prices continuing to rise in 2022. Because assets are not included in inflation measures, the rise in asset prices has no direct effect on inflation. Nonetheless, rising asset prices could have added to inflationary pressures. This connection is most direct in residential housing. If home prices rise, that may cause rents to go up, which would cause owners' equivalent rent and hence inflation to rise. More broadly, there can be a "wealth effect" on consumption when owners of assets, such as stocks, that have risen in value decide to spend more in response to their newfound wealth, which can add to inflationary pressures.

Potential Causes of Current Inflation

The fact that high inflation has persisted ultimately indicates a mismatch between aggregate supply and aggregate demand in the economy, as described above. In the case of current inflation, the roots of inflation can be found in the specific supply disruptions caused by the sudden and widespread changes in consumer behavior, spread of the virus, and mandated restrictions.

However, once inflation became widespread throughout goods and services in the economy, the concept of supply disruptions as the sole cause of inflation was no longer a convincing one.

Supply disruptions cause relative price changes: When all prices are rising simultaneously and persistently, it indicates that current demand is too high relative to current supply—regardless of whether current supply is constrained.[47] While supply constraints remain in the economy, stimulative monetary and fiscal policy also remain, although both have been tightened in recent months. This section discusses both why inflation started rising in 2021 and why it continues to be high in 2022.

---

[47] See Adam Hale Shapiro, *Decomposing Supply and Demand Driven Inflation*, September 22, 2022, Federal Reserve Bank of San Francisco, https://www.frbsf.org/wp-content/uploads/sites/4/wp2022-18.pdf; Julian di Giovanni, "How Much Did Supply Constraints Boost U.S. Inflation?," Federal Reserve Bank of New York, August 24, 2022, https://libertystreeteconomics.newyorkfed.org/2022/08/how-much-did-supply-constraints-boost-u-s-inflation/.

Roots in Pandemic Disruptions

The pandemic initially caused reductions in both aggregate supply and aggregate demand that were larger and more sudden than the economy had experienced before.[48] Fears of the virus and social distancing measures resulted in decreased spending[49] and increased unemployment,[50] resulting in a negative shock to aggregate demand. On the supply side, disruptions to the production process—owing to health constraints on operations and workers, capacity limits on customers, and prohibitions on attendance at certain activities[51]—contributed to a negative supply shock as well.

Additionally, demand for certain goods and services such as gasoline and dining away from home fell as workers began to telework at unprecedented rates and people stayed home. At the same time, demand for other products rose quickly, and supply chains could not keep up. Grocery stores experienced shortages in food, toilet paper, and cleaning supplies, and personal protective equipment became scarce.[52] Many of these specific supply issues cleared over time, although several other specific bottlenecks have cropped up and continue to cause supply problems in the economy.[53]

Periodic surges in COVID-19 cases have also caused labor shortages at times that have hobbled production. For example, the Omicron-variant surge led to employee absences that caused new supply disruptions in the winter of 2021-2022, including to flights and passenger rail.[54] The U.S. Bureau of Labor

---

[48] For more information, see CRS Report R46606, *COVID-19 and the U.S. Economy*, by Lida R. Weinstock.

[49] Real personal consumption expenditures fell by 33.4% in the second quarter of 2020, largely driven by a 42.4% drop in services expenditures.

[50] In April 2020, employment fell by 22,279,000 workers.

[51] See, for example, Brent Meyer and Mark E. Schweitzer, *The Impact of the Pandemic on US Businesses: New Results from the Annual Business Survey*, Federal Reserve Bank of Atlanta, March 2022, https://www.atlantafed.org/-/media/documents/research/publications/policy-hub/2022/03/22/03—impact-of-pandemic-on-us-businesses—new-results-from-annual-business-survey.pdf.

[52] Ana Swanson, "Global Trade Sputters, Leaving Too Much Here, Too Little There," *New York Times*, April 10, 2020, https://www.nytimes.com/2020/04/10/business/economy/global-trade-shortages-coronavirus.html.

[53] For example, see Stephanie Yang and Jiyoung Sohn, "Global Chip Shortage 'Is Far from Over' as Wait Times Get Longer," *Wall Street Journal*, October 29, 2021, https://www.wsj.com/articles/global-chip-shortage-is-far-from-over-as-wait-times-get-longer-11635413402.

[54] Eli Rosenberg, "Workers Are Out Sick in Record Numbers, Exacerbating Labor Shortage Woes," *Washington Post*, January 20, 2022, https://www.washingtonpost.com/business/2022/01/20/workers-out-sick-omicron-census/; Luz Lazo, "Amtrak to Reduce Train Service Amid Omicron Surge," *Washington Post*, January 20, 2022,

Statistics reported that 3.6 million employed individuals were unable to work at some point in January 2022 (when Omicron peaked) because of illness—more than twice as high as the pre-pandemic high.[55] In the same month, 6 million individuals were unable to work because their employers closed or lost business due to COVID-19. Absences and loss of business because of illness have been consistently above average throughout the pandemic.[56]

These earlier disruptions are still affecting the economy today in ways that are contributing to high inflation. Earlier shutdowns and shifts in demand led to extremely large layoffs in certain industries, such as the leisure and hospitality industry, and spikes in demand in other areas, such as consumer durables, that could not be easily met. After those shutdowns ended and demand began recovering, businesses were unable to quickly ramp their production and workforces back up, causing labor and supply chain shortages that continue to the present.

Although the economy has become less affected by the pandemic, supply and demand continue to be affected to varying degrees. For the past several months, the economy has been in a state where demand has significantly recovered from the COVID-19 shock with the help of fiscal and monetary stimulus (discussed in the next section), but supply has remained constrained by COVID-19-related problems (see the section below entitled "Supply Disruptions in 2022") and low labor force participation (see the section below entitled "The Post-Pandemic Labor Market").

Fiscal and Monetary Stimulus in the Pandemic

In response to the pandemic and subsequent economic downturn, unprecedentedly large monetary and fiscal stimulus was put in place. This contributed to the rapid recovery in economic activity after the initial

---

https://www.washingtonpost.com/transportation/2022/01/20/amtrak-cuts-service-virus-surge/.

[55] BLS, *Absences from Work*, https://www.bls.gov/cps/absences.htm. Census also collects data in its experimental Pulse survey on people who reported that they were "caring for someone or sick myself with coronavirus symptoms" and workers who reported that they were not working due to COVID. See U.S. Census Bureau, "Household Pulse Survey Data Tables," Employment Table 3, https://www.census.gov/programs-surveys/household-pulse-survey/data.html.

[56] BLS, "2.5 Million Unable to Work in March 2022 Because Employer Closed or Lost Business Due to COVID-19," April 6, 2022, https://www.bls.gov/opub/ted/2022/2-5-million-unable-to-work-in-march-2022-because-employer-closed-or-lost-business-due-to-covid-19.htm.

contraction and was not inflationary at that point, because the economy was well below full employment. However, continued stimulus—both fiscal and monetary policy remain expansionary, although to a lesser degree than early in the pandemic—may be contributing to the mismatch between supply and demand. Fiscal and monetary policy are expected to continue to provide less stimulus to the economy, but not return to a neutral or contractionary stance, in 2022.

Stimulus is not always inflationary, but stimulus can lead to high inflation if it causes the economy to overheat. Stimulus helped stabilize an economy where output fell by about one-third in the first half of 2020 without causing inflation to rise. But now that the economy is at full employment and prices have been rising, expansionary fiscal and monetary policy may be exacerbating the rise in prices.

Fiscal Policy

In FY2020 and FY2021, Congress passed several laws to provide economic stimulus and assistance to the American people, including the Coronavirus Preparedness and Response Supplemental Appropriations Act, 2020 (P.L. 116-123); the Families First Coronavirus Response Act (P.L. 116-127); the Coronavirus Aid, Relief, and Economic Security (CARES, P.L. 116-136) Act; the Paycheck Protection Program and Health Care Enhancement Act (P.L. 116-139); the Consolidated Appropriations Act, 2021 (P.L. 116-260); and ARPA (P.L. 117-2).[57]

The easiest way to gauge the size of the fiscal stimulus is through its effect on the budget deficit.[58] Deficit-financed government spending on goods and services boost total spending directly. Deficit-financed tax cuts or transfers to individuals (which is recorded as government spending) boosts their income,

[57] The Infrastructure Investment and Jobs Act (P.L. 117-58) was enacted in November 2021 but had little short-term stimulative effect, because its outlays will occur mostly in future years. See CBO, *Senate Amendment 2137 to H.R. 3684, the Infrastructure Investment and Jobs Act*, Cost Estimate, August 5, 2021, at https://www.cbo.gov/publication/ 57406. The effect of P.L. 117-58 on budget deficits is smaller than its increase in spending because of offsetting provisions.

[58] The COVID relief legislation included unusual temporary measures taken to prevent economic hardship, including forgivable loans to small businesses and moratoria on foreclosures, evictions, and student loan payments. As a result, the increase in the deficit does not fully capture the magnitude of fiscal stimulus provided.

inducing private spending.[59] Based on Congressional Budget Office (CBO) data (shown below in Table 1), the stimulus acts increased projected deficits by roughly a combined $2.3 trillion in FY2020 (of which $1.6 trillion is attributable to the CARES Act), $2.6 trillion in FY2021 (of which $1.2 trillion is attributed to ARPA), and $0.6 trillion in FY2022 (mostly attributed to ARPA).[60]

Table 1. Timing of fiscal stimulus

trillions of dollars

	FY2020	FY2021	FY2022	10-Year Total	Debt Service Included?
FY2020 Legislation	$2.3	$0.6	-$0.08	$2.8	Yes
Divisions M and N of the CAA	$0	$0.8	$0.07	$0.9	No
ARPA	$0	$1.2	$0.5	$1.9	No
Total	$2.3	$2.6	$0.5	$5.6	

Source: CRS calculations using CBO data.

Notes: See text for details of stimulus legislation. Negative numbers reduce the deficit. CAA = Consolidated Appropriations Act, 2021.

As a result of this fiscal stimulus and the decline in economic activity,[61] FY2020 and FY2021 budget deficits were unusually large by historical standards. The FY2020 federal budget deficit totaled $3.1 trillion, more than

[59] In economic theory, an increase in government spending would need to be deficit financed to have a significant stimulative effect. If it were offset by higher taxes or reductions in other spending, that would offset most or all of its stimulative effect.

[60] See CBO, The Budgetary Effects of Laws Enacted in Response to the 2020 Coronavirus Pandemic, March and April 2020, June 16, 2020, at https://www.cbo.gov/publication/56403; CBO, An Update to the Budget Outlook: 2020 to 2030, September 2, 2020, p. 29, https://www.cbo.gov/system/files/2020-09/56517-Budget-Outlook.pdf; CBO, Preliminary Estimate of the Effects of H.R. 748, the CARES Act, P.L. 116-136, Revised, with Corrections to the Revenue Effect of the Employee Retention Credit and to the Modification of a Limitation on Losses for Taxpayers Other Than Corporations, April 27, 2020, https://www.cbo.gov/system/files/2020-04/hr748.pdf; CBO, Estimated Budgetary Effects of H.R. 1319, American Rescue Plan Act of 2021, https://www.cbo.gov/system/files/2021-03/Estimated_Budgetary_Effects_of_HR_1319_as_passed_0.pdf; CBO, Summary Estimate for Divisions M Through FFH.R. 133, Consolidated Appropriations Act, 2021, January 14, 2021, https://www.cbo.gov/system/files/2021-01/PL_116-260_Summary.pdf; and CBO, The Budget and Economic Outlook: 2022 to 2032, May 2022, https://www.cbo.gov/ system/files/2022-05/57950-Outlook.pdf.

[61] Without policy changes, tax revenues automatically fall and means-tested spending automatically rises, causing the deficit to automatically increase when economic activity declines. These are referred to as "automatic stabilizers."

triple its FY2019 value, and the FY2021 budget deficit totaled nearly $2.8 trillion. As a percentage of GDP, these deficits were equal to 15% in FY2020 and 12.4% in FY2021, compared to 4.7% in the year before the pandemic (FY2019).[62] These were the largest deficits as a share of GDP since World War II, as shown in Figure 4.

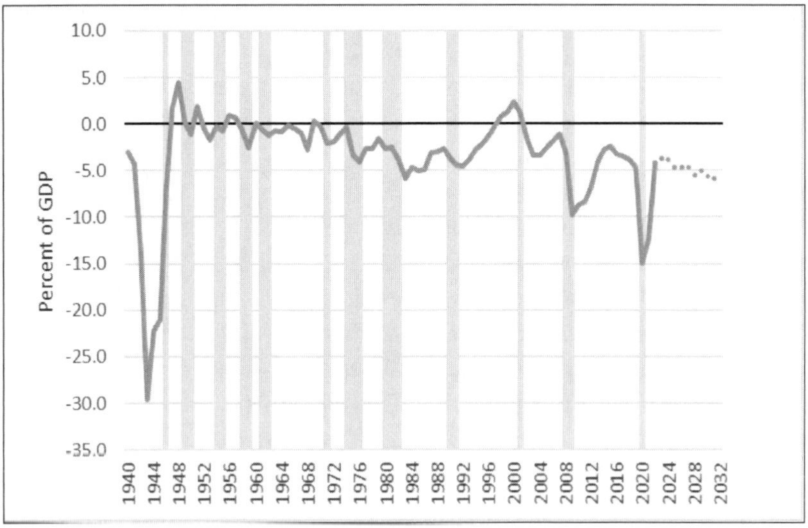

Source: Office of Management and Budget, Budget of the U.S. Government Fiscal Year 2023; and CBO, Budget and Economic Outlook, 2022-2032.

Notes: Data for FY2022-FY2032 are projections using current law. Gray bars denote recessions.

Figure 4. Deficit-to-GDP Ratio. FY1940-FY2032.

Reflecting its emergency nature, COVID relief was designed to be mostly temporary and delivered quickly, so much of it had expired or been exhausted by FY2022. As a result, CBO projects that the budget deficit as a share of GDP will decline by more than half to 4.2% of GDP between FY2021 and FY2022.[63] In other words, deficits are still large by historical standards but have been shrinking, providing less support to overall demand. Nonetheless, fiscal policy is still expansionary and therefore continues to put upward pressure on demand. Goldman Sachs estimates that fiscal stimulus since 2020

[62] CBO, *Monthly Budget Review: Summary for Fiscal Year 2021*, November 8, 2021, https://www.cbo.gov/system/ files/2021-11/57539-MBR.pdf.

[63] CBO, *The Budget and Economic Outlook: 2022 to 2032*, May 2022, https://www.cbo.gov/ system/files/2022-05/ 57950-Outlook.pdf.

boosted GDP by 6% in (calendar year) 2021 and 2.25% in 2022 but will boost GDP by less than 1% beginning in the second half of 2023.[64]

The extent to which current inflation can be tied specifically to pandemic stimulus is not agreed upon.[65] The initial COVID response, including the CARES Act (which had the largest budgetary impact), occurred when inflation was falling and the economy was in freefall. Given that much of the spending and revenue reductions in the FY2020 legislation was projected to be spent in FY2020 (see Table 1), when inflation was still low, it is not likely that those acts would still be causing inflation. By contrast, ARPA was enacted about halfway through FY2021 and had its main budgetary effects in that fiscal year and FY2022. Combined with the remaining stimulus from earlier bills, a total of $2.6 trillion in stimulus was projected to be delivered in FY2021 (ofwhich at least $1.2 trillion was delivered in the second half of the year through ARPA) and an additional $0.5 trillion in FY2022, whereas inflation started rising about halfway through FY2021 and continued to rise in FY2022. (CBO does not provide a breakdown of which months the projected budgetary effects occur within the fiscal year.[66]) In short, fiscal stimulus was large enough to have a significant effect on demand in FY2021, although much of it may have occurred before inflation started rising. Stimulus in FY2022 was smaller and so would have had a smaller effect on demand, although inflation may have been more sensitive to changes in demand at that point.

Economists and policymakers have debated ARPA's contribution to inflation, among other things. Proponents of the law said that the stimulus was necessary for the economy to fully recover from COVID-19, while skeptics expressed concern that it was too large relative to the output gap at the time

---

[64] Alec Phillips, "How Much Fiscal Drag?" Goldman Sachs, *US Economics Analyst*, April 11, 2022. Goldman Sachs reports that the contribution of proposed legislation not already enacted to their estimates is modest.

[65] For a working paper finding relatively large effects of fiscal policy on inflation, see Francois de Soyres, Ana Maria Santacreu, and Henry Young, *Demand-Supply Imbalance During the Covid-19 Pandemic: The Role of Fiscal Policy*, International Finance Discussion Papers Number 1353, August 2022, https://www.federalreserve.gov/econres/ifdp/files/ifdp 1353.pdf.

[66] BEA provides data on the effects of pandemic-relief income transfers on personal income, which were a major category of pandemic fiscal stimulus. Its data shows most transfers occurring in the first quarter of 2021 (of which the largest category was Economic Impact Payments) and dropping off steeply after that. However, such transfers were lower in the first quarter of 2021 than in the last quarter of 2020, so personal disposable income declined in the first quarter. See BEA, *Effects of Selected Federal Pandemic Response Programs on Personal Income, 2022Q2 Advance*, July 28, 2022, https://www.bea.gov/recovery.

and would therefore increase aggregate demand too much, causing inflation.[67] Indeed, as discussed above, after the passage of ARPA, inflation did rise, giving credence to the argument that it would boost aggregate demand by more than aggregate supply could keep up with.[68] The question remains, after the initial outlay, whether ARPA has continued to cause inflation. CBO projected that ARPA would continue to increase deficits through FY2025 (and decrease them thereafter), so, in theory, that deficit spending could be contributing to increased demand, exacerbating the current inflation problem. However, given that the effects on deficits decrease each fiscal year and are small after FY2022, these projections also indicate that ARPA should likely have a decreasing effect on inflation over time.[69]

Relatedly, some have pointed to large increases in government transfers included in pandemic relief legislation as potentially causing inflation to rise.[70] Notably, the three rounds of economic impact payments (popularly called "stimulus checks") contributed notably to increases in personal income. (These payments represented 12.3%, 7.7%, and 16.7% of total personal

---

[67] The difference between actual and potential GDP is known as the output gap. See, for example, Lawrence H. Summers, "The Biden Stimulus Is Admirably Ambitious. But It Brings Some Big Risks, Too," *Washington Post*, February 4, 2021, https://www.washingtonpost.com/opinions/2021/02/04/larry-summers-biden-covid-stimulus/; Olivier Blanchard, "In Defense of Concerns over the $1.9 Trillion Relief Plan," Peterson Institute for International Economics, February 18, 2021, https://www.piic.com/blogs/realtime-economic-issues-watch/defense-concerns-over-19-trillion- relief-plan; and Jason Furman, "Why Did (Almost) No One See the Inflation Coming?," *Intereconomics*, vol. 57, no. 2 (2022), pp. 79-86, https://www.intereconomics.eu/contents/year/2022/number/2/article/why-did-almost-no-one-see-the- inflation-coming.html. The IMF projected that if the American Rescue Plan, American Jobs Plan, and American Families Plan had all been enacted, inflation would have risen from below 2% to above 3% in 2021 before falling below 3% in 2022. The IMF also projected that GDP would be higher and unemployment would be lower. IMF, *United States 2021 Article IV Consultation—Press Release*, https://www.imf.org/en/Publications/CR/Issues/2021/07/22/ United-States-2021-Article-IV-Consultation-Press-Release-Staff-Report-and-Statement-by-the-462540.

[68] Regis Barnichon, Luiz E. Oliveira, and Adam H. Shapiro, "Is the American Rescue Plan Taking Us Back to the '60s?," Federal Reserve Bank of San Francisco, October 18, 2021, https://www.frbsf.org/economic-research/publications/economic-letter/2021/october/is-american-rescue-plan-taking-us-back-to-1960s/.

[69] CBO, *Estimated Budgetary Effects of H.R. 1319, American Rescue Plan Act of 2021*, https://www.cbo.gov/system/files/2021-03/Estimated_Budgetary_Effects_of_HR_1319_as_passed_0.pdf.

[70] Òscar Jordà et al., "Why Is U.S. Inflation Higher Than in Other Countries?," Federal Reserve Bank of San Francisco, March 28, 2022, https://www.frbsf.org/economic-research/publications/economic-letter/2022/march/why-is-us-inflation-higher-than-in-other-countries/.

incomein April 2020, January 2021, and March 2021, respectively.[71]) As a result, personal income exceeded its pre-pandemic trend beginning in April 2020, although GDP was still far below trend at that point. The three rounds of payment were all one-time transfers, and therefore the effects on income dropped off quickly, however. Furthermore, inflation did not begin to rise in earnest until March 2021, meaning that only the last of these transfers occurred when inflation was high.

If these transfers were spent when they were received, they would not have any effect on inflation after the fact when inflation was high. But the personal income growth during the pandemic was also associated with an unprecedented increase in the personal saving rate, reaching 34% in April 2020. While the saving rate subsequently returned to pre-pandemic levels, households amassed a large stock of savings during the pandemic. The difference between that savings and a baseline of what would have been saved in the absence of the pandemic can be thought of as excess savings. If that excess savings was drawn down once the health situation improved, it could be contributing to inflation after the fact. For example, households may be temporarily consuming (at above-trend rates) certain goods or services, such as personal travel, that were forgone in the early stages of the pandemic. How large this effect might be is uncertain. Estimates of excess savings range between \$2.2 trillion and \$2.7 trillion.[72] Most of this excess savings is estimated to be held by higher-income households with lower spending propensities, leaving it unclear if this glut of savings will contribute to inflationary pressures moving forward.[73]

---

[71] For related data, see BEA, *Personal Income and Outlays*, https://www.bea.gov/data/income-saving/personal-income.

[72] A TD Economics report estimates this stock of excess savings at \$2.7 trillion. See Maria Solovieva, *Where the Road of Excess [Saving] Leads*, TD Economics, September 16, 2021, https://economics.td.com/us-excess-savings. A Goldman Sachs newsletter estimates that this excess saving is being held predominantly in bank accounts—which can easily be spent at any time—as opposed to less liquid investments or having been used to pay down household debt. See Joseph Briggs, "The Good and the Bad About the Consumer Spending Outlook," Goldman Sachs, *U.S. Economics Analyst*, March 20, 2022. A Brookings study puts excess saving at \$2.5 trillion and also finds that it is being held predominantly in bank accounts. See Mitchell Barnes et al., *Bolstered Balance Sheets: Assessing Household Finances Since 2019*, Brookings Institution, March 22, 2022, https://www.brookings.edu/research/bolstered-balance-sheets- assessing-household-finances-since-2019.

[73] Joseph Briggs, "The Growth Boost from Excess Savings Is Probably Mostly Behind Us," Goldman Sachs, *U.S. Daily*, August 16, 2022.

Monetary Policy

The Fed has a statutory mandate to achieve maximum employment and stable prices, which it defines as 2% inflation as measured by the PCE. It provides monetary stimulus when employment or prices are below their mandated goals and tightens policy when they are higher. When the pandemic first hit, the unemployment rate spiked and the economy experienced some month-over-month deflation, spurring the Fed to quickly provide monetary stimulus.

The Fed provided monetary stimulus in the spring of 2020 by lowering the FFR (the overnight interbank lending rate and the Fed's main monetary policy tool) to a range of 0%-0.25%, purchasing assets (mainly Treasury securities and mortgage-backed securities), reviving and creating new emergency credit facilities, and encouraging use of the discount window.[74] As a result of these actions, the Federal Reserve's balance sheet expanded from $4.7 trillion on March 19, 2020, to $7 trillion on May 20, 2020, to almost $9 trillion before the Fed started reducing it in June 2022.[75] Thus, the Fed continued to add extraordinary stimulus and liquidity to the economy even as economic conditions significantly improved.

As the economy improved, the Fed waited unusually long to begin withdrawing monetary stimulus that was historically large. Emergency lending facilities were mostly closed at the end of December 2020 or March 2021. The Fed's asset purchases (called "quantitative easing" or "QE") continued at a pace of $120 billion per month until November 2021. Between November 2021 and March 2022, it "tapered" (reduced the pace of) its asset purchases before ending those purchases in March 2022. The Fed began a series of increases in the FFR target on March 16, 2022—the first time that rates were raised above the zero range since the onset of the pandemic. The Fed began gradually reducing the size of its balance sheet in June 2022.

The decision to not begin withdrawing stimulus until March 2022 in reaction to inflation that was already above its 2% target underlines how its strategy for achieving price stability has changed. From the 1980s to the financial crisis, the Fed's strategy for achieving price stability was to tighten monetary policy preemptively before higher inflation had emerged. It believed that this was necessary because of lags in the time it took for a change in

---

[74] For more information on the Federal Reserve's response to the COVID-19 pandemic, see CRS Report R46411, *The Federal Reserve's Response to COVID-19: Policy Issues*, by Marc Labonte.

[75] Federal Reserve, *Credit and Liquidity Programs and the Balance Sheet: Recent Balance Sheet Trends*, https://www.federalreserve.gov/monetarypolicy/bst_recenttrends.htm.

monetary policy to affect inflation and in order to keep inflationary expectations contained. Now, the Fed decided to wait until after higher inflation had proven to be persistent to raise rates.

The decision to wait until March 2022 to start withdrawing stimulus had at least three motivations. First, the Fed did not want to jeopardize the fledgling recovery. Second, it initially believed that inflation was caused by supply disruptions that would prove transitory. Finally, it reflected a strategy announced in 2020 to achieve an average inflation target of 2% that features periods of above 2% inflation to compensate for periods of below 2% inflation. Because inflation was below 2% by the Fed's preferred measure (PCE) in most years since the 2007-2009 financial crisis, the Fed saw a period of inflation modestly above 2% as desirable to help break the cycle of persistently low inflation. As part of this strategy, the Fed also stated that it would no longer tighten monetary policy in response to unemployment that was below the natural rate.[76] Through December 2021, when the unemployment rate was 3.9%, the Fed stated that it did not intend to raise interest rates above zero "until labor market conditions have reached levels consistent with the committee's assessments of maximum."[77]

While the Fed was focused on risks to withdrawing stimulus too soon, there were also risks of waiting too long that are now making it harder to control inflation today. Arguably, inflation had become embedded in the economy before the Fed decided to start withdrawing stimulus. While expectations of inflation in five years are fairly stable (the median five-year ahead expected inflation rate was 2.35% in July 2022), one-year expectations remain high (at 6.2% in July 2022),[78] which could signal that lowering inflation might prove challenging in the short term (and costly if Fed actions result in a recession). If individuals stop believing that the Fed is committed to low inflation, it makes it harder for the Fed to achieve low inflation, because it keeps inflationary expectations anchored.

---

[76] Federal Reserve, "Review of Monetary Policy Strategy, Tools, and Communications," https://www.federalreserve.gov/monetarypolicy/review-of-monetary-policy-strategy-tools-and-communications.htm.

[77] Federal Reserve, *Federal Reserve Issues FOMC Statement*, press release, December 15, 2021, https://www.federalreserve.gov/monetarypolicy/files/monetary20211215a1.pdf.

[78] Federal Reserve Bank of New York, *Survey of Consumer Expectations*, https://www.newyorkfed.org/ microeconomics/sce#/.

Money Supply Growth and Inflation

Some commentators attribute high inflation to monetary policy based on a "monetarist" explanation of inflation— that inflation rises when the money supply persistently and significantly outpaces the demand for money. The Fed's policies during the pandemic have been mostly financed by a rapid increase in the monetary base (currency and bank reserves), notably its monthly purchases of Treasury securities and mortgage-backed securities until March 2022. Increases in the monetary base can lead to increases in the broader money supply, and one measure of the money supply (M2) increased 27% from February 2020 to February 2021 and an additional 11% in the 12 months after that. Since then, the growth rate of M2 has been around its historical average.[79] However, rapid increases in the money supply (albeit not as rapid as the growth between February and May 2020) did not result in higher inflation during the Great Recession, and the Fed has introduced new tools, such as paying interest on bank reserves and the Overnight Reverse Repurchase Agreement Facility, to contain inflationary pressures caused by growth in the monetary base.[80] In the Fed's view, the growth in the money supply to date has few implications for inflation.[81]

Supply Disruptions in 2022

As mentioned above, the pandemic has disrupted the production of many goods and services. Various indicators show a surge in labor shortages, supply shortages, and logistic/transport constraints causing U.S. manufacturers to operate below capacity.[82] Although those disruptions have greatly waned since spring 2020, some continue to constrain production, exacerbating inflationary pressures. In 2021, 60% of small businesses surveyed reported supply chain

---

[79] M1, a narrower measure of the money supply, cannot be used over this time period, because a definitional change to include savings accounts caused it to quadruple.

[80] The Fed's goal in expanding the monetary base was to put downward pressure on interest rates and, in the spring of 2020, prevent a liquidity crisis by flooding the financial system with liquidity. It does not assess its policies based on their effect on the money supply.

[81] Federal Reserve, *Historical Approaches to Monetary Policy*, https://www.federalreserve.gov/monetarypolicy/historical-approaches-to-monetary-policy.htm.

[82] Federal Reserve, *Monetary Policy Report*, June 2022, p. 8, https://www.federalreserve.gov/monetarypolicy/files/ 20220617_mprfullreport.pdf.

issues to be one of their top operational challenges.[83] The belief that supply disruptions would prove transitory did not come to fruition, as in 2022 alone, supply has been constrained by ongoing labor shortages (discussed in the next section), temporary business disruptions linked to COVID- 19 outbreaks, and commodity shortages linked to the 2022 Russian invasion of Ukraine.

Pandemic-related shutdowns and production delays worldwide have caused a chain reaction of delays in the availability of products across a wide range of industries. Product availability has been disrupted for both final products sought by consumers and inputs used by American producers. Earlier shutdowns created backlogs that have taken months to unwind.

Supply chains are global, and a product can pass through several countries before reaching the United States.[84] A delay or disruption in any one of those countries can therefore cause supply problems for the United States. Different countries have experienced different kinds of production disruptions and at different times compared to the United States, with some countries lifting or re- imposing lockdowns and other work restrictions at different times than when such changes occurred in the United States. Global supply chain disruptions have improved significantly since peaking in December 2021 but remain higher than at any period before the pandemic.[85]

Shipping and U.S. port disruptions have also caused delays in imports arriving and being processed in the United States.[86] This could raise the cost of imports, which could feed through to overall inflation.[87] After falling early in the pandemic, import prices have risen more quickly than overall inflation has (13.2% compared to 8.9% in the second quarter of 2022).[88]

The complexity of global supply chains has led to unexpected problems—for example, disruptions in semiconductor (microprocessor) production. With the proliferation of smart devices, microchips are now found in numerous

---

[83] Federal Reserve, *Small Business Credit Survey*, 2022, https://www.fedsmallbusiness.org/medialibrary/ FedSmallBusiness/files/2021/2022-sbcs-employer-firms-report.

[84] See CRS Report R46641, *Global Value Chains: Overview and Issues for Congress*, coordinated by Rachel F. Fefer; and IMF, "Global Trade and Value Chains During the Pandemic," in *World Economic Outlook*, ch. 4, April 2022.

[85] See Federal Reserve Bank of New York, "Global Supply Chain Pressure Index," https://www.newyorkfed.org/ research/policy/gscpi#/interactive. Their series starts in 1998.

[86] See CRS Insight IN11800, *Supply Chain Bottlenecks at U.S. Ports*, by John Frittelli and Liana Wong.

[87] Maggie Isaacson and Hannah Rubinton, *Shipping Prices and Import Price Inflation*, Federal Reserve Bank of St. Louis, August 2022, https://doi.org/10.20955/wp.2022.017.

[88] BEA, *Gross Domestic Product (Second Estimate), Corporate Profits (Preliminary Estimate), Second Quarter 2022*, August 25, 2022, https://www.bea.gov/sites/default/files/2022-08/gdp2q22_2nd.pdf.

types of consumer goods, including household appliances and vehicles. As a result, supply disruptions have emerged across a range of products. For example, microchip shortages contributed to a 2.3 million shortfall in new automobiles produced in 2021 in North America, because each automobile contains an average of 298 semiconductors.[89] As a result, demand for new automobiles outpaced supply, causing a spillover into the used auto market, and 12-month inflation peaked at 45% for used automobiles in June 2021 and 13% for new automobiles in April 2022. Disruptions have since eased somewhat, with used auto prices declining (but still above pre-pandemic prices) in 2022. New auto prices have continued to rise rapidly in 2022, however.

The 2022 Russian invasion of Ukraine has resulted in a new set of supply shocks, increasing the world prices of energy and certain foods, metals, and other commodities and disrupting trade patterns.[90] While the war continues, some of the initial supply shocks have had lessening effects on inflation over time and could eventually become deflationary if they continue to fall. For example, after spiking in the immediate aftermath of the invasion, gas prices fell by 7.7% in July 2022 and 10.6% in August 2022.[91] Nonetheless, this conflict may still result in relatively long- lasting supply shocks that complicate efforts to achieve low inflation and full employment.[92]

Individual supply disruptions, supply shocks, and bottlenecks are, by their nature, likely to be temporary and therefore would cause only a temporary increase in inflation. Many specific problems have already shown

---

[89] See CRS In Focus IF12000, Semiconductor Shortage Constrains Vehicle Production, by Manpreet Singh.

[90] Of note, the CPI does not directly include the price of most raw materials such as metal or other commodities, as these are not goods typically purchased by consumers. However, the prices of raw materials faced by producers tend to be reflected in the prices of final goods and services purchased by consumers.

[91] BLS, *Consumer Price Index Summary*, August 10, 2022, https://www.bls.gov/news.release/cpi.nr0.htm.

[92] Initial estimates of the effects of the Russian invasion of Ukraine vary. The Organisation for Economic Co-operation and Development (OECD) projected that if the supply shocks lasted for one year, they would reduce U.S. growth by almost one percentage point and raise U.S. inflation by almost 1.5 percentage points in the first full year. See OECD, "Economic and Social Impacts and Policy Implications of the War in Ukraine," March 2022, https://www.oecd.org/ economic-outlook/#gdp-inflation-impact. Other research from the Federal Reserve suggests that, compared to a scenario in which the invasion did not take place, the war may reduce the level of global GDP about 1.5% and increase global inflation by about 1.3 percentage points. See Dario Caldara et al., "The Effect of the War in Ukraine on Global Activity and Inflation," *FEDS Notes*, May 27, 2022, https://www.federalreserve.gov/econres/notes/feds-notes/the-effect-of-the-war-in-ukraine-on-global-activity-and-inflation-20220527.htm.

improvement. A close look at the price of any one good or servicetends to be explainable by certain unique factors. But nearly every major category in the CPI has shown an above-average increase at some point. When added together, these various factors that are ubiquitous and persistent indicate that in the aggregate they are actually being driven by a supply-demand imbalance and point to a more general and longer lasting overheating of the economy.

The Post-Pandemic Labor Market

Another sign of the current supply-demand imbalance in the economy is the tight labor market and labor shortages. Labor demand is high—employment has increased at a rapid pace in all but one month since May 2020—yet employers are still unable to fill job openings and retain employees at a more historically normal rate. Their struggles are caused in part because the labor supply is low by historical standards. As of July 2022, the unemployment rate and level of payroll employment had returned to pre-pandemic levels.[93] However, as a percentage of the population, both employment and labor force participation are still lagging, resulting in a relatively smaller labor force than before the pandemic began.

Ultimately, the divergence between the unemployment rate and the employment/population ratio reflects the decline in labor force participation. The pandemic caused an unusually large decline in the labor force participation rate (LFPR), which is the percentage of the working-age population that is either working (employed) or actively looking for work (unemployed). The LFPR was 63.4% in February 2020 before the pandemic began and fell to 60.2% in April 2020. It has rebounded more slowly than the unemployment rate since and has only partially recovered to 62.1% as of July 2022, which is still lower than at any point between the 1970s and the start of the pandemic. This suggests that if workers could be brought back into the labor force, there appears to be significant room for employment to grow. However, the likelihood of this occurring is highly uncertain. For example, much of the decline is driven by retirements, which for many workers is a permanent decision, so it is uncertain if many older workers will reenter the

[93] BLS, *Employment Situation Summary*, August 5, 2022, https://www.bls.gov/news.release/empsit.nr0.htm.

labor force.[94] Worryingly, the LFPR has shown no upward trend in 2022 despite the booming job market.

The relatively low supply of available workers (i.e., low unemployment rate and low LFPR), combined with the relatively high demand for labor by businesses, has resulted in a tight labor market.[95] The job openings rate and worker quits rate additionally both remain considerably elevated compared to pre-pandemic rates and significantly higher than when unemployment reached lows in 2000, 2007, and 2020.[96] As of June 2022, the job openings rate was 6.6%, and the quits rate was 2.8%, compared, respectively, to 4.4% and 2.3% in February 2020.[97] Since May 2021, there has been more than one job opening per unemployed worker, as shown in Figure 5. In 2021, 60% of small businesses surveyed reported hiring or retaining qualified employees to be one of their top operational challenges.[98]

Labor market tightness may be contributing to inflationary pressures. Some commentators have warned of a "wage-price spiral."[99] Wage growth has accelerated since 2021 but to date has been lower than overall inflation (although wage growth has been notably stronger than average for periods in certain industries such as leisure and hospitality). For example, the Federal Reserve Bank of Atlanta wage growth tracker reached its highest growth rate

---

[94] A recent Goldman Sachs newsletter attributed 1.9 million of the labor force shortfall to retirements and 1.4 million to workers under age 55. David Mericle, "Taming Inflation Without a Recession: A Progress Report," Goldman Sachs, August 14, 2022, https://publishing.gs.com/content/research/en/reports/2022/08/15/85315ba4-5859-41ea-b7d7- cf2a654d4fda.html.

[95] For a more in-depth analysis of current labor market trends and labor market tightness, see CRS Insight IN11770, *Labor Market Tightness and the Economic Recovery, Part 1*, by Marc Labonte and Lida R. Weinstock; and CRS Insight IN11771, *Labor Market Tightness and the Economic Recovery, Part 2*, by Marc Labonte and Lida R. Weinstock.

[96] These data series begin in December 2000, so today's data can be compared only to the very end of the 1991-2001 expansion. For more information, see CRS Insight IN11770, *Labor Market Tightness and the Economic Recovery, Part 1*, by Marc Labonte and Lida R. Weinstock; and CRS Insight IN11771, *Labor Market Tightness and the Economic Recovery, Part 2*, by Marc Labonte and Lida R. Weinstock.

[97] For data on job openings and turnover, see BLS, *Job Openings and Labor Turnover Survey*, https://www.bls.gov/jlt/.

[98] Federal Reserve, *Small Business Credit Survey*, 2022, https://www.fedsmallbusiness.org/medialibrary/FedSmallBusiness/files/2021/2022-sbcs-employer-firms-report.

[99] For example, a recent BIS paper discusses the potential for a wage-price spiral and several factors affecting the likelihood of such an event, including the relatively low current correlation between wage growth and inflation, declines in bargaining power and cost-of-living-adjustment coverage, increases in pricing power on the part of firms, and increasing inflation expectations. See Frederic Boissay et al., "Are Major Advanced Economies on the Verge of a Wage-Price Spiral?," *BIS Bulletin*, vol. 53 (May 4, 2022), https://www.bis.org/publ/bisbull53.pdf.

since data was first collected in 1997 (6.7% for the three-month average for June 2022), but that is still lower than the PCE for June (6.8%).[100] In other words, although nominal wages are rising, inflation-adjusted wages are falling. But if all employers continually raise wages beyond the productivity gains of workers, it could eventually result in a wage-price spiral that could make it harder to restore price stability. In that regard, the recent decline in productivity growth could be problematic if it continues. Labor productivity has declined in three of the past four quarters.

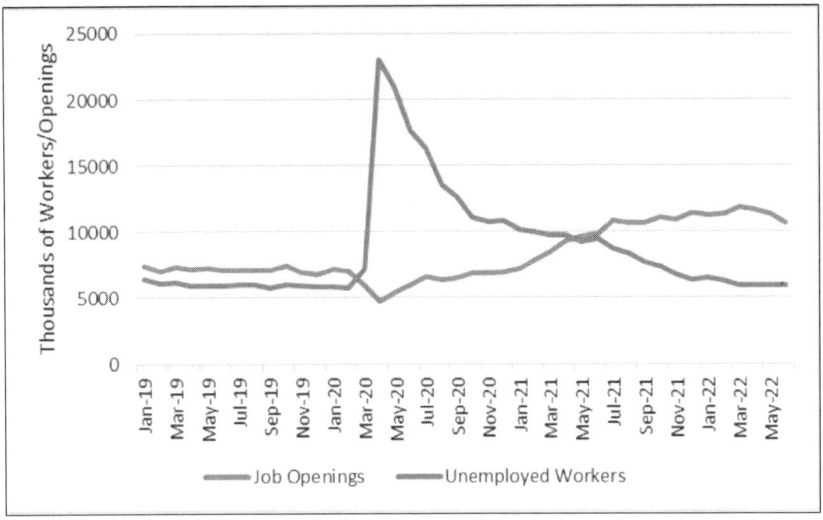

Source: Bureau of Labor Statistics, Current Population Survey and Job Openings and Labor Turnover Survey.

Notes: Data are seasonally adjusted.

Figure 5. Job Openings vs.Workers. January 2019 to June 2022.

Demand in 2022

If high inflation is attributable to a supply-demand imbalance, how much of that imbalance is being caused by rising demand? Several indicators suggest that aggregate demand bounced back strongly after collapsing during the onset of the pandemic. A large part of that aggregate demand recovery was due to a

[100] There are several different measurements of wage growth. The Atlanta Fed's measure was chosen because it tracks wage growth for the same individual over time. Available at https://www.atlantafed.org/chcs/wage-growth-tracker? panel=1.

bounce back in private demand, some of which may still be occurring. As the economy reopened and health restrictions were removed, real final sales to private domestic purchasers (i.e., spending by U.S. businesses and households) grew at an annualized rate of almost 17% from the third quarter of 2020 through the second quarter of 2021. Much of this represented "catch up" growth after the large decline in output in the second quarter of 2020. As discussed above, personal income and personal saving rose during the pandemic as a result of fiscal stimulus, which created pent-up demand that was later released when economic conditions normalized and households could spend on a full range of goods and services again. Spending was also stimulated by low interest rates, as discussed above. It is difficult to disentangle how much of private demand growth was spurred by fiscal and monetary stimulus compared to growth that occurred independently because of the rebound in economic prospects and sentiment.

Since that catch up growth was completed, real final sales growth has averaged less than 2% over the past four quarters. This slowdown is seen across consumption and investment categories, with the exception of spending on services, which continues to grow rapidly, as it was the last category to rebound from the pandemic due to social distancing. In the second quarter of 2022, real final sales to private domestic purchasers grew at 0.5%, which may indicate that the removal of fiscal and monetary stimulus and deteriorating consumer and business confidence are starting to weigh on spending. The most interest-sensitive categories of spending—consumer durables, business fixed investment, and residential investment—all declined in the second quarter of 2022. If demand is cooling, it may begin to relieve inflationary pressures, assuming that inflationary expectations have not become unmoored and the economy does not experience further supply shocks.

The interaction of demand and inflation can be seen when comparing real to nominal data— nominal final sales to private domestic purchasers has continued to grow rapidly in the past four quarters, averaging almost 9% annualized. In other words, U.S. households and businesses have continued to increase spending at a rapid rate over the past four quarters, but inflation has reduced their purchasing power.

How quickly reduced demand can translate into lower inflation depends in part on how much the economy has "overheated," which can be measured in terms of how much the economy overshot potential GDP (i.e., how much the economy is capable of producing at full employment). This is hard to ascertain, because it is difficult to determine how much the pandemic might have reduced potential GDP and how long it would take for potential GDP to recover from pandemic disruptions.[101] If potential GDP had been unaffected by the pandemic, it would not appear that GDP had risen enough to cause significant overheating. The fact that the economy nonetheless seems to have overheated suggests that potential GDP may have reduced. In terms of the labor market, the historically low unemployment rate coupled with the decades-low LFPR (as discussed above) would also indicate overheating in the presence of reduced potential.

Policy Options for Congress

Given that inflation results from an imbalance between aggregate supply and aggregate demand, ultimately the two ways to rein in inflation through policy are to increase aggregate supply or decrease aggregate demand (or a combination of both). Aggregate demand is generally easier to adjust in the short term than is aggregate supply. For this reason, historically, the most effective policy tool to combat inflation has been monetary policy, specifically increasing interest rates. In the words of Fed Chair Powell, "The first lesson [from the history of inflation] is that central banks can and should take responsibility for delivering low and stable inflation."[102] However, fiscal policy can also lower aggregate demand by decreasing the budget deficit. Monetary policy can typically be enacted much more quickly than fiscal policy can, allowing the Fed to raise interest rates whenever it chooses. However, interest rates are a fairly blunt tool, and their use to control inflation in the past has often resulted in recession. The fact that inflationary problems are partly caused by supply shocks that reduce output (relative to trend) unfortunately means that policies that try to offset the reduction in growth and income can inadvertently make inflation worse. This section reviews policy options and considerations from the perspective of economic theory and current conditions. The success of historical policies aimed at lowering inflation is also discussed. One theme of this review is that, as economic theory would predict, policies that do not or cannot reduce supply-demand imbalances have either failed to reduce inflation or only temporarily restrained

---

[101] John Fernald and Huiyu Li, "The Impact of COVID on Productivity and Potential Output," Federal Reserve Bank of San Francisco, September 2022, https://doi.org/10.24148/wp2022-19.

[102] Jerome H. Powell, Chair, Federal Reserve, "Monetary Policy and Price Stability," August 26, 2022, https://www.federalreserve.gov/newsevents/speech/powell20220826a.htm.

price pressures, which then caused a surge in inflation when the policies were lifted.

Removing Fiscal and Monetary Stimulus

Fiscal and monetary stimulus helped expedite a return to full employment when unemployment was high in 2020 and 2021. Yet, despite labor market tightness and low unemployment indicating the economy has been at—or close to—full employment since late 2021, policy remains stimulative at present.[103] Although the removal of fiscal and monetary stimulus has already begun, the decision to "wait and see" rather than tighten when inflation first emerged in 2021 meant that the remaining monetary stimulus will not be removed until at least 2023 and the budget deficit remains relatively large under current policy.

Stimulative policy is inconsistent with returning to price stability—regardless of why inflation is high—at full employment. At full employment with low inflation, a neutral fiscal and monetary policy (i.e., a policy that neither stimulates nor constrains demand) may be appropriate. At full employment with high inflation, contractionary fiscal and monetary policy that curbs demand may be required to reduce inflation, especially if expectations of high inflation have become endemic.

Policymakers still express hope (and forecast) that inflation will be relatively easy to reduce on the grounds that, after 40 previous years of persistently low inflation, households will view the last year as an anomaly and will therefore be easy to convince to keep their expectations of future inflation low. This was not the case in the 1970s, however, when inflation remained high even during economic slowdowns. Once expectations incorporate higher inflation as permanent, inflation would be expected to stay high even if the economy were no longer growing rapidly and unemployment were not unusually low.

The recently enacted Inflation Reduction Act (P.L. 117-2) is aimed at reducing inflation by reducing budget deficits, among other goals. CBO projected that under an earlier version of the bill, "In calendar year 2022,

---

[103] Although overall employment is still relatively low because of the low LFPR, in this context unemployment may be a better gauge of full employment, as it indicates excess demand for labor. The low LFPR, by contrast, appears to reflect an inadequate supply of labor.

enacting the bill would have a negligible effect on inflation, in CBO's assessment. In calendar year 2023, inflation would probably be between 0.1 percentage point lower and 0.1 percentage point higher under the bill than it would be under current law."[104] That is because, in part, the earlier bill's effect on the deficit in 2022 and 2023 was small relative to GDP, although according to CBO, the bill was expected to reduce deficits over the 2022-2031 period.[105]

This points to the challenge of addressing inflation using fiscal policy: Economic models suggest that very large changes in short-term deficits are needed to generate significant reductions in inflation. For that reason, the mainstream consensus among economists is that fiscal policy takes a secondary role to monetary policy in achieving price stability. Monetary policy changes can be made more quickly and precisely than fiscal policy changes can (in theory and practice) and have a more direct relationship with inflation, as the Fed directly influences the money supply, so the Fed is widely seen as taking the leading role in addressing inflation.

The Federal Reserve and Interest Rates

Since the Fed began raising interest rates and stopped purchasing assets in March 2022, monetary policy has become less stimulative, but it nevertheless remains highly stimulative at present. The Fed waited longer than usual after a recession to start tightening and waited to raise rates until it had very gradually phased out asset purchases. As a result, to move to a neutral or contractionary monetary stance, it must now first make up lost ground.[106] The Fed started its planned gradual reduction in its $8.9 trillion balance sheet in June, but liquidity will likely remain abundant for some time. Meanwhile, by historical standards, interest rates remain unusually low.

After adjusting for inflation, the FFR is currently negative in real terms, meaning investors' compensation when repaid has less real purchasing power than did the amount initially lent out. In fact, as inflation rose, real rates became more negative and thus more expansionary through March 2022, as economic activity is generally influenced by real rates. Since then, rates have risen but remain negative. Because inflation varies by measure, the size of the

---

[104] CBO, *Letter to Honorable Lindsey Graham*, August 4, 2022, https://www.budget.senate.gov/imo/media/doc/58357- Graham.pdf.

[105] CBO, Estimated Budgetary Effects of H.R. 5376, the Inflation Reduction Act of 2022, as Amended in the Nature of a Substitute (ERN22335) and Posted on the Website of the Senate Majority Leader on July 27, 2022, August 5, 2022, https://www.cbo.gov/system/files/2022-08/hr5376_IR_Act_8-3-22.pdf. To date, CBO has not provided a budget estimate of the version of the bill that was signed into law.

[106] See CRS Insight IN11868, *The Federal Reserve and Inflation*, by Marc Labonte.

difference between nominal interest rates and real interest rates today depends on the measure used. If inflation (as measured by PCE) stays at 6%, with a FFR of 3% currently, the real rate would be -3%.

Alternatively, if inflation for the year meets the Fed's projection of 5.5%, then the real rate would currently be -2.5%.[107]

Economists have theorized that there is a neutral rate of short-term interest rates where monetary policy is neither stimulative nor contractionary. Prior to the 2007-2009 financial crisis, the neutral rate was thought to be about 2% after adjusting for inflation (i.e., 2% plus the prevailing inflation rate.) Following the financial crisis, there was evidence that the neutral rate was variable over time and had fallen in the past decade.[108] One well-known estimate has it falling to around 0.5% during the pandemic.[109] Using the inflation assumptions above, the Fed would need to raise interest rates from 2.3% to between 4.8% and 7.5% just to achieve a neutral monetary policy— assuming the real neutral rate is still 0.5%—or 6.3% to 9.0% if the neutral rate returned to 2% as pandemic-related factors waned.[110] If contractionary policy is needed instead to reduce inflation, interest rates need to be higher than the neutral rate to restore price stability.

By contrast, Fed leadership is now projecting that an appropriate FFR in real terms would be negative at the end of 2022 and almost 2% at the end of 2023. In other words, Fed officials believe monetary policy should still be stimulative—but less so than it is today—through 2022. Although monetary policy would remain stimulative in this projection, they project that this will cause inflation to fall to a range of 2.4% to 4.1% in 2023 with little increase in unemployment— the "soft landing" scenario.[111] Critics have questioned how the Fed expects inflation to fall so quickly without a sizable increase in unemployment.[112] Gradual policy changes are more likely to result in a soft landing but are also more likely to fail to put a dent in inflation given the

---

[107] Federal Open Market Committee, *Summary of Economic Projections*, June 15, 2022, https://www.federalreserve.gov/monetarypolicy/files/fomcprojtabl20220615.pdf.

[108] For more information, see CRS Insight IN11056, *Low Interest Rates, Part 2: Implications for the Federal Reserve*, by Marc Labonte.

[109] Federal Reserve Bank of New York, *Measuring the Natural Rate of Interest*, at https://www.newyorkfed.org/ research/policy/rstar.

[110] Because CPI is higher than PCE, if CPI is a more accurate measure of "true" inflation, rates need to be higher than these estimates to achieve the same economic outcomes.

[111] Federal Open Market Committee, *Summary of Economic Projections*, September 21, 2022, https://www.federalreserve.gov/monetarypolicy/files/fomcprojtabl20220921.pdf.

[112] Laurence Ball, Daniel Leigh, and Prachi Mishra, *Understanding U.S. Inflation During the COVID Era*, Brookings Institution, August 2022, https://www.brookings.edu/wp-content/uploads/2022/09/Ball-et-al-Conference-Draft-BPEA- FA22.pdf.

amount of tightening still required at this point just to return policy to neutral. Thus, there is the risk that successfully avoiding a mild recession now could lead to worse outcomes down the road.

Alternatively, if expectations of high inflation have become entrenched and inflation enters a wage-price spiral, so much tightening could be required to restore price stability that a "hard landing," where the economy enters a recession, would result. The Fed could also inadvertently trigger a hard landing by tightening too quickly, even if high inflation expectations are not endemic. It remains to be seen whether the Fed would be willing to continue to pursue low inflation if the economy were to return to recession. For more information, see CRS Insight IN11963, *Where Is the U.S. Economy Headed: Soft Landing, Hard Landing, or Stagflation?* by Marc Labonte and Lida R. Weinstock.

Targeting Supply Chains

Another option for policymakers to address current inflation is to increase aggregate supply. However, policy options to alleviate supply disruptions can be ineffective at reducing inflation in the short run because they are time-consuming to implement, frequently require the private sector to respond to incentives to be successful, and, depending on how they are financed, could even make inflation worse by adding to aggregate demand.

Capacity constraints causing bottlenecks can typically be relieved through new infrastructure investments. However, by nature, those investments are long-term projects that cannot bring new capacity on line quickly. At the same time, increased infrastructure investment could exacerbate labor and supply shortages in the short run, as the infrastructure projects themselves require labor, commodities, and other inputs. In 2021, the Infrastructure Investment and Jobs Act (P.L. 117-58) was enacted to boost public infrastructure investment, and the Administration has set goals to increase investment in port and waterway infrastructure.[113]

Firms with bottlenecks in production and distribution caused by labor shortages face the same hiring and retention challenges as other firms do. Reversing historically low U.S. labor force participation rates has been a

[113] The White House, *FACT SHEET: The Biden-Harris Action Plan for America's Ports and Waterways*, November 9, 2021, https://www.whitehouse.gov/briefing-room/statements-releases/2021/11/09/fact-sheet-the-biden-harris-action-plan-for-americas-ports-and-waterways/.

challenging policy issue.[114] While COVID-related constraints on participation may have been driving much of the decrease earlier in the pandemic, at this point, much of the drop in participation is due to retirements that have traditionally proven hard to reverse.[115]

Current supply chain problems are also difficult for U.S. policy to address due to their global nature. Lockdowns in China and the Ukraine invasion demonstrate that foreign supply disruptions due to the pandemic, foreign governments' policies, or both are largely beyond U.S. influence.

Policy options to work around these disruptions are more long-term in nature. Unfortunately, disruptions caused by the invasion could reduce growth without constraining price inflation.

The Biden Administration has implemented some targeted micro-policies and plans to alleviate supply chain bottlenecks but is limited legally in what it can do without statutory changes. For more information, see CRS Insight IN11926, *Supply Disruptions and the U.S. Economy*, by Marc Labonte and Lida R. Weinstock.

Income Relief Policies

When prices of key goods such as food or gasoline rise, policymakers sometimes suggest providing broad relief to affected households through gas tax holidays, rebates, temporary tax cuts, and so on. These proposals are sometimes made on equity grounds, which is beyond the scope of this report to evaluate. However, they disrupt market adjustment, thereby reducing economic efficiency. Price increases in the marketplace signal greater scarcity and induce a reduction in demand to adapt to that scarcity. In terms of their effect on inflation, they are doubly counterproductive—they further stimulate demand by boosting after-tax incomes and, when targeted to the product that has risen in price, they increase demand for the commodity whose price rise contributed to inflation in the first place. Since the commodity's price has risen because of increased scarcity, an increase in demand would be likely to

[114] For more information, see CRS Insight IN11711, *The Post-Pandemic Labor Market and Rising Inflation*, by Lida R. Weinstock.

[115] Federal Reserve, *Monetary Policy Report*, February 25, 2022, https://www.federalreserve.gov/monetarypolicy/files/20220225_mprfullreport.pdf.

translate largely into further price increases, because supply has already proven to be unable to increase in response to higher prices.[116]

Corporate Profits

Some commentators have argued that inflation has risen in part because corporations have raised prices to increase profits.[117] (Although the debate is often framed in terms of corporate profits, it should be noted that many businesses are unincorporated.) In general, theory and evidence suggest that corporations seek to maximize profits and will charge the price that does so based on various factors. Given that corporations are typically always seeking to maximize profits, it is unclear in this explanation why they would choose to wait until inflation is high to raise prices sufficiently to increase profits and not have done so previously. Some commentators have suggested that corporations have taken advantage of the high inflation environment to raise prices more than necessary to cover increased costs while being shielded from criticism.[118]

Higher prices alone are not sufficient evidence to establish that profits have risen. Corporations could also be raising prices with no increase in profits because their inputs of labor, capital, and raw material have risen in cost because of inflation. Finally, sustained inflation represents continually rising prices, but corporations cannot continually raise prices to boost profits without reducing demand for their products, inducing competitors to undercut their sales, and so on. Thus, higher profits could potentially explain a one-time increase in prices but not the continual increase in general prices that occurs in a sustained inflationary period like the present.

---

[116] For more information, see CRS Insight IN11879, *Potential Impacts of a Federal Gasoline Tax Moratorium*, by Anthony A. Cilluffo and Robert S. Kirk.

[117] Josh Bivens, *Corporate Profits Have Contributed Disproportionately to Inflation. How Should Policymakers Respond?*, Economic Policy Institute, April 21, 2022, https://www.epi.org/blog/corporate-profits-have-contributed-disproportionately-to-inflation-how-should-policymakers-respond/.

[118] One study found that while increased prices in an industry are often associated with increasing corporate profits, it did not find evidence that higher inflation resulted in higher profits. See Mathias Andler and Anna Kovner, *Do Corporate Profits Increase When Inflation Increases?*, Federal Reserve Bank of New York, July 13, 2022, https://libertystreeteconomics.newyorkfed.org/2022/07/do-corporate-profits-increase-when-inflation-increases/.

Trade Liberalization

The United States and its trading partners have imposed a number of new trade barriers, such as tariffs, on each other in recent years, many of which remain in place at present.[119] Trade barriers work by raising the prices of imports, directly or indirectly, which in turn may raise the prices of import-competing goods or domestic goods and services that use imports as intermediate inputs. All of these goods and services appear in the baskets of different inflation indices, so when their prices rise, overall inflation rises, if other prices are assumed to stay constant.[120]

Conversely, reducing import barriers could theoretically reduce the prices of these goods and services. Thus, some have proposed trade liberalization as a policy option to reduce U.S. inflation.[121] As a practical matter, using trade policy to reduce inflation would be limited in size because imports are equal in value to about 16% of GDP (and so make up a limited amount of any price index basket), and tariffs and trade barriers vary by product type but are mostly low, so there are limits on potential reductions. Further, reducing trade barriers would result in only a one-time reduction in prices, whereas current inflation can be characterized as a continual increase in prices.[122]

Harder to quantify, liberalizing trade could increase competition in domestic markets and among domestic producers. This could boost the supply side of the economy in the long run, helping to alleviate the supply-demand imbalance that is driving high inflation. For example, a Peterson Institute for International Economics study estimates that a 2 percentage point tariff-equivalent reduction would result in a one-time 1.3 percentage point reduction in CPI, comprised of a 0.2 percentage point direct effect through lower import prices and a 1.1 percentage point reduction in domestic prices through its

---

[119] See CRS Report R45529, Trump Administration Tariff Actions: Frequently Asked Questions, coordinated by Brock R. Williams.

[120] See Mary Amiti, Sebastian Heise, and Noah Kwicklis, "The Impact of Import Tariffs on U.S. Domestic Prices," Federal Reserve Bank of New York, January 4, 2019, https://libertystreeteconomics.newyorkfed.org/2019/01/the- impact-of-import-tariffs-on-us-domestic-prices.html.

[121] Jeffrey Frankel, "How Liberalizing Economic Trade Could Reduce Inflation and Supply Chain Woes," *Los Angeles Times*, June 21, 2022, https://www.latimes.com/opinion/story/2022-06-21/trade-inflation-tariffs-supply-chain.

[122] How quickly the tariff reduction resulted in lower consumer prices would depend on how quickly businesses passed through lower prices to consumers.

effect on competition.[123] Although beyond the scope of this report, liberalizing trade would have other positive effects on overall economic growth and efficiency, as well as redistributive effects on different actors within the economy (i.e., there would be "winners" and "losers" from policy changes).

Historical Policies

Over the years, policymakers have taken several kinds of policy action to lower inflation, but few have ultimately proven successful. Several of the policies discussed in this section were enacted during the Great Inflation era. However, it was not until the Federal Reserve began aggressive monetary policy tightening under the leadership of Paul Volcker (1979-1987) that inflation fell and remained low. As a result, most economists credit monetary policy with ending the Great Inflation.

Price Controls

Office of Price Administration

Executive Order 8734 established the Office of Price Administration and Civilian Supply (OPACS) on April 11, 1941.[124] The title of OPACS was changed to the Office of Price Administration (OPA) by Executive Order 8875 on August 28, 1941.[125] The purpose of OPA was to stabilize prices and rents by establishing price ceilings for commodities (except agricultural commodities) and rents. Additionally, OPA was authorized to implement rations and subsidies for scarce and essential commodities. OPA was abolished effective as of May 29, 1947.[126]

---

[123] Gary Clyde Hufbauer, Megan Hogan, and Yilin Wang, *For Inflation Relief, the United States Should Look to Trade Liberalization*, Peterson Institute for International Economics, March 2022, https://www.piie.com/sites/default/files/ documents/pb22-4.pdf.

[124] UC Santa Barbara: The American Presidency Project, *Executive Order 8734 Establishing the Office of Price Administration and Civilian Supply*, https://www.presidency.ucsb.edu/ documents/executive-order-8734-establishing-the-office-price-administration-and-civilian-supply.

[125] UC Santa Barbara: The American Presidency Project, *Executive Order 8875 Establishing the Supply Priorities and Allocations Board*, https://www.presidency.ucsb.edu/documents/ executive-order-8875-establishing-the-supply-priorities-and-allocations-board.

[126] National Archives, *Records of the Office of Price Administration*, https://www. archives.gov/research/guide-fed- records/groups/188.html.

The effectiveness of OPA is debated.[127] Average annual inflation between 1941 and 1947 (and for a few years thereafter) was relatively high, although significantly lower than during World War I.

Annual inflation was relatively low throughout most of the 1950s, although this was likely a result of a recession in the late 1940s, as opposed to actions taken by the OPA before it was abolished. Of note, during the time period in question, the Federal Reserve was working under a different context and without the congressionally mandated goal of price stability (which Congress mandated in 1977). It was not until 1951 that interest rate controls were ended and the Fed was given more freedom to control inflation via monetary policy.[128] Finally, the primary purpose of OPA was to support the war effort, which required major disruptions in economic activity. Therefore, the economic and policy context in which OPA was created is not necessarily analogous to the context of today.

Nixon-Era Controls

In an attempt to lower inflation without causing an increase in unemployment, the Nixon Administration enacted price controls. Pursuant to the Economic Stabilization Act of 1970 (P.L. 91-379),[129] which gave the President the authority to impose price controls to fight inflation, President Nixon signed Executive Order 11615 to impose a 90-day freeze on prices, rents, and earnings.[130] The controls were then extended by Executive Order 11627, which specified that the authority to stabilize rents, wages, and salaries would remain "for so long as the Economic Stabilization Act, as amended, is in effect or until such other time as the President may hereafter prescribe."[131] These controls artificially put a price ceiling on most goods and services, rents, and

---

127 Meg Jacobs, "'How About Some Meat?:' The Office of Price Administration, Consumption Politics, and State Building from the Bottom Up, 1941-1946," *Journal of American History*, vol. 84, no. 3 (December 1997), pp. 910-941, https://www.jstor.org/stable/2953088; Andrew Bartels, "The Office of Price Administration and the Legacy of the New Deal, 1939-1946," *Public Historian*, vol. 5, no. 3 (1983), pp. 5-29, https://www.jstor. org/stable/ 3377026.

128 Federal Reserve, *Overview: The History of the Federal Reserve*, https://www.federal reservehistory.org/essays/ federal-reserve-history#wwii.

129 Amended by P.L. 92-210.

130 UC Santa Barbara: The American Presidency Project, *Executive Order 11615—Providing for Stabilization of Prices, Rents, Wages, and Salaries*, https://www.presidency.ucsb.edu/ documents/executive-order-11615-providing-for-stabilization-prices-rents-wages-and-salaries.

131 UC Santa Barbara: The American Presidency Project, *Executive Order 11627—Further Providing for the Stabilization of the Economy*, https://www.presidency.ucsb.edu/ documents/executive-order-11627-further-providing- for-the-stabilization-the-economy.

earnings until 1973, when the controls began to be removed in stages. While the controls were in place, inflation did fall but then spiked to double-digit rates after the controls were dismantled.

During the period of prize freeze, demand grew and supply fell as consumers and producers reacted to the artificially low prices. Ultimately, this period led to pent-up demand in the economy that supply could not keep up with once the controls ended, leading to the increase in inflation.

Whip Inflation Now

During the Great Inflation era, the economy experienced several energy supply shocks, which gave rise to a series of policies aimed at rationing oil and bringing down energy prices. The energy price shocks also contributed to already high inflation during this period. In late 1974, following one of these shocks, President Ford set out on a public relations campaign to "Whip Inflation Now," known as the WIN program. The WIN program was a set of voluntary measures to encourage higher saving and lower spending, and while it initially had public support, the program was not taken up at a rate high enough to lower aggregate demand significantly.[132]

Humphrey-Hawkins Act

Popularly known as the Humphrey-Hawkins Act, the Full Employment and Balanced Growth Act of 1978 (P.L. 95-895) was enacted in 1978 as an amendment to the Employment Act of 1946. The Humphrey-Hawkins Act had several goals, including the reduction of inflation, provided that its reduction did not interfere with employment goals.[133] Some policy recommendations included establishing stockpiles of agricultural commodities, increasing exports, and enforcing antitrust and patent laws to improve the "economic climate" for small businesses.[134] The act set goals and a 3% or below target for inflation (with a goal of zero inflation by 1988)[135] but required additional legislative or executive actions to accomplish them, and thus the law provided no tangible measures to reduce inflation. Inflation continued to rise in 1978

---

[132] Amy Farber, "Historical Echoes: Whip Inflation Now … and Then," Federal Reserve Bank of New York, July 13, 2012, https://libertystreeteconomics.newyorkfed.org/2012/07/historical-echoes-whip-inflation-now-and-then/.

[133] Federal Reserve, *Full Employment and Balanced Growth Act of 1978 (Humphrey-Hawkins)*, https://www.federalreservehistory.org/essays/humphrey-hawkins-act.

[134] Federal Reserve Bank of St. Louis, *Full Employment and Balanced Growth Act (Humphrey-Hawkins Act)*, https://fraser.stlouisfed.org/title/full-employment-balanced-growth-act-humphrey-hawkins-act-1034.

[135] Federal Reserve, Full Employment and Balanced Growth Act of 1978 (Humphrey-Hawkins).

and 1979, reaching an average annual inflation rate of 7.6% and 11.3% in those years as measured by the CPI and 7% and 8.8% as measured by the PCE index, respectively.[136]

Credit Controls

In 1980, under the authority of the Credit Control Act (12 U.S.C. §§1901 et seq.), President Carter enacted credit controls via Executive Order 12201.[137] The 1980 credit controls restrained spending and investing via credit in an attempt to lower spending in the economy. During the months in which the credit controls were in place (March-July), consumer spending did drop notably and interest rates became very volatile, resulting in a brief recession from February to July. As with price controls, once the credit controls were removed, pent-up demand resulted in an increase in spending, increasing inflationary pressures in the economy once more.[138]

---

[136] During this time, the Carter Administration additionally put in place some deregulatory measures, such as the Airline Deregulation Act of 1978 (P.L. 95-504), aimed at reducing inflation by removing unnecessary costs. Such measures did not prove impactful on inflation, as evidenced by the high inflation of the late 1970s and early 1980s. For an overview, see Council of Economic Advisers, Economic Report of the President, January 1979, ch. 2.

[137] UC Santa Barbara: The American Presidency Project, Executive Order 12201—Credit Control, https://www.presidency.ucsb.edu/documents/executive-order-12201-credit-control.

[138] Stacey L. Schreft, "Credit Controls: 1980," Federal Reserve Bank of Richmond, pp. 25-55, https://www.richmondfed.org/~/media/richmondfedorg/publications/research/economic_review/1990/pdf/ er760603.pdf.

Chapter 3

Inflation: A Preventable Crisis*

Committee on Oversight and Accountability

Thursday, March 9, 2023
House of Representatives Committee on Oversight and Accountability
Subcommittee on Health Care and Financial Services
Washington, D.C.

The Subcommittee met, pursuant to notice, at 2:06 p.m., in room 2247, Rayburn House Office Building, Hon. Lisa McClain [Chairwoman of the Subcommittee] presiding.

Present: Representatives McClain, Comer, Foxx, Grothman, Fry, Langworthy, Burlison, Porter, Balint, Lee, Casar, and Crockett.

Mrs. MCCLAIN. The Subcommittee on Health Care and Financial Services will come to order. Welcome, everybody.

Without objection, the Chair may declare a recess at any time. I recognize myself for the purpose of making an opening statement.

Welcome to the first hearing of the Subcommittee on Health Care and Financial Services for the 118th Congress. To the witnesses, thank you very much for your attendance and participation in today's hearing on the inflation crisis.

I think it is most important to understand how we got here so we don't make the same mistakes going forward, and we can do better going forward. We first have to agree that we have a problem before we can fix it and move forward for the American people. When the pandemic began in March 2020,

---

* This is an edited, reformatted and augmented version of Hearing Before the Subcommittee on Health Care and Financial Services of the Committee on Oversight and Accountability, House of Representatives, Serial No. 118–9, dated March 9, 2023.

In: Inflation: Background, Causes and Current Policies
Editor: Julie Taylor Lowe
ISBN: 979-8-89530-696-3

Congress and Federal agencies took quick action to deliver financial relief to the American people. Congress quickly enacted a series of five laws providing over $3.1 trillion in Federal funds to mitigate the economic and public health impact of the COVID–19 pandemic.

President Trump's pro-growth and pro-worker economy, created by the Tax Cuts and Job Act, and investing in American manufacturing, combined with the unparalleled response to the pandemic, created the fastest economic recovery in history. As a result, only $1.9 trillion of the COVID relief funds were spent by January 2021, leaving over a trillion dollars for further relief.

Between the start of the pandemic in March 2020 and March 2021, inflation rose 2.6 percent. The Food Index rose 3.5 percent. Energy services increased by only 4.1 percent, and gasoline prices increased by $0.67 to $2.89 a gallon. Instead of allowing these policies to continue supplementing the successful economic recovery efforts, Democrats jammed through Congress another $1.9 trillion, claiming it was for pandemic relief.

I want to remind everyone that we still had at that time $1 trillion leftover from the relief packages that we hadn't spent yet, and the definition of "inflation" is too many dollars chasing too few goods. Republicans and economic leaders of both parties, including Larry Summers, Greg Mankiw, and Michael Strain, warned that this completely unnecessary spending would put the economy at risk of inflation and possibly recession. Congressional Democrats simply did not listen to the experts. They were determined to spend more money. Government clearly has a spending problem. Then exactly what Republicans and economic experts predicted actually happened.

In 2020, inflation rose to a 40-year high. The price of groceries went through the roof, gas prices soared, and retirement accounts plummeted. Between March 2021 and March 2022, inflation rose 8.5 percent. The Food Index rose 8.8 percent, the largest increase since 1981. Welcome back, Jimmy Carter. The Energy Services Index rose by 13 percent, more than triple the rate it did the year prior under Trump despite the COVID–19 pandemic, and gasoline prices increased $1.43 to $4.32.

What was the Democrats' response? More spending. They pushed through the wrongly named, I might add, Inflation Reduction Act, another $740 billion boondoggle which did nothing to fight inflation, but it did spend more than $360 billion on climate policies and funded 87,000 IRS agents. I am not sure how that helps the pandemic, but this is on top of $3.1 trillion and $1.9 trillion. Democrats decided to spend even more money, and let me remind you that we still have left over money to this day from those relief packages.

Democrats' spending spree over last Congress drove the prices of groceries up by more than 11 percent. Their spending spree and attack on American energy caused Americans across the country to pay 27 percent more to heat their homes this winter. Inflation driven by Democrat policies made Michiganders choose between heating their homes and buying groceries. I don't know if you all know, but it gets cold in Michigan, especially this winter.

Then what was President Biden's solution to the skyrocketing energy inflation? He told Americans to buy expensive electric vehicles. Now, mind you, in Michigan, we didn't have the infrastructure, the charging stations, nor the money to buy these electric vehicles. But President Biden's "let them eat cake" response illustrates just how little he and congressional Democrats care about the impact of the reckless spending policies have had on working Americans.

This Committee stood on the sidelines for too long while Americans across the country were feeling the pressure of inflation brought on by the Biden administration and congressional Democrats. Today, we hear from experts to better understand how inflation could have been prevented and what this administration and Congress must do to address it. I thank you and look forward to your testimony.

I yield now to Ranking Member Porter, for her opening statements. Thank you.

Ms. PORTER. Thank you very much, Madam Chairwoman. It is great to join you at our first Subcommittee hearing together, and I look forward to working across the aisle to oversee and strengthen our capitalist economy.

Today, we begin our work by discussing inflation. My Republican friends titled this hearing, "Inflation: A Preventable Crisis." So, I think our first task is to dig into what they think was preventable. Let's rule a few things out. We all know that Congress couldn't have prevented a once-in-a-century pandemic or Putin's illegal war in Ukraine. We all know Congress couldn't have prevented the strain on our supply chains when people started trading consumption of services for goods during COVID, and we all know Congress couldn't have immediately fixed our strained supply chains to reduce inflation. After all, it took decades for Washington to crack our supply chains by underinvesting in infrastructure, ignoring price gouging monopolies, and letting corporations offshore manufacturing.

So, we have ruled out Congress preventing the economic shocks and the resulting effects that led to inflation, but still, our Republican friends are suggesting that something about inflation was a choice. Well, I suppose it was a choice to help people suffering the economic impacts of COVID, but to me, that help wasn't really a choice. It was a necessity, but it seems like today's hearing could turn into a forum to blame American fiscal policy for the global phenomenon of inflation. If American fiscal policy created inflation as a crisis that is being felt in countries across the globe, then American fiscal policy should equally be able to solve that crisis. So, what policies do Republicans think will solve global inflation? Is it deep cuts to social programs like Social Security and Medicare that would devastate our seniors and working families, or maybe it is just the REIN IN Act, which Republicans passed last week, which requires the President to consider the inflationary impact of executive orders. The problem is the REIN IN Act commissions a report. It is not a comprehensive look at the costs and benefits of executive orders. Does that really help us make more informed fiscal decisions, or is it just designed to discourage executive orders? Either way, the REIN IN Act still just commissions reports. It takes no real action. If that was House Republicans' secret plan to fight inflation, it is going to be a long two years for American families. Either Republicans don't have a plan to address inflation while making life better for families, or they are too afraid to admit that their plan is to take away deeply popular and needed programs from the American people.

Let's contrast that with what Democrats have been up to. We passed the Inflation Reduction Act, which would cap the price of insulin for seniors, allow Medicare to negotiate drug prices, lower the cost of health insurance, and lower the cost of renewable energy, all while reining in inflation by paying down the national debt. We passed the Bipartisan Infrastructure Law to invest billions in our ports and airports to stop the supply chain bottlenecks that have spiked prices during the pandemic. We passed the CHIPS for America Act that will bring back domestic manufacturing that Washington let move overseas for decades, injecting competition and resiliency into our markets that lowers prices. And perhaps most importantly, we have had a President who has taken executive action to break up monopolies, chipping away at the power big corporations have enjoyed to gouge huge profit margins and raise prices on consumers. These are the kinds of actions that contain inflation, make life better for families, and shore up our economic resiliency.

Today, I am calling on House Republicans to please put forward your own plan to fight inflation that is at least as detailed as the Inflation Reduction Act. It is time the American people see where you stand, not see you grandstand. I yield back.

Mrs. MCCLAIN. Thank you, Ms. Porter. I am pleased to introduce our three witnesses today, who are experts in fiscal and monetary policy and can speak to the causes and long-term consequences of the current inflation crisis. Dr. Douglas Holtz-Eakin is the president and founder of the American Action Forum. From 2003 to 2005, he was the sixth Director of the nonpartisan Congressional Budget Office, which provides the budgetary and policy analysis to the U.S. Congress. He has a Ph.D. in economics from Princeton University. Welcome.

Dr. John Taylor is the Mary and Robert Raymond Professor of Economics at Stanford University and George P. Shultz Senior Fellow in economics at the Hoover Institute. He is known for his research on the foundations of modern monetary theory and policy, which has been applied by central banks and fiscal market analysts around the world. He has a Ph.D. in economics from Stanford University.

And Mr. Michael Konczal—did I say that correct? I am always struggling with names, so I apologize in advance—is the director of macroeconomic analysis at the Roosevelt Institute. A former financial engineer, he holds a B.A. in math and computer science and an M.S. in finance from the University of Illinois at Urbana Champaign.

Pursuant to the Committee Rule 9, the witnesses will please stand and raise their right hands.

Do you solemnly swear or affirm that the testimony that you are about to give is the truth, the whole truth, and nothing but the truth, so help you God?

[A chorus of ayes.]

Mrs. MCCLAIN. Let the record show that the witnesses all have answered in the affirmative.

We appreciate all of you being here today, and we look forward to your testimony. Let me remind the witnesses that we have read your written statements, and they will appear in full on the hearing record. Please limit your oral statements to five minutes. And as a reminder, please press the button on your microphone in front of you so that it is on and the Members can hear you. When you begin to speak, the light in front of you will turn green. After four minutes the light will turn yellow. When the red light comes on, your five minutes is expired, and we would ask that you please try and wrap it up as soon as possible.

I recognize the first witness to begin their opening statement.

Statement of Douglas Holtz-Eakin, President and Founder, American Action Forum

Mr. HOLTZ-EAKIN. Well, thank you, Chair McClain, and Ranking Member Porter, and Members of the Committee for the privilege of being here today. You have my written statement. Let me say three things briefly, and then I look forward to answering your questions.

Point No. 1 is that inflation really took root in 2021. At the beginning of 2021, in January, year-over-year CPI inflation was 1.4 percent. One year later, in January 2022, it was 7.5 percent. This marks one of only three years in which CPI inflation grew by six percentage points in a single year in the postwar United States. So, what are the sources of this sharp run up in 2021? Well, the Chair alluded to some of them in her opening remarks. One was excessive monetary stimulus. The Federal Reserve responded aggressively to the arrival of the pandemic recession, cut rates to zero, made an open-ended commitment to provide liquidity to markets, and, importantly, started buying $90 billion a month of Treasuries and mortgage-backed securities, and it continues to do so in 2021. Even as inflation started to creep up, it maintained this pace through the entire year.

In addition, there was excessive fiscal stimulus, the American Rescue Plan, $1.9 trillion in stimulus, was enacted in March 2021 at a time when the U.S. economy was growing at 6.5 percent. It was plain in the data, things like GDPNow at the Atlanta Fed showed that. At a time when the measured output gap between what GDP was running at and what its potential was, as calculated by my old shop, the Congressional Budget Office, that budget gap was $400 billion to $600 billion. You don't need a $1.9 trillion bill to close a $400 billion to $600 billion output gap, so it was just much too big and destined to cause macroeconomic disruptions.

And there were, as well, supply chain constraints from around the globe, but to the extent that you recognize supply constraints, you should be even more restrictive in your fiscal stimulus because it is only demand relative to supply that matters. So in 2021, inflation really, really ramped up, and that, I think, is the period that was most crucial and where the biggest policy errors were made. Point No. 2 is that once inflation gets embedded in the economy, policymakers have essentially no good choices. Choice No. 1 is live with the inflation. When it got to 10 percent, that was clearly unpalatable. American households were deeply dissatisfied and being harmed by the inflation. The alternative is to live with the things necessary to bring it back into control, and that is a steady stream of bad news in the terms of house prices start going down, retail sales declining, slower growth in jobs in the labor market. And as a result, that initial policy, it gets compounded into further costs down the line as you deal with taking the inflation out of the system.

Point No. 3 is we are hardly done with this episode. In the most recent readings, CPI inflation was 6.4 percent year-over-year, well above two-percent target. The core, taking out the volatile food and energy components, was still at 5.6, but for me, the really striking numbers are food, energy, and shelter are 50 percent of the CPI. That is because they are about 50 percent of the typical family budget, and food, energy, and shelter still rising at 8.5 percent year-over-year. Go to the gasoline station, go to the grocery, go home and be reminded that your paycheck is nearly 10 percent less valuable than a year before.

And inside that, shelter is really the poster child for the inflation problem. Shelter is a third of the CPI. Year-over-year inflation, shelter inflation is 7.9 percent. It has risen every month since February 2021. We have yet to see a peak, and shelter isn't something that has a supply chain. It is in the United States. Shelter is a service, and services are the U.S. inflation problem right now. Goods price inflation has been, in fact, addressed to some extent, and the Federal Reserve, in particular, will need to do more to address the inflation problem.

I will just close with something which I find sort of slightly depressing on the inflation front. The Fed's preferred measure of inflation is a geeky thing called the market-based Price Index for personal consumption expenditures. We don't want to talk about that in public, but I will be happy to answer questions later. But it is really just indicative of what transactions are actually happening in the economy right now. When they started their tightening in April 2022, year-over-year market-based core PCE was 4.9 percent. In January 2023, it was 4.9 percent. That is very little progress on the underlying inflation, which means that as the tightening the Fed has done so far gets into neutral, there is more to do to really address the inflation.

So, I thank you for the chance to be here today, and I would be happy to answer your questions.

Mrs. MCCLAIN. Thank you, sir. I appreciate your opening statement. I now recognize Dr. Taylor.

Statement of John B. Taylor, Mary and Robert Raymond Professor of Economics, Stanford University, and George P. Shultz Senior Fellow In Economics, Hoover Institute

Mr. TAYLOR. Thank you, Chairwoman McClain and Ranking Member Porter, for inviting me to this important Subcommittee meeting. Inflation is such an important topic. I am going to focus most of my remarks on that, in particular, the monetary policy aspects of that.

For several years, starting back in 2017, the Fed began to move to a more rules-based monetary policy, and it worked well for the United States in 1980's, 1990's, and in other years. Many papers were written at the Fed and other places showing the benefits of the so-called rules-based policies. In July 2017, when Janet Yellen was the Chair of the Fed, a whole section on rules-based monetary policy was put in the monetary policy report. The target inflation rate was only two percent.

Many monetary policy experts made favorable comments about the rules-based policy. J. Powell, for example, said, "I find these rule prescriptions helpful." Evidence was that with the move toward rules-based policy was beneficial, economic performance improved. Unfortunately, this moved toward monetary policy rules was interrupted when the pandemic hit in 2020. First, rules were removed from the Fed's report. They were put back in in February 2021. Then rules were taken out again in February 2022. But Chair Powell, in answer to complaints from Members of Congress about rising inflation, said he would put the rules back in. And in the report released on June 17, 2022, policy rules were back.

This approach of including rules in the report has continued, and it appeared last Friday, in the March 3, 2023 report. A copy of the table is in my prepared testimony, but let me just mention the Taylor rule was first on the list. And the Fed admitted that throughout 2021 and 2022, the target range for the Federal funds rate was below the prescriptions of most simple rules. I think it is good that rules are back in the Fed's monetary policy report. It would be more helpful if the Fed formally incorporated rules into its actual decisions and apparently has been trying to do this recently. At first, only small changes were seen in actual monetary policy as inflation rose sharply, as you just heard. This was the case of the Fed and other central banks who are behind the curve. So, we are still living in a high inflation era, unless monetary policy actions are taken.

Events in Ukraine raised inflation, but not the basic story. Figure 1 in my prepared testimony shows the effective Federal funds rate through late 2022 through the present. The rate moved from 25 basis points to 4-and-a-half percent, but that is still probably too low. While the gap between the rules and the effective rate has narrowed, the huge discrepancy still exists.

During March 2022, the actual Federal funds rate was well behind the curve. Why? If we use the Taylor Rule, which is in the Fed's report, the most recent monetary policy report in particular, you plug in an inflation rate over the past four quarters of only four percent, a target inflation of two percent, which the Fed says we are still taking it to, an equilibrium interest rate of one percent, which is a consensus at this point, lower than I assumed originally, and the gap between real GDP and its potential of zero—we are pretty close to zero, low unemployment—then you get a Federal funds rate of six percent. These are mild assumptions. So, even with these mild inflation numbers, the Fed is still behind the curve, though, as Chair Powell indicated this week in testimony, they are still trying to catch up, so we will see.

My written testimony shows that the Fed got way behind the curve in detail compared to the rules-based monetary policy, and it says this is why inflation rose so much. The Fed has started on a method to get inflation back down. By reviewing the years leading up to the present situation, the formal testimony provides the background needed for analyzing the current and future monetary policy decisions.

There are now more reasons than ever for central banks, including the Fed, to use the more rules-based policy, to keep inflation at the two-percent target range. Central banks should start now on procedures or rules that markets understand. The policy interest rate would increase as inflation rises, as has now just begun to happen. It would, of course, be a contingency plan, as are all rules. This would greatly reduce the chances of a large, damaging change later. Thank you.

Mrs. MCCLAIN. Thank you. I appreciate your testimony. I now recognize Mr. Konczal.

Statement of Michael Konczal, Director of Macro- Economic Analysis, Roosevelt Institute, Washington, D.C.

Mr. KONCZAL. Chair McClain, Ranking Member Porter, and distinguished Members of Subcommittee, thank you for inviting me to testify at this hearing.

My name is Mike Konczal, I am the director of macroeconomic analysis at the Roosevelt Institute.

Today I am going to speak about the causes of inflation that have been unique to this recovery, the progress we have made so far, and what policymakers can do to bring down inflation further. But first, it is important to remember this recovery has been remarkable. The economy has added more than 500,000 jobs each month for the past two years. There are now 4 million more jobs in the February 2021 CBO projection of what would have happened without the American Rescue Plan. In contrast to previous recessions, real GDP is recovering to projections of where it would have been without the pandemic, but we have also experienced inflation has been higher and more sustained than financial markets and the Federal Reserve projected.

There has been four key contributors to inflation during the past two years, and we have heard stories about people canceling gym memberships and buying home gym equipment instead. And the first contributor, the shift in demand from services to goods, has been aggregated across the entire economy. Second, vulnerabilities in our supply chains, many of which already lacked resiliency pre- COVID, led to skyrocketing prices for goods in summer of 2021, yet during this time, the prices for services did not fall. As the economy reopened, inflation and services picked up even as supply chains were still normalizing. This all mechanically increases inflation.

Third has been the change in demand for housing resulting from remote work, which now covers over a quarter of the work force. One study by the San Francisco Fed found that these shifting patterns of demand for housing explain half of the overall increases in house prices and rents during the past two years, all of which has been a major contributor to inflation. And fourth, Russia's invasion of Ukraine in February 2022 also increased inflation, especially through energy and food prices. Thanks to U.S.-led domestic and international efforts, especially the financial commitments in deploying and restocking the U.S. Strategic Petroleum Reserve, the CPI for inflation has come down to rates near the beginning of the war in recent months.

Now, what we don't see is if these explanations are sufficient to explain most of the shifts in inflation over the past two years. But if inflation was primarily the result of the Biden administration's policy, we would have expected to see certain things in the data, but we see the opposite. First, if too much demand was the main contributor of inflation, we would expect to see potential output, real GDP, or real consumption exceed pre-pandemic projections or trendlines. Where we would expect the big difference is the composition of them have changed.

Second, we would expect the United States to be globally unique, but instead, we see inflation increasing across the globe. All of the 40 countries the OECD collects data on saw higher core inflation across 2022 than in 2019. Of those 40, 28 of those 40 had higher inflation increases relative to 2019 than the United States. United States' increase in inflation has been lower than many European countries, like the U.K. and Germany, but also lower than countries not in Europe, such as Canada and Israel. Our inflation increase has been about the same as South Korea. This inflation is truly a global phenomenon. Now, our inflation picked up earlier in 2021 than peer countries, driven by price breaks and automobiles particularly, but our reopening growth started earlier and stronger as well. The IMF estimates that the U.S. growth will be twice the average of the Eurozone from 2020 to 2023.

A third thing is instead of seeing people not working, we have seen a rapid recovery in the labor force. Prime age employment to population ratios are near pre-pandemic levels and still growing. There are more workers working today than the CBO projected in 2019 that there would be at this point. Fourth, if unemployment was below a natural rate of unemployment, we expect nominal wages to be increasing and increasing fast. Instead, wages decelerated across 2022 to rates that, while still especially strong, are more consistent with lower inflation.

Now, there has been a lot of progress. Inflation is down almost half across the past three months compared to the first half of 2022 across a variety of metrics, roughly six percent to four percent, depending on what you are looking at. However, inflation is still higher than we want it to be, and there are still policy options we can use to speed its decline.

First is to raise or eliminate the debt ceiling. A financial crisis would be devastating to this economy, I don't need to say much more about that. Second is to recognize that a lot of tightening has taken place. Federal Reserve raised interest rates rapidly in 2022, almost five percent, close to the six percent, as the Taylor rule might suggest, and economists agree that these hikes slow the economy in long and variable lags. We don't want to administer too much medicine if we think we haven't seen all the effects of the previous around yet. Measures of housing inflation, in particular, which we know will fall from private sector analysts, take a long time to be incorporated in the official statistics.

Third is to look at corporate profit margins. Non-financial profits as a percent of GDP are at record levels. If corporate profits fall, it means we can have lower inflation while still keeping a strong job market. Fourth, we need to build more. Our infrastructure needs to become more resilient through successful deployment of the Inflation Reduction Act. And also, we need more housing, which was a challenge even before the pandemic. And fifth, we need to expand the labor force from everything, through higher immigration to expanded childcare. There are many job openings available, and this would make our economy stronger.

Thank you for your time, and I look forward to your questions.

Mrs. MCCLAIN. Thank you very much for all of your testimony and opening statement.

I am going to recognize myself for five minutes.

Dr. Holtz-Eakin, yes or no. Did the American Rescue Plan increase inflation?

Mr. HOLTZ-EAKIN. Yes.

Mrs. MCCLAIN. Was it predictable that the American Rescue Plan would drive inflation so significantly?

Mr. HOLTZ-EAKIN. Yes. People said so at the time, notably Larry Summers, former Secretary of the Treasury, also an economist. History has given us examples just like the American Rescue Plan. In 1951, the U.S. economy was growing at 10.5 percent, quite rapid growth. Federal spending was increased by about 50 percent. That is roughly the American Rescue event, $2 trillion on a $4 trillion race, and inflation jumped by six percentage points that year. So, you get the big fiscal stimulus, and an accommodative Fed, and the high growth environment, you get inflation.

Mrs. MCCLAIN. Thank you. Were the Democrats warned about these risks?

Mr. HOLTZ-EAKIN. Yes, there were public comments made by people about how undesirable this was and how large it was. There was testimony. I testified at the Senate Banking Committee about the risks of the American Rescue Plan and made the points I made today about how it is the wrong time for stimulus. We are growing rapidly. It is too big compared to the problem. I had some issues with the design. It wasn't really focused on COVID-related fallout in the economy. And so, there were lots of people who had expressed some concern over the scale and composition of the bill.

Mrs. MCCLAIN. So, Democrats passed the legislation they knew would likely drive the country into its worst inflationary period in 40 years?

Mr. HOLTZ-EAKIN. I don't have any idea what the motivation is.

The bill passed, and we have now seen the policy error.

Mrs. MCCLAIN. And it is good to learn from our past mistakes. Mr. HOLTZ-EAKIN. It would be nice if we did.

Mrs. MCCLAIN. In your opinion, I would like to understand your definition of inflation.

Mr. HOLTZ-EAKIN. Inflation is a broad-based increase in the price level so that the dollar price of goods and services broadly in the economy rising.

Mrs. MCCLAIN. OK. Thank you. In 2021, President Biden's then chief of staff, Ron Klain endorsed a tweet saying, "Inflation is a high-class problem." From Jason Furman, a Democrat who was President Obama's Chair of the Council of Economic Advisers, inflation is a high-class problem. Doctor, doesn't inflation affect middle-income and low-income Americans as well?

Mr. HOLTZ-EAKIN. You got a couple of doctors.

Mrs. MCCLAIN. I got a couple of doctors. We will start with you.

Mr. HOLTZ-EAKIN. Yes, certainly. In my written testimony, I pointed out that if you look at the median income in the United States and you say 50 percent, it is going to food, energy and shelter. That is a $3,000 tax on food, energy, and shelter at current inflation rates. It is a real loss in purchasing power for other purposes because you have to devote it to those core elements.

Mrs. MCCLAIN. Dr. Taylor, would you agree?

Mr. TAYLOR. Yes. I think the effects of inflation on a broad population are completely understated. That is why this two percent or whatever, I thought it should be 1.5 percent before they chose two. That is why I think it is so important.

Mrs. MCCLAIN. Thank you, and a follow-up. In fact, according to several research institutions in the Fed, the inflationary crisis brought on by the Biden and congressional Democrats' reckless spending has disproportionately impacted low-income individuals. Shouldn't the Biden administration be forcing more help on Americans in need by actually addressing the inflationary crisis rather than minimizing the real pain inflation caused by their reckless actions? We can't fix a problem unless we first admit we have a problem.

Mr. HOLTZ-EAKIN. I think we all know we have an inflation problem. The question now is what is the best route to fixing it. My own opinion is that the Federal Reserve is, in fact, correct when Chairman Powell said that this is the Fed's problem. We have a mandate for price stability and full employment, and the only way to get to full employment is to restore price stability.

Within the Fed's strategies, I want to just note what Dr. Taylor said about the fact that their discretionary decisions thus far have left them way behind the curve. There was a large discussion about the uptick in inflation in the first half of 2021. They continued with the foot on the gas through the whole year and didn't begin tight- ening until early in 2022, and tightened too slowly.

Mrs. MCCLAIN. I agree. Dr. Holtz, the Biden administration continues to claim that 70 percent of the increased inflation was due to Russia's invasion of Ukraine. Is that true? Big percentage?

Mr. HOLTZ-EAKIN. You can find a window where you can make that true, and they did. It was one month earlier last year. But broadly, the inflation problem really did take root in 2021, prior to the invasion, and I don't think explanations that point toward an invasion of Ukraine as the problem of inflation are correct.

Mrs. MCCLAIN. Well, I am just looking at the facts. So, if I understand the facts correctly, and please correct me if I am wrong, when the President took office in January 2021, inflation was at 1.4 percent. By December of that year, inflation had risen, right, to seven percent, six percent jump, kind of a big jump in my opinion, but the war in Ukraine didn't start till the following February. So, those are the facts, right? I am not distorting the reality, and I am looking at the global picture.

Mr. HOLTZ-EAKIN. That is right, and that was in my written testimony as well.

Mrs. MCCLAIN. So, how much of the inflation is due to Biden's policies versus how much is caused by Putin's invasion of Ukraine? I mean, we have to start talking about facts.

Mr. HOLTZ-EAKIN. So, a crude decomposition, as you put aside the invasion, which happens later, you compare Europe to the United States, as many people want to do. In 2021, European consumer price inflation rose about a percentage point each quarter, went from zero percent to four percent. That is because they shared the same supply chain problems the U.S. had. U.S. inflation got well above seven percent, and so there is part which is attributable to the impact of supply chain difficulties, but there is another part that is unquestionably excessive demand stimulus in the U.S.

Mrs. MCCLAIN. Thank you. The Chair would like to recognize Mr. Casar. Did I say that right, Casar?

Mr. CASAR. Yes, thank you. Thank you so much. There is this false presumption that I think is talked about here in Congress that government spending always necessarily equals inflation, and my understanding is that that is just wrong. I want to go back to some basics here that we heard today. Prices can go up for a variety of reasons—supply demand mismatch, corporate greed, supply chain issues, war—and when prices go up, smart government interventions can have a role in bringing those prices down.

And I want to talk about one example, for example, investing in childcare when there is a smart investment by the Federal Government or local government to make sure that there is more childcare available for people, something I hear from my constituents, they need all the time, if we bring people back into the childcare work force, raise their wages, make sure that there is more small childcare operators available. Mr. Konczal, can you talk to us about whether smart, targeted government investments like this one to provide people more childcare options could actually bring prices down as opposed to driving them up?

Mr. KONCZAL. Yes, absolutely. So, a strong characteristic of this recovery has been a lot of job openings. Though the labor market has recovered quite rapidly to pre-pandemic levels, we knew pre- pandemic, we were still missing millions of people who could be working as a result of lack of access to childcare and lack of other kinds of care infrastructure, and that problem is still with us even after the pandemic. We also know that declines in immigration are probably putting pressure on labor markets and making it harder for employers to find workers that they could be filling the jobs.

Mr. CASAR. So, on top of potentially bringing childcare costs down by the government, subsidizing childcare, and helping open more childcare centers, what you are saying is also by having folks send their kids to that childcare, they could reenter the work force, increase productivity overall, overall increase supply, and, therefore, also drive prices down?

Mr. KONCZAL. Yes, absolutely. We knew this was a problem in 2019, and it still remains with us.

Mr. CASAR. And then long term, when you have those children participate in high-quality childcare, we know that their overall productivity goes up, their ability to innovate and find the career of their choice goes up in their adult life, and long term, that also increases our overall productivity, the overall strength of our economy, and that is anti-inflationary as well?

Mr. KONCZAL. In the long and medium term, it allows us to be much more productive and have a much higher level of output.

Mr. CASAR. I think that is really important because the false narrative that I think needs to not be constructed is that we shouldn't help folks when they are in need. The government shouldn't intervene and spend in smart ways, because the answer to any time congressional Democrats or the Biden administration want to do something good is that it is going to further inflation, then the answer is let's just not do much at all. But I, as a city council member, saw how the American Rescue Plan not only created millions of jobs, but saved people's lives. And if we make sure we make smart investments that actually support the American worker and bolster our economy, we can make those kinds of investments in ways that actually bring prices downward, and I think that your testimony makes that really clear. I appreciate that.

Mr. KONCZAL. Thank you.

Mr. CASAR. Thank you, and I yield my time back to Representative Balint.

Mrs. MCCLAIN. Thank you, Mr. Casar. OK. The Chair recognizes Dr. Foxx for five minutes.

Ms. FOXX. Thank you very much, Madam Chair, and thanks for our panelists being here, particularly Doug Holtz-Eakin. We haven't seen you in a little while. It is nice to see you, Dr. Taylor. Thank you very much to all of our panelists.

Dr. Holtz-Eakin, Federal officials and members of academia have used the term "transitory" to describe the current trend of inflation. Now, they have been saying that lately, but do you want to explain a little bit more about what you think they mean by that?

Mr. HOLTZ-EAKIN. Early in 2021, as inflation started rising from that 1.4 percent, I noted it. At the start of the year, there was a discussion about whether this was something that was transitory, would take care of itself and return toward 1.4 percent within the year, or if this was part of a longer trend that was more permanent and something the Fed would have to actively lean against to get back to the two percent target. For at least six months, perhaps longer, many Fed officials and analysts stuck to the notion that it was transitory and that no change in Federal reserve policy was necessary. By the second half of 2022, essentially, everyone had been in this notion. Inflation was clearly high, rising, and not a transitory phenomenon.

Ms. FOXX. Thank you. Dr. Taylor, last Congress, I introduced the Spending Safeguard Act, which would tamp down mandatory spending increases by establishing specific caps for new or reauthorized programs. How would legislation like this affect America's inflation?

Mr. TAYLOR. I think it would be a step in the right direction. This is in focus on the budget deficit. In my testimony, I focus on monetary policy, which I have looked at a lot, but the deficit is an issue. And you can wish it away, but it is there, and it is a very, very important factor, so actions like this are very important to take. Monetary policy is complicated. The tendency is, it is always easy to think about fiscal policy, but it is such a difference now in terms of monetary policy. That is why I focused on that.

Ms. FOXX. And you mentioned the deficit just now, so I will follow up. Do you think that really could be effective in lowering the deficit and the debt as well?

Mr. TAYLOR. Oh, yes. I think a policy is monetary, is fiscal, is regulatory, is international. We are focusing a lot on fiscal now because it is such a mess. We are focusing on monetary because it is such a mess, but don't forget the regulatory stuff. Don't forget the international stuff. It is very important. But I always say, yes, the fiscal side is so important, and it has exploded and needs to be brought back to normal.

Ms. FOXX. Yes. For my colleagues, we have agencies that have money that they can spend under mandatory spending, and an estimate comes from CBO, it is going to cost $100 million, and then they go out and spend $200 million because there is no cap. And so, my bill put a cap on it saying if it goes above 10 percent, you have to come back to us to get approval for it. It may not be trillions, but pennies add up. So, Dr. Taylor, in your opinion, is allocating trillions more in spending toward liberal initiatives like the Green New Deal an effective approach to addressing inflation?

Mr. TAYLOR. I don't think it is an issue really. It would be counterproductive to do this. In fact, it doesn't really matter too much of what you are spending on. It is a deficit itself, and it has caused a lot of problems. I think it is too big by any stretch of the imagination. It interferes with other kinds of policy, so that should be the focus, and I think what you describe, limits mandates, is an important part of this. We used to have thought about a balanced budget amendment at one point, so this is in that direction.

Ms. FOXX. OK. For both you and Dr. Holtz-Eakin, when do you anticipate inflation to return to pre-COVID levels, and what actions should the Biden administration, Congress, and the Federal Reserve be taking to meet that timeline?

Mr. TAYLOR. So, we can't predict inflation very well, but the stated goal of the Fed is to get it back to two. They will probably raise rates a little bit more. I know that has concerned people, but it is the best thing that I know that they could be doing. If they do that, then inflation will come down gradually, and that could be instantly—be lucky to be instantly—but come back to this two percent, which is the target we shouldn't give up on.

Mr. HOLTZ-EAKIN. At the time that the Fed launched this tightening cycle, Chairman Powell addressed the National Association for Business Economics and said it would take three years to get back to the two-percent target. In the interim, inflation has proven more stubborn than he had anticipated, and the terminal rate are going have to get to higher than they had anticipated. So, I think it will probably take longer than he anticipated.

Ms. FOXX. Thank you, Madam Chair. I apologize for going over. I yield back.

Mrs. MCCLAIN. Thank you. The Chair recognizes the gentlelady from Pennsylvania, Ms. Lee.

Ms. LEE. Thank you, Madam Chair. So, we have all seen personally back in our communities, right, how they are hurting. I have never seen eggs costing you $7 at Giant Eagle. Rents are rising, housing costs are only getting worse, but we know why. Inflation is hurting everyone globally because the pandemic was global. A war in Europe is impacting everyone. We know the reasons, but today, we really want to focus on solutions. So, Mr. Konczal, what policies could Congress pursue to further tackle inflation, in your opinion?

Mr. KONCZAL. I believe things that help us build more and expand our capacity would be very helpful, particularly in the housing sector. I think things that might raise taxes on rich people, in particular, to bring down the deficit to pay for important targeted investments, I think, would be very useful. I think letting the tightening that has already happened, seeing the impacts of it, I think that is actually quite important. And things that increase our labor force supply, such as childcare, immigration, other things I think would really help our work force.

Ms. LEE. Yes. Similarly, I think that listening to testimony and about the different causes of inflation, I think the one thing that we didn't maybe hear a lot about is corporate greed and price gouging. Gasoline prices now average more than $5 a gallon in Pittsburgh, and oil companies posted record profits this year, leading me to suspect price gouging at the pump. Pennsylvania has among the weakest laws in the Nation when it comes to investigating and preventing price gouging. What actions do you believe we can take at the Federal level to address corporate greed impacting my constituents?

Mr. KONCZAL. I think broadly speaking, we had a competition problem in 2019, and I think that competition problem is here now. It is important to remember that the labor share has fallen during this recovery; that is, workers' wages have gone up less than the prices. Workers are not driving the inflation. The inflation has been reflected in corporate profits. And so, I think things like competition coming online, that would bring down margins. Particularly we see prices that businesses pay have increased less than the prices consumers pay, which has shown up in these corporate profits. I think competition bringing that down and increasing the labor share, I think could do a lot to help alleviate inflation at the margins.

Ms. LEE. Thank you. In the wake of historic pandemic, ideally war, inflation rates now, is not the time to simply point fingers. I want to ensure we are doing work to get money back into the pockets of all the people in this country. I yield back, Madam Chair.

Mrs. MCCLAIN. The gentlelady yields.

Ms. BALINT. If I may, Madam Chair? One of the premises of this hearing is that the Biden policies have been reckless, that the policies of the Biden Administration have added to the deficit. And I just want to really be rooted in fact here, which is that the new budget that has been proposed will actually cut the deficit by nearly $3 trillion over the next 10 years. And that is really a stark contrast to what I am hearing from my colleagues, the Republicans' proposal, which would actually increase the national debt by $3 trillion over the next 10 years, and would continue to give big handouts to the rich, to big corporations, to special interests. And I just want to make sure that we are always keeping that fact at the center of this. We are here to try to work toward solutions, and I think it is really important that we are rooted in reality. I yield back.

Mrs. MCCLAIN. Thank you. The Chair now recognizes the gentleman from Wisconsin, Mr. Grothman.

Mr. GROTHMAN. Thank you. I am going to kind of follow up on some of the things Ms. Foxx said. Could you comment on the current Federal deficit or the total amount of Federal debt as to where it is historically as far as percentage GDP? Whichever one of you guys. You seem pretty bright. We will give you another shot.

Mr. HOLTZ-EAKIN. We are at roughly 100 percent of GDP, and we will shortly exceed the highest level relative to GDP in the history of the country.

Mr. GROTHMAN. Right, and I don't think people realize how much we are exceeding it. We were near 100 percent, I think, only for like one year, but have we been anywhere near 100 percent, say, for the last 75 years?

Mr. HOLTZ-EAKIN. The only comparable period was World War II, and so we are now even going to surpass the levels in World War II.

Mr. GROTHMAN. Right. We are around 100 percent, you are right. For most people on this panel, for most of our life, what were we around, 40 to 50 percent through the 1970's and 1980's?

Mr. HOLTZ-EAKIN. About 35 coming into the financial crisis, jumped to about 70 after the financial crisis. We are now at 100.

Mr. GROTHMAN. Right, so easily the most. Next thing I want to comment about GDP itself. We calculate that GDP is supposed to be a measure, I guess, of the wealth in society, OK? But if the government spends money on something, say that government spends money on childcare, the government spends money on some green initiative, something that not by itself is increasing the wealth of American society, or the government just spends more money on government bureaucrats, the government spends more money on IRS agents, what effect does that have on GDP?

Mr. HOLTZ-EAKIN. So, GDP is actually not a wealth measure. It is a measure of the——

Mr. GROTHMAN. I mean——

Mr. HOLTZ-EAKIN [continuing]. Production and goods and services in a year.

Mr. GROTHMAN. Right.

Mr. HOLTZ-EAKIN. It is an income——

Mr. GROTHMAN. Measure of income, right?

Mr. HOLTZ-EAKIN. It is an income measure, and one way to measure the income is to add up how it is spent. And so, if it is spent on government bureaucrats, or childcare, or something, that is one way to get a measure of it. Another way to get a measure of it is to look at all the people who are contributing to producing it, look at their wages, and their profits, and their rents, and things like that. So, those measures are just accounting classification.

Mr. GROTHMAN. Right. I guess the point I am trying to make is, normally when you say a country's GDP is expanding, you think of more cars, more houses, more dinners out or something, not just expanding government bureaucrats, but for the purpose of GDP, we are including things like hiring new bureaucrats, that sort of thing.

Mr. HOLTZ-EAKIN. Correct.

Mr. GROTHMAN. OK. Well, just kind of question here for you on just the Fed in general and something that the press has not adequately reported. When this COVID thing broke, we met with the Fed, or at least with Powell, and we were encouraged to spend as much as we could. And we were told that that would not lead to inflation, which I thought was preposterous at the time, but that is what we were told. Could you comment on that philosophy that spending recklessly, at least when we are in a—what do they call it, depression, recession, whatever—could not lead to inflation?

Mr. HOLTZ-EAKIN. I think that reflects two things. One was really the, I think, the recent history of the Fed coming out of the financial crisis where it felt that fiscal policy was not being used, and that all of the responsibility was up to the Fed to generate growth. And it simply can't do that, and it was unable to do that, and so it wanted some help in the face of a downtrend. That is point No. 1. Point No. 2 is, the Fed had publicly been quite celebratory of its tactic of keeping monetary policy quite accommodative, in like 2019, late in the cycle, and having unemployment get to record-low levels without generating inflation. And I think it believed that it was going back to a war world inflation, just wasn't going to where it said, but it was an error, and they have since admitted it was an error in judgment.

Mr. GROTHMAN. OK. Quick other things. In this budget, we have an increase in a variety of taxes, so I am going to ask you to comment on two things, first of all, because capital moves about. When we raise marginal rates in this country compared to other countries, what effect does that have on GDP?

Mr. HOLTZ-EAKIN. We lose capital to produce goods and services, and so it diminishes future GDP on the supply side.

Mr. GROTHMAN. So, it affects growth, right?

Mr. HOLTZ-EAKIN. Yes.

Mr. GROTHMAN. Rates, marginal rates and affects growth. Next thing along those lines, if we increase marginal rates, what effect does that have on wealth within the country? In other words, say, on an individual, and I am just kind of speaking the Laffer Curve here, that sort of thing. I wonder if you could comment on the effect of increased rates, be it on corporate business level or individual level?

Mr. HOLTZ-EAKIN. Well, I would be happy to get back to at length on the individual pieces, but I would just point out the corporate rate reverses something which is an undisguised success. Getting the U.S. rate down has changed the situation formula. We lost 10 headquarters a year on average in the decade leading up to 2017. We haven't lost a single U.S. headquarters since, and, indeed, the one company that was leaving then came back. So, these do affect location decisions, and we should be cognizant of that.

Mr. GROTHMAN. Thank you.

Mrs. MCCLAIN. Thank you. I want to thank my colleagues for pointing out that the President's budget reduces the deficit by $3 trillion. Another interesting fact I would like to add is the President's budget actually increases taxes by 4.5 trillion. Interesting, it only reduces the deficit by 3 trillion. But with that said, I would like to recognize the gentlewoman from Texas, Ms. Crockett.

Ms. CROCKETT. Thank you so much, Madam Chair, and thank you so much to all of you for being here. You definitely make me so happy that I did not do the economist side of things as I was supposed to do as a business major. So nevertheless, I just want to be clear about a few things because I feel as if the conversation is veering off in a couple of different ways. Can I have each of you agree with me or just say you disagree that inflation is a multifaceted issue? Yes or no.

Mr. HOLTZ-EAKIN. I am not even sure I understand the question, but I will say yes.

Ms. CROCKETT. OK. Dr. Taylor?

Mr. TAYLOR. It is multifaceted, but there are a few things that we know is a big factor in inflation, is the Fed.

Ms. CROCKETT. OK.

Mr. KONCZAL. Multiple causes to our current inflation.

Ms. CROCKETT. OK. Perfect. Along with that, would you all agree with me that the inflation that we are experiencing in the United States is not solely because of one person being in the White House, but this is inflation that has affected the entire world? Yes or no. I will start it this way.

Mr. KONCZAL. As of 2022, U.S. is not an outlier. There is an increase in inflation.

Ms. CROCKETT. Thank you so much.

Mr. TAYLOR. So, I think it is the Federal Reserve, and they have been followed now too slowly by the ECB and the other countries in Latin America. It is a global phenomenon.

Ms. CROCKETT. Thank you so much.

Mr. HOLTZ-EAKIN. It is global.

Ms. CROCKETT. Thank you so much, and I would agree with you that it is global. And I had the privilege of traveling on our last district work weekend, and I left the country, and I had some conversations about what they were experiencing economically, as well as conversations about how, say, those that threatened not to raise the debt ceiling, which I know we are not here to talk about that. But we have conflated the budget with debt ceiling conversations continually, so I just decided I will go ahead and conflate, continue on with the tradition of this House.

But in talking to them, I was curious to know, what did inflation look like to you, and surprisingly, it looked a lot like what it looked like here. They talked about supply chain issues as it relates to food. They talked about the war in Ukraine. I will admit that they did not talk about healthcare as much because, you know, in fact, I believe, in your opening statement, you mentioned Europe. Europe actually has universal healthcare. So, when you look at, say, a pandemic, we didn't have as many people that did not have health coverage. And I know about lacking in health coverage because in the great state of Texas, we have over 5 million people that are not covered. That tends to drive costs up when we increased the demand so much on the system that was really already on the brink and we weren't providing coverage, but that is yet another issue for another day.

I know there was just mention about tax cuts, and I will go to you. I am not going to slaughter your name. So, I am going to just go like this, right? So, the Trump tax cuts not only devastated this country's finances with deficits, but it also set the stage for inflation even before the pandemic. Would you agree with this statement or disagree?

Mr. KONCZAL. I am not sure. I need to know more context. It did not provide any kind of increase in investment that economists have found, which have left us in a worse position for our infrastructure and for our ability to produce.

Ms. CROCKETT. Absolutely. Thank you so much, and you would agree with me that it is important to invest. And let me ask you all this again because I like having all three of you all participate. You would agree with me that no one had a playbook for what to do in the midst of a pandemic, correct, in order to make sure we didn't suffer from the inflation that we are seeing?

Mr. HOLTZ-EAKIN. I guess I would tend to disagree. I think that in March 2020, what the Fed saw very clearly was across the economy—cash-flow crunches, liquidity crunches in the lingo—because the customers disappeared while hiding from the virus. And the Fed knows how to deal with liquidity shortages, and it dealt with them, and that was a playbook they ran from the financial crisis.

Ms. CROCKETT. I didn't want to get into it back and forth. I guess I am not going to get to you all because we only got 40 seconds. But for instance, I live in Dallas, and I believe that there is housing crisis all over the country. There are plenty of people we know right now. Commercial businesses are still complaining about the fact that people aren't going into the businesses, right? And so, we know that our work force has actually morphed into something else.

There are people that saw an opportunity to be able to take care of their children, and stay at home and work, and save that money. Would you not agree that there had been actually a shift? Right now, what I hear from small business owners is they don't have a work force, so I don't think that the Fed can fix that or fix that person that, say, has a preexisting condition and decides, I don't want to risk my life by going to work. Do you think that changing the Fed rate can fix those types of things that were going on, which is why my first question was? Do you not agree that this was a multifaceted issue?

Mr. HOLTZ-EAKIN. So, the Fed can't control supply issues, and labor force participation is part of the aggregate supply issues. It can only control demand issues through the quantitative tightening, buying back the bond, selling off the bonds, and raising rates.

Mrs. MCCLAIN. Thank you. The Chair recognizes the gentleman from South Carolina, Mr. Fry.

Mr. FRY. Thank you, Madam Chair, for having this hearing today. Thank you to the panel for your time and your testimony. I really appreciate that. I am glad that we are having this hearing. I think it is really important.

I am a freshman and when we are running, we talk to people in our districts about what they face, and they are seeing 40-year high inflation. They are seeing gas prices are up, grocery prices are through the roof, pantry staples such as eggs, butter, milk, chicken, have skyrocketed. And what is even worse, I think, is that in the district that I represent, that is home to 163,000 retired seniors, 1 in 6 seniors in America are considering returning to work because they can no longer afford the rising cost of living. I think about that. I think about the middle-income Americans on fixed incomes. I think about seniors who are on fixed incomes. Dr. Holtz-Eakin, you previously testified in February 2021 that the American Rescue Plan injected too large of a stimulus into the American economy. Can you elaborate on that?

Mr. HOLTZ-EAKIN. Certainly. The bill, when proposed, came at a time when the weekly and monthly data that we received suggested the economy is growing quite rapidly. A good summary of this is something produced by the Atlanta Fed known as GDPNow, which sort of gives you an estimate of what is the current growth rate is in the quarter for GDP, and it was at 6.5 percent. So, this was not the same as March 2020 when the economy was falling at a rate that ultimately contracted by nearly 10 full percentage points in a single quarter, was extraordinary. So, we are in a completely different situation. We are growing quite rapidly, and we are getting close to full employment. We are getting close to potential GDP, and there is no reason to have a nearly $2 trillion stimulus. It is way too big for whatever problem you might have imagined remained, and so it was going to be a big macroeconomic error.

Mr. FRY. Do you still two years later maintain that same assessment that the American Rescue Plan overstimulated the economy?

Mr. HOLTZ-EAKIN. Absolutely.

Mr. FRY. Is there anything from your original assessment to now that has changed in that?

Mr. HOLTZ-EAKIN. Oh yes, I got one piece badly wrong. I thought the biggest fallout would be to repeat what we had seen in 2020. We passed the CARES Act, $2.5 trillion spending, and in May 2020, the U.S. savings rate went to 33 percent. That is positively un-American. We do not save a third of every dollar, and that then flowed into asset classes, and we saw, broadly, equities were up. Housing was up. That is when crypto first became a big deal. Every asset class got inflated. Saw the same phenomenon after the December 2020, $900 billion stimulus.

And so, I was afraid, on the heels of that, with all of this money flow into asset price inflation, the Fed would take a look at a whole bunch of asset bubbles, and have to just pull the plug on them and raise rates sharply, and we would have a recession in the immediate aftermath of a terrible pandemic downturn. I thought that was sort of lining up to do that. I was wrong because the economy opened up at roughly the same time, the vaccines came online, and the money came out of the asset classes and into the consumer purchases and became consumer price inflation instead.

Mr. FRY. Do you think that the Inflation Reduction Act, in fact, reduced inflation?

Mr. HOLTZ-EAKIN. No single act reduces inflation. Its contribution was minimal. At best, it was $300 billion in deficit reduction backloaded, so it was going to be five years off, and we hope the Fed has got us at two percent well before that. At the same time the Inflation Reduction Act was being considered, Congress passed the CHIPS and Science Act, $300 billion of pure deficit-financed spending, the PATH Act, up to $600 billion dollars by CBO's estimate of pure deficit finance spending. It is the cumulative spending and tax cuts by the Congress that matter for inflation, and in 2022, it continued to produce inflationary pressures.

Mr. FRY. So, will the subsidies—you are testifying, your testimony is that the subsidies included in those packages increase those inflationary pressures?

Mr. HOLTZ-EAKIN. They pale in comparison to doing $2 trillion in a month, but they are of the same type.

Mr. FRY. Right, but all three of those collectively and even individually cause that inflationary pressure?

Mr. HOLTZ-EAKIN. Continually. No question.

Mr. FRY. Madam Chair, thank you, and I yield back the balance of my time to you.

Mrs. MCCLAIN. Thank you. The Chair recognizes the gentlelady from Vermont, Ms. Balint.

Ms. BALINT. Thank you, Madam Chair. Last year, as so many Vermont families like mine saw their grocery bills, their gas bills skyrocket, we know that many American companies were posting record profits. And according to a staff analysis by the Subcommittee on Economic and Consumer Policy this past fall, there is clear evidence that shows record price hikes, record profits, profit margins that not only helped to drive inflation, but are also continuing to keep prices high.

So, from 1979 to 2019, profits contributed to only 11 percent— 11 percent—of price growth in the United States, but from the second quarter of 2020 through the end of 2021, profits accounted for roughly 54 percent of price increases. Four of the largest meatpacking companies saw profits increase by 134 percent between 2019 and 2021. The two largest public companies and the rental car industry enjoyed a 597 percent increase in profits. Three of the biggest shipping companies saw profits raise by—wait for it because I couldn't believe it, had to go back and check—nearly 30,000 percent—nearly 30,000 percent. I know that the Vermonters, because Vermonters watch C-SPAN—Vermonters watch this, they are howling at 30,000 percent. It is not in their minds that they are being fleeced. They are absolutely being fleeced. The Subcommittee analysis detailed numerous instances in which companies were using inflation as an excuse to justify jacking up their prices and forcing consumers to pay more to pad their profit margins.

So, Mr. Konczal, am I pronouncing your name right? Mr. Konczal, why did we see such a significant unconscionable increase in excess corporate profits in this time period?

Mr. KONCZAL. I think inflation was reflected in corporate profits for a couple of different reasons. One was the shift from services to goods. I think when you have the kind of supply chain problems we have that ends up with higher prices, it is moderated through prices. I think there is some evidence, or at least there is certainly something worth looking at more formally, about whether or not firms have used the opportunity of this crisis and reopening to raise prices a little bit higher than they would have otherwise.

I think a lot of economists and certainly a lot of financial analysts are a little surprised that the margins, corporations, their profit margins have not declined throughout 2022 and still seem like they might not even decline for quite some time. Even a little bit of a decline in those margins through competition, through proper regulatory scrutiny, would allow inflation to come down while the labor markets still stay strong. I think it is in general, and also, I think it is worth noting that we don't see workers or wages really leading this inflation, like some argue that happened in the 1970's. This is really being reflected on the corporate side. Ms. BALINT. I really appreciate that. I have to bring up what I hear when I travel around Vermont. We have a lot of general stores in Vermont. These are little mom-and-pop shops. They are trying to sell groceries in these tiny rural communities. And I talked to them, and they say what is happening at the corporate level is disgusting. These are not necessarily Democrats that are saying this. There are people across the political spectrum who are trying to feed the people in their communities.

And so, I wanted to go back to something that I saw. Again, it is really hard to believe some of this stuff. The Subcommittee analysis also found examples of corporate executives essentially admitting to using inflation as a cover for massive price hikes. We had one executive, make sure I get this right, executive from Kroger saying, "Hey, a little bit of inflation is always good in our business." We had another one saying, this one was from industrial sealants, "We don't reduce prices on the back of these increases. We are going to see what the consumer will bear." Other people said that. I could go on and on.

So, the question to you is when we are trying to convey to our constituents back home why it is that they are still seeing incredible inflation right now, like, how do you articulate for them, regular people, because that is why I ran for office, to show up as a regular person here. How do I explain to them a 30,000 profit increase? How do I explain that?

Mr. KONCZAL. I think it is very hard to explain. I mean, in that specific case, I would explain that the ports have been disinvested in for decades, that our infrastructure is not the capacity it needs. And that is why we needed to make important investments to be able to have the access to ports and capacity that we need to handle those specific problems. More generally, people are going to debate why inflation went up, but the fact that corporate profits remained so high and so elevated, it is part of the reason inflation is not going to come down as quickly as it should.

Ms. BALINT. Thank you. I yield back.

Mrs. MCCLAIN. Thank you. The Chair recognizes the gentleman from New York, Mr. Langworthy.

Mr. LANGWORTHY. Well, thank you so much, Madam Chairwoman, and thank you so much for our witnesses and the testimony that you have presented here today.

One of the great areas of concern in my district, in the 23d congressional District in New York, which is large swaths of agricultural territory in the New York-Pennsylvania line along with the suburbs of Erie County and in Buffalo, is the high cost of energy. And, Dr. Holtz-Eakin, are you aware that the prices of American home heating this year rose by more than 27 percent?

Mr. HOLTZ-EAKIN. Sounds about right, yes.

Mr. LANGWORTHY. It has been something that people across upstate New York have been gravely concerned about while they are struggling with some of the proposals at the state and Federal level of reforms and changes to the way we heat our homes. The other concern is mandates on electric vehicles into the future. I have questions. Do you think that President Biden's recommendation to Americans that one of their ways to reduce energy prices is for them to go out, buy an electric car? Do you think that that is a legitimate solution for most Americans?

Mr. HOLTZ-EAKIN. A, the price point on electric cars is well above mass penetration. It is not going to happen that fast, so the magnitudes are all wrong. It is not going to do anything substantial. It is a single price. Again, the inflation phenomenon is prices across the economy, all goods and services rising at the same time.

And so, picking out individual items and focusing on them, which is something people do a lot, misses the larger point. We have prices going up everywhere.

Mr. LANGWORTHY. Right. I think you bring up a great point. I mean, estimates have the cost of an electric vehicle between $45,000 and $50,000, on average. A median household income is $50,000 to $55,000, and that is with Federal subsidy involved. Instead of recommending that Americans spend almost every single penny of their income on an electric vehicle, do you believe that the Biden administration should instead be focused on increasing American energy production at all different levels?

Mr. HOLTZ-EAKIN. I think the strategy which they have undertaken on the climate front is an extremely unwise one and quite risky. I mean, it basically says we are going to have the cleanest electricity sector on the globe. And we are going to send that electricity across the grid that doesn't exist to power every home, industrial plant, vehicle in the United States, and that is betting the ranch on one solution, which isn't smart. If you let markets decide things, they will diversify and come up with lots of solutions, so I think it is not a wise strategy.

It is also quite troubling from a sort of matching it up to the research literature, in any serious study of the economics of climate change. Natural gas is the bridge fuel, and natural gas is a focus for decades during the transition to cleaner energy portfolio. So, to take it off the table in 2021, 2022, makes no sense whatsoever.

Mr. LANGWORTHY. I am glad that you brought up natural gas because in my state of New York, in my actual congressional district, the Marcellus Shale runs right under the ground in the southern tier counties of New York and Pennsylvania does safely——

Mr. HOLTZ-EAKIN. As a native of Pittsburgh, we want to thank New York for their policies.

Mr. LANGWORTHY. But, unfortunately, you are right. In 2015, our former Governor, Andrew Cuomo, announced a moratorium on the safe pumping of natural gas, making New York as the first state with this significant shale resources to do so. In your opinion, could ending bans on fracking in states like New York, could that increase American energy production?

Mr. HOLTZ-EAKIN. It would. We have actually already seen this from about 2008 to 2012. The hydraulic fracturing and horizontal drilling revolution generated a North American energy supply expansion that made us the preeminent source on the globe, and it was also an enormous source of economic growth at that time.

Mr. LANGWORTHY. That is right. Do you believe that the jobs created by domestic production of oil and natural gas could benefit Americans in the economy as a whole, and can it actually bring down inflation?

Mr. HOLTZ-EAKIN. Now, again, it is energy. It is energy prices, not oil prices, but it is a crucial input. When we see global oil prices go up, we see fertilizer costs go up, we see all sorts of cost pressures that have to get passed along to consumers, so it can contribute.

Mr. LANGWORTHY. OK. Do you believe that the anti-fossil fuel, political leaders that are restricting the supply of oil by opposing oil investment, oil production, oil transport, that they are causing energy prices to rise?

Mr. HOLTZ-EAKIN. Global oil markets are always tightly balanced, and so small variations in supply and demand produce big price swings. And so that certainly has had an impact over the past several years.

Mr. LANGWORTHY. Very good. Thank you very much, and I yield back.

Mrs. MCCLAIN. Thank you. The Chair recognizes the gentleman from Missouri, Mr. Burlison.

Mr. BURLISON. Thank you, Madam Chair. Thank you for coming. I really appreciate it.

I think that when we are looking at this situation with all this unbelievable inflation that we are experiencing, right, and consumers are suffering, the question is, what do we do about it? To me, the answer is, how do we grow our way out of this, right? How do we increase productivity, increase the production of eggs so that the price per egg drops? I mean, this is simple supply and demand economics, right? So, the question is what do we need to do as policymakers to figure out how to motivate, whether it is a farmer that wants to invest in more chicken production or someone who wants to invest in more energy production? What kind of things can we do as a policy to ramp up productivity?

Mr. TAYLOR. First of all, you don't increase taxes. That is maybe the first thing and that will——

Mr. BURLISON. Wait. Wait. Can you repeat that?

Mr. TAYLOR. You don't increase taxes.

Mr. BURLISON. OK. And elaborate on that?

Mr. TAYLOR. Well, taxes are a drag. It reduces productivity. It is not a good thing to do, especially in a situation we are now. We have a productivity problem.

Mr. BURLISON. So, if we were to decrease taxes, then all of those evil companies that have profit, they would, instead of investing that profit into future production, future mining operations, future chicken farms, they would hoard the money, right, hoard the profits, or they are more likely to do that, right?

Mr. TAYLOR. They are interested in making profit, so use the money most effectively.

Mr. BURLISON. Right.

Mr. TAYLOR. Let me say because you began by saying inflation is a problem, and so many of your colleagues have said inflation is a problem. It is a problem, but it is not necessarily related to these profits. It is a different subject.

Mr. BURLISON. Right.

Mr. TAYLOR. It is monetary policy.

Mr. BURLISON. Right.

Mr. TAYLOR. I mean, you can see it, such as the U.S. is all over the place. So, this Congress used to have efforts to try to have the Fed report more on what it is doing. That seemed to disappear. I think it should come back because in a sense, I am not the best person to answer your questions. I am not at the Federal Reserve Board. Those are the people who can answer your questions, and if you had a specific requirement that they say what they are doing, it will be much easier for you.

Mr. BURLISON. But going back to my question, though, is other policies. Mr. Konczal?

Mr. KONCZAL. That was right.

Mr. BURLISON. How do we increase productivity?

Mr. KONCZAL. There are a lot of ways. To increase overall growth, I think increasing the labor force, that is through immigration, through bringing more people into the work force. There are a lot of different ways to do that. I think housing has been a real lag on productivity, so ways that we can intervene to make it easier to build more housing, particularly in places that are pretty housing constrained.

Mr. BURLISON. So, what would that mean? Reducing regulations, reducing the tax burden on people who are developing?

Mr. KONCZAL. I mean, it is fundamentally a local zoning issue, so it is very hard to do at the Federal level, but I know a lot of policymakers who are thinking very hard about this.

Mr. BURLISON. OK. Dr. Holtz-Eakin, your comments on that? How do we ramp up productivity in the United States?

Mr. HOLTZ-EAKIN. You don't, but firms have every interest in being more productive.

Mr. BURLISON. I guess I should ask, how do I, how do we incentivize private actors to ramp up productivity?

Mr. HOLTZ-EAKIN. You want to have an environment which has good incentives for the deployment of risky capital into innovation, physical capital accumulation, human capital accumulation. That means setting the tax rules and keeping them, not moving around. Having sunsets is a bad idea.

Mr. BURLISON. Creating certainty.

Mr. HOLTZ-EAKIN. The regulatory burden, I think, is an under-appreciated issue, and at AF, we keep track of the cost of every regulation issued by the Federal Government, and there have been some remarkable changes over the years. In the Obama Administration, the average cost to regulation, $1.1 per day every day for eight straight years, $890 billion of self-reported regulatory costs. That is a $900 billion still tax increase. Trump administration, essentially zero over four years. First year, the Biden administration, $200 billion regulatory costs. That cost goes somewhere, and it goes into inflation. It comes at the expense of productive investments. So, having a more sane regulatory environment, having a stable set of tax rules all would help firms decide what will be productive, and the productivity will take care of itself.

Mr. BURLISON. I appreciate it. Thank you.

Mrs. MCCLAIN. Thank you. The Chair recognizes the Chairman of the full Committee from Kentucky, Mr. Comer.

Chairman COMER. Thank you, Madam Chairman. Dr. Holtz- Eakin, do you agree that inflation is reflected more in corporate profit or corporate greed, as some of our friends on the other side of the aisle would refer, than it is for labor cost?

Mr. HOLTZ-EAKIN. No, I don't agree with that. We have done some work at AF on the sort of favorite measures of concentration and do they lead to higher prices. They do not. Do they lead to reduced competition in the form of entry? They do not. So, this line is at odds with the data.

Chairman COMER. Can you explain why corporate profits are increasing in recent decades?

Mr. HOLTZ-EAKIN. I haven't done a specific study on that. I would be happy to get back to you.

Chairman COMER. Would there be repercussions for reducing corporate profits for the sake of reducing inflation?

Mr. HOLTZ-EAKIN. Yes. The profit motive drives business decisionmaking, so you would be interfering with a lot.

Chairman COMER. Dr. Taylor, would you advise the Fed to take a wait-and-see approach raising interest rates because of the tightening labor market?

Mr. TAYLOR. No, I think it is pretty clear they need to move ahead. They began to talk about it recently. The question is how far. I say six percent in my testimony. I think that is a place to go, and it would be beneficial to the economy. It will increase growth and reduce the chances of a serious recession later.

Chairman COMER. So, what would you say the most important way to fight inflation would be? What is the silver bullet there because the media wasn't as interested in inflation during the last administration, and they came to the summary, many in the media, that the Inflation Reduction Act actually would reduce inflation. Obviously, it has not. So, what would you say the most important way to fight inflation would be?

Mr. TAYLOR. So, I think that the problem is the Federal Reserve. And globally, you have the European Central Bank, you have other central banks around the world, which are tending to follow the Fed to some extent as they have in the past. That is an important thing, so the focus should be the Fed. And as I mentioned, this Congress used to have policies that will require more reporting. That is why the Fed has reported a little bit more, but that could go further so you would get explicit answer from them. Why did you have the interest rate zero for so long? It was the feeling, that kind of thing, and they haven't answered that.

Chairman COMER. I couldn't agree more. I couldn't agree more. So, last question, just to follow up, does investing in infrastructure and housing reduce inflation because I think that is something the President has implied. Like if we invest more money in housing and infrastructure, will that reduce inflation?

Mr. TAYLOR. So, it will reduce inflation for some goods, but it might increase otherwise. I think you have to think about inflation, as Doug indicated, it is a measure of all prices, and this two percent just doesn't choose a few. And so, all the things that have been mentioned in this hearing are hoping there is one particular issue, but it is a broader set of issues.

Chairman COMER. And talking about having to raise interest rates, obviously, one reason you raise interest rate is to fight inflation. But when you raise interest rates, that reduces new home builds, new housing starts. That makes housing less affordable as opposed to more affordable just simply by supply and demand. I think that is something to point out. Go ahead, Dr. Taylor, you can finish, and then Dr. Holtz, you can.

Mr. TAYLOR. What we have learned about monetary policy, if it is clear what is happening, it doesn't have to be these crunches. People realize that interest rates will be a little higher, but that will be good because inflation comes down, so they think about this whole process. The more communicative the Fed can be, the more you can participate in this discussion, the better this will work, and you wouldn't have the bad circumstance you are referring to.

Mr. HOLTZ-EAKIN. So, I want to agree with that. I mean, the idea is to have them look past what is happening right now toward a rule that will show a path of future interest rates, and they can plan the whole lifecycle, the construction, and the sale, and all of that. In the absence of that, the idea that right now, if the Federal Government just goes out and engineer a residential construction boom, that will somehow be effective in fighting inflation, misses the fact that the Fed is trying to stop residential construction.

And if you start trying to build it, they will raise rates more because when they reduce residential construction, that transmits monetary policies to a big swath of the economy. You don't buy refrigerators to put in the houses, you don't buy furnaces to put in them, you don't carpet them, and that is a traditional route for the Fed to influence the demand for goods, especially in the economy. So, to fight the Fed, when you are asking it to deal with inflation is not good policy.

Chairman COMER. Right. Exactly. Madam Chair, I yield back. Thank you for this very substantive Committee hearing.

Mrs. MCCLAIN. Thank you, and now the Chair recognizes the gentlewoman from California, Ms. Porter.

Ms. PORTER. Thank you very much.

If we want to understand the multifaceted root causes of inflation, it is important we lay out some basic economics. You all know this, but I want to make sure the American people do, and we have a great panel to help us learn.

So, Mr. Konczal, I am going to have you help me with this basic economics 101, supply and demand situation. So, here is the basic model on economics that helps us determine how much real GDP an economy produces, and at what price level. So, what are these lines on the graph? The supply line, long-range aggregate supply shows us how much real GDP an economy can supply at different price levels. And the demand curve, aggregate demand right here, shows us how much real GDP people are willing to consume at different price levels. Where these curves intersect, that shows how much real GDP our economy generates and what prices people are going to face. So, what causes inflation? What happens when we change this intersection? Let's demonstrate. So, Mr. Konczal, what does increased government spending do to the demand curve?

Mr. KONCZAL. It would increase. It would move it to the right. Ms. PORTER. It would move it over here, so this is what happens when you increase government spending. Everyone see? Prices go up. All right. What happens to the demand curve if the government, say, increases taxes on wealthy Americans?

Mr. KONCZAL. It would move the demand curve to the left and decrease the price level.

Ms. PORTER. Prices would go down. OK. So, let's combine these two effects. What would happen if you increased government spending, but you paid for it all with taxes on the wealthy?

Mr. KONCZAL. In general, it would not have an effect.

Ms. PORTER. So unclear, but indeterminate, could balance each other out depending on the scope and size of those spendings. So, when you have legislation that puts money in the hands of people who need it, say, during a pandemic, but you make sure you are getting at least that much back from taxes on rich people, you should not see much aggregate meaningful inflation. Now, it is even more promising for inflation when the legislation generates surplus tax revenue that might even be able to help cool inflation. Can you raise your hand, all three of you, if you agree that the Inflation Reduction Act followed the basic anti-inflationary principle of putting money in people's hands, but raising taxes on the wealthy? Anybody? One. Mr. Konczal.

So, Mr. Holtz-Eakin, you are here to advise Congress about how to contain inflation, and the best hint I got from your testimony is on page one. You said, "Congress should not further exacerbate inflation through excessive spending," and you said there is no good option. When we get to inflation, it is all tough. So, what is next? How are we going to reduce inflation without inflicting pain on working families and seniors?

Mr. HOLTZ-EAKIN. So, I say this lovingly, but please don't try. I think that this is the Fed's problem that you have delegated to the Fed and given it a mandate for full employment price stability, and you should let them pursue that mandate, review their efforts with oversight hearings. That is exactly the right thing to do. And you should think about setting the parameters for fiscal policy, the tax structure, the tax levels, the kinds of spending programs we have to maximize long-run economic growth, and not move them back and forth quickly to try to respond to whatever is going on this year, next year. Congress is not well suited for that. It is much more suited for the long-run growth potential for the economy, and so that is an allocation of roles, I think, would be preferable.

Ms. PORTER. So, for example, investing in things like infrastructure, that is a long-term growth?

Mr. HOLTZ-EAKIN. Where appropriate, yes. Where appropriate, yes.

Ms. PORTER. Where appropriate to invest in that. So, I think as we sort of wrap up this, I think, really productive hearing with an amazing all-star, and let me just say, intimidating witness panel. I want to sort of go through what I think are the key takeaways. It doesn't cause inflation to make paid-for investments in working families. If you pay for them, if you take the money out of the economy with taxes, and you put it back in other places, that is allocative, but on aggregate, if you get it right, it shouldn't cause inflation. That is what that curve, that chart was showing. It is a good idea to make wealthy pay their fair share, to pay off the national debt, and help cool inflation. We take some of that surplus tax revenue, we can actually use it to cool inflation.

Democrats' Inflation Reduction Act, you two didn't agree, but I think it basically met that basic principle of doing those two things: making investments in families and making the wealthy pay their fair share. And the fourth thing is, I don't think, and I really appreciate your honesty, Dr. Holtz-Eakin, there really isn't a secret Republican plan or Democratic plan for that matter, to fight inflation. There is no easy way to do this without punishing hardworking American families, so the solution here isn't to cut spending programs that people rely on. The solution here is to try to support families as we get through this really difficult economic period and let our economy try to find its way back to a level of inflation. That is less painful than where we find each other today. So, I yield back and thank the Chairwoman for her indulgence.

Mrs. MCCLAIN. I thank my colleague for her comments, and right now, I will recognize the Ranking Member, Ms. Porter, for her closing statement.

Ms. PORTER. Thank you again, Madam Chairwoman, and thank you again, for all of our witnesses. I think you probably know that I don't flatter witnesses unnecessarily. You really are an all-star panel, and we really are grateful for you being here today.

Look, I am a single mom with three school-aged kids, and like all of you, I am tired of what is happening at the grocery store. It used to be fun, and now it is just tough to go in there. I am tired of feeling the sticker shock and putting the cereal back on the shelves because we can't afford it. I am tired of searching for coupons and finding that there aren't any to help me bring down prices. I am deeply invested in trying to rein in inflation for constituents and for my own family. But when we talk about inflation, we need to do it justice by not oversimplifying. And today, what many Democrats have tried to do is demonstrate that calling inflation a preventable crisis is an oversimplification.

Now, it is our job in Congress to set aside the partisan games and try to get to work. Inflation is complex. It is multifaceted, and there are certainly tools that government, sometimes Congress, but, as you suggested, often not Congress, can use to try to address inflation. We can keep making our tax code more fair. We can crack down on tax cheats so that we increase tax revenue, can pay down debt, can cool inflation. We can keep fighting corporate monopolies so that our markets can be more competitive and can deliver lower costs. That is really the promise of a capitalist economy. We can keep shoring up supply chains, bringing manufacturing back home, and helping smooth the transport of goods to market. We can invest in long-term structural investments that will do right by our economy, things like infrastructure, things like renewable energy, because these investments pay off in the long run with lower costs for families and a stronger, more stable, more resilient economy that is less vulnerable to inflationary shocks.

It is possible to do all of these things together, but we can't use inflation as a convenient scapegoat to cut programs that seniors and kids and families rely on. Wherever Committee Republicans land, and I hope the chairwoman will address that, the American people should know that Committee Democrats are going to continue to work tirelessly toward thinking about how to navigate this inflationary period while honoring our commitment to make life better for the American people. I yield back.

Mrs. MCCLAIN. Thank you, Ms. Porter, and thank you for conducting my first oversight hearing with me. I appreciate it. I look forward to working with you in the future to come up with some commonsense solutions to help the American people move forward.

I now recognize myself for the closing statements.

I would agree that we are not here to talk about cuts. That is not our plan, but I first feel that we need to start talking about the causes of what got us in this situation. So, we are not going to repeat the same thing over and over again because if we can learn from the past, we can have a brighter future, and I think that is what both sides of the aisle are trying to do for the American people. I can assure you that is what I am trying to do, but we must learn from our mistakes so we are not deemed to repeat them in the future.

Today's hearing has illustrated how important actually facts are over fiction, and we need to stop with the messaging and take a look at the facts. When the pandemic hit in March 2020, inflation was 1.5 percent as compared to the prior year. When Biden took office in January 2021, inflation was at 1.4 percent, compared to the previous year. That is just a fact. On March 11, 2021, Democrats jammed through $1.9 trillion American Rescue Plan. By April, inflation had risen from 1.4 percent to 4.2 percent. By December, inflation was at seven percent. By June 2022, inflation was at 9.1 percent. The Biden administration and congressional Democrats did not stop there. On August 16, 2022, the $740 billion Inflation Reduction Act was signed into law, again, inflation. Too many dollars chasing too few goods.

We are just doubling down on the American people, yet Democrats have spent this entire hearing denying that inflation exists, claiming inflation is a high-class-only problem and blaming the corporations, who I might add, those corporations pay massive, massive amount of taxes. And what would happen to the taxes if corporations, because there is a third option, the corporations could just stop producing? And then who would pay the massive amount of taxes that the corporations pay because there is another option. We just don't ever want to talk about that.

We cannot fix a problem of inflation until our colleagues recognize what all hard-working Americans recognize and what we are dealing with, and that is, inflation exists. The truth is Democrats' reckless spending caused the dramatic inflation, hurting millions of Americans. This isn't an opinion, this is a fact, and we need to learn from this fact, to not double down and make the same mistakes again.

The data clearly illustrates that despite the destructive economic impacts of the pandemic, President Trump had the economy on a rapid path to recovery, 1.4 percent inflation, with his pro-growth and pro-economic policies. Yet Democrats choose to flood the economy with unnecessary—unnecessary—remember, we passed, we infused money into the economy. We didn't spend it all, and we passed two more policies that put more money into the economy. I mean, we flooded the economy with unnecessary and wasteful spending, causing inflation to spike at a 40-year high and put the economy, I might add, on the brink of recession, no matter how you want to change the definition of a recession. My colleagues across the aisle must acknowledge that it is their inflationary crisis and recognize that Congress needs to immediately address it.

So, I thank the witnesses for your time. You have been remarkable, all three of you. The wealth of knowledge that you three bring is amazing.

And without objection, the Members will have five legislative days to submit materials and to submit additional written questions for the witnesses which will be forwarded to the witnesses for their responses.

Mrs. MCCLAIN. If there are no further business, without objection, the Subcommittee stands adjourned. Thank you so much.

[Whereupon, at 3:45 p.m., the Subcommittee was adjourned.]

Chapter 4

Prices on the Rise: Examining of Inflation on Small Businesses*

Committee on Small Business

Wednesday, June 7, 2023
Washington, DC.

The Committee met, pursuant to call, at 2:01 p.m., in Room 2360, Rayburn House Office Building, Hon. Roger Williams [chairman of the Committee] presiding.

Present: Representatives Williams, Luetkemeyer, Stauber, Meuser, Mann, Ellzey, Molinaro, Alford, Bean, Hunt, LaLota, Vela´zquez, Golden, Mfume, Phillips, Landsman, McGarvey, Gluesenkamp, Perez, Scholten, Thanedar, Davids, and Pappas.

Chairman WILLIAMS. Good afternoon to everybody. And before we begin, we're going to take a moment and ask Congressman Meuser of the great state of Pennsylvania to lead us in our opening prayer in the Pledge of Allegiance.

Mr. MEUSER. Please stand for the Pledge of Allegiance.

Chairman WILLIAMS. I now call the Committee on Small Business to order without objection. The Chair is authorized to declare recess of the committee at any time. I now recognize myself for my opening statement. I'd like to welcome everyone to today's hearing, where we will be examining the detrimental effects inflation has had on main street America. I also want to thank our witnesses for joining us today. Your time is greatly valuable and we appreciate you being with us.

---

* This is an edited, reformatted and augmented version of Hearing Before the Committee on Small Business United States, House of Representatives Publication, dated June 7, 2023.

In: Inflation: Background, Causes and Current Policies
Editor: Julie Taylor Lowe
ISBN: 979-8-89530-696-3

According to almost every small business economic survey, inflation has been ranked as the owner's biggest concern going back to 2021. They have been seen utility payments increase because of skyrocketing energy prices, distributors charging more to source materials because of supply chain disruptions, and labor costs rising because of not being able to find qualified workers. In all these instances, small businesses are left with 2 options pass along these price increases to the consumer, or absorb the cost and watch your operating profit margins shrink.

The COVID-19 pandemic started this inflationary cycle that we are still experiencing, but we have seen it prolonged by reckless levels of government spending. The Federal Reserve Bank of San Francisco did a study after the passage of the partisan American Rescue Plan that showed government spending made inflation in the United States spike more than other developed economies. This should not come as a surprise to anyone. There are going to be consequences when the Government continues to stimulate the economy further than what is necessary. This has led to a prolonged period of high prices that has forced the Federal Reserve to raise interest rates to tamper demand.

High interest rates have led to many additional problems that are being faced by small businesses. The cost of getting a loan has greatly increased, and now even the average SBA loan is approaching 10 percent interest. This is forcing banks to tighten their lending standards as they evaluate if it will make sense to even extend the loan, and is forcing many business owners to delay expansion plans because it simply is too expensive in this environment.

There are a few things that I think will stop the runaway inflation problem. First, we must stop reckless government spending, as we say. We all know this was not a transitory issue like so many people claimed when this started in 2021. And we must get the Government's fiscal house in order. Second, we must stop passing burdensome regulations when businesses are forced to hire compliance officers, it is nothing but a drag on a company's bottom line. And a third, we must find ways to secure our supply chains and expand our domestic manufacturing base, whether it be energy or food supply. We must reduce our reliance on foreign influences.

In this hearing, I hope we will explore how each of your businesses and industries have been dealing with this pressing issue that has been affecting every American for the last few years. As the voice for main street here in Washington, the House Committee on Small Business will be working to create an environment where businesses can thrive and where businesses can grow. We are eager to find solutions that will help pave the path towards success for both now and in the future. So, I want to thank all of you again for being here with us today, and I'm looking forward to today's conversation. With that, I want to yield to our distinguished Ranking Member from New York, Ms. Velázquez.

Ms. VELÁZQUEZ. Thank you, Mr. Chairman. The effect of inflation on small businesses is no secret. It can dig into margins and contribute to tighter monetary conditions, limiting access to capital and the ability to grow and expand. However, inflation is not a single threaded issue. It is a complex dynamic of global events. The COVID-19 pandemic, supply chain disruptions, labor shortages, monopolistic price gouging, and geopolitical tensions have created a perfect storm of inflationary pressures that are impacting main street. It is a disservice to our nation's small firms to oversimplify this issue, as a mere consequence of federal spending. We stand in the middle of the global pack in terms of inflation rates.

Yet our recovery from the pandemic has been unparalleled. Fiscal stimulus, like the Cares Act and the American Rescue Plan, turned the deepest post World War II recession into the shortest. Projections from Moody's Analytics predict that without this relief U.S. GDP would have fallen 3 times its actual rate, and we would have experienced a double dip recession in early 2021. Today, we now enjoy unemployment rates at 50 year lows, with GDP recovering to its prerecession trend, something not seen in decades. According to the Federal Reserve, the entire $5 trillion worth of fiscal stimulus deployed in response to the pandemic contributed to only about a third of total inflation. Therefore, we must consider the many other drivers of inflation to create a comprehensive policy response, not play political games.

First, our country has a history of outsourcing and supply chain consolidation. While this made a few shareholders a lot of money in good times, it made us increasingly vulnerable to disruptions. Additionally, the increasing concentration of industries over the past 30 years enabled corporate monopolies to exploit their market power and dramatically increase margins. Democrats focused on enhancing our domestic productive capacity by passing the Infrastructure Investment and Jobs Act to revitalize and bolster our supply chains. We passed the Chips and Science Act to invest in innovation and create resilient domestic supply chains. Finally, the Inflation Reduction Act was enacted to lower health care and energy costs for small businesses while making the U.S. a world leader in clean energy and reducing our dependence on volatile global energy markets. Clearly, there is more to be done, but we are seeing encouraging signs of lower inflation, nearly cut in half from last summer's peak.

While the only Republican plan to fight inflation is draconian cut to our social safety net, democrats have recognized the need to invest in the future to bring long term stability to our small businesses. I thank all the witnesses for their participation and look forward to hearing your testimony. Mr. Chairman, I yield back.

Chairman WILLIAMS. Thank you very much, and I will now introduce our witnesses. Our first witness this afternoon is Mr. Gordon Gray. Mr. Gray is the Vice President for Economic Policy at the American Action Forum, located in Washington, DC. Prior to joining the American Action Forum, he was a Professional Staff Member for the Senate Budget Committee before working for Senator Rob Portman as a Senior Policy Advisor.

Mr. Gray's portfolio includes the federal budget, taxes, the macronomic outlook, and general economic policy. He has testified as an expert witness before the multiple committees in Congress on domestic and economic issues. Mr. Gray is a graduate of Tufts University and has a degree in Political Science. Mr. Gray, thank you for being here today, and we look forward to hearing from you.

Our next witness here with us today is Silvia Saldana Lee. Ms. Lee is the Executive Vice President and Chief Lending Officer of the First Community Bank in Corpus Christi, Texas, and she previously served a 3 year term on the Texas Bankers Association board of Directors. Ms. Lee has worked in the banking for over 31 years and has been with First Community Bank since 2000.

In her current position, she manages all aspects of First Community Bank's lending portfolio, including risk selection, underwriting, and loan production, making her uniquely qualified to discuss the important topic at hand today. Ms. Lee is a graduate of Texas A and M University in Kingsville, Texas, where she received her Bachelor of Business Administration Finance. So, Ms. Lee, thank you for being with us today, and we also look forward to your testimony.

I now recognize my colleague, Mr. Molinaro from New York, the great state of New York, to briefly introduce our third witness who is appearing before us today.

Mr. MOLINARO. Thank you, Mr. Chairman. The great state of New York is happy to welcome Mr. David Zittel. A graduate of Cornell University. Mr. Zittel is president of Ammo. Zittel and Sons, inc. In Eden, New York. The

Zittels have been farming in Eden Valley for six generations, since 1897. Producing vegetables on about 400 acres.

The farm primarily focuses on vegetable production. To sustain operations, the farm heavily relies on a labor force comprising over 100 seasonal workers, some of whom have dedicated more than 2 decades to working at the farm. However, rising inflation rates have driven up prices and wages, which cut into profit margins, making today's hearing all the more relevant and pressing.

Given Mr. Zittel's extensive experience and long-standing ties to the community, his testimony provides invaluable insight into how the current economic conditions are affecting the economic mainstays of local communities like his and his business. Mr. Zittel, thank you for being here today, and we look forward to hearing from you, and I yield back.

Chairman WILLIAMS. Thank you. I now recognize the Ranking Member, Ms. Vela´zquez, to introduce the minorities witness for today's hearing.

Ms. VELA´ ZQUEZ. Thank you, Mr. Chairman. Our final witness today is Dr. Josh Bivens. Dr. Bivens is the Chief Economist at the Economic Policy Institute. His areas of research include macroeconomics inequality, social insurance, public investment, and the economics of globalization. He has been published in both peer reviewed journals, like the Journal of Economic Perspective, as well as in popular print outlets like The New York Times and Wall Street Journal. He is the author of the books Failure by Design: The Story of America's Broken Economy and Everybody Wins Except Most of Us: What Economics Really Teaches Us About Globalization. He holds a PhD in Economics from the New School of Social Research and a BA in Economics from the University of Maryland. Thank you, Mr. Bivens, for joining us on such short notice. Your attendance is greatly appreciated. Thank you and welcome.

Chairman WILLIAMS. Thank you again to all of you for being here today. So before recognizing the witnesses, I'd like to remind them that their oral testimony is restricted to 5 minutes in length. So if you hear this and you're still talking, that means you're talking too long, okay? And if you see the light turn red in front of you, it means your 5 minutes have concluded, and you should wrap up your testimony. So with that, I now recognize Mr. Gray for his 5 minute opening remarks.

Statements of Gordon Gray, Vice President For Economic Policy, American Action Forum; Silvia Saldana Lee, Executive Vice President and Chiel Lending Officer, First Community Bank; Dave Zittel, President, Amos Zittel & Sons, Inc.; Josh Bivens, Chief Economist, Economic Policy Institute

Statement of Gordon Gray

Mr. GRAY. Chairman Rogers, Ranking Member Vela´zquez, and Members of the Committee. It is a privilege to be before this committee again, to join my fellow witnesses and to discuss a matter of National significance: inflation and its effects on the beating heart of American commerce, Small Businesses. In my testimony, I wish to make 3 basic observations: The United States is experiencing persistent inflation that is taxing America's families and businesses.

Policy choices have contributed to the recent rapid acceleration in price levels. Federal policies should be oriented around reducing inflationary pressures, and the record has been mixed at best. I'll briefly discuss these observations in turn. According to the U.S. Census Bureau, the median age of the United States is about 39, which means a little bit more than half the United States population has never experienced inflation like what we've seen over the last couple of years. Not since 1980 has the consumer price index grown as rapidly as was observed in June of 2022, when yearly inflation topped 8.9 percent. Stripping out more volatile food and energy price components to isolate core price growth reveals a similar story of rapid, historically aberrant inflation.

Notably, one can observe a significant divergence between the 2 indices around the time of the Russian invasion of Ukraine that significantly disrupted energy markets. It is clear that event moved food and energy prices, but the fundamental story of U.S. price growth is not about the Russian invasion, but the laws of supply and demand. These laws are in force, and they are taxing small businesses and the households that support them.

Over the last 2 years, yearly price inflation has averaged about 2 percentage points higher than yearly wage growth. Wage growth has been substantially elevated over the same period but has nevertheless failed to keep pace with price growth. Put another way, small business and households are falling behind. While inflation is down off of the recent peak, it remains stubbornly elevated at well above the average of recent decades and more than twice the target rate set by the Federal Reserve. Thus, even though the U.S. inflation outlook has improved, enduring inflation is nevertheless a significant tax on household finance that will diminish the US standard of living. At the current rate of 5 percent, a family with a median income of about $71,000 is paying over $3,500 in price growth.

Food, energy and shelter inflation, which tends to be more volatile but nevertheless represents about half the average household budget, has been more elevated and serves as a uniquely regressive tax. It is worth acknowledging the rocky road that led us here. In March of 2020, the COVID-19 Pandemic precipitated a historic shuttering of the economy. The public policy response was robust, with combined monetary, fiscal and administrative actions estimated to be on the order of $11 trillion. Most notable was the series of bipartisan measures that were enacted in 2020. Through a combination of public policy, effective vaccines and more than a fair amount of grit from the American public, the nation and the economy recovered rapidly. Subsequent policy changes marked a break from the bipartisan tradition that largely characterized the Congressional response to the Pandemic.

One conspicuous example, though not the only one, is the $1.9 trillion American Rescue Plan Act. Despite a chorus of warnings from a diverse range of economists that the act would give a massive injection of fiscal stimulus at a time when it needed, at least the law was passed and sure enough, within 2 months, inflation had nearly doubled before doubling again in the subsequent months. It is important to note that while other global economies faced rapid inflation, the United States was a conspicuous frontrunner, subsequent to the enactment of the American Rescue Plan. To be sure, there are economic forces at work that can and eventually do swamp the effects of temporary legislation. Many of these challenges are beyond the direct control of policymakers.

Accordingly, while I want to emphasize that no single policy change is responsible for the current inflation challenge, to the extent legislation is within the direct control of policymakers, American Rescue Plan stands out as a significant policy error. The Federal Reserve's rapid tightening of monetary policy and eventually improved public comments on the likely course of monetary policy have done and will continue to do most of the work in bringing stubborn inflation under control. But as any household or business relying on credit markets knows this is not costless. Congress should therefore help the Fed by pulling in the same direction. Congress has a somewhat uneven record since the enactment of the American Rescue Plan. The Inflation Reduction Act, for instance, was found to have no effect on inflation by CBO and Penn Wharton. Policies such as the Chips Act and the infrastructure bill must be balanced against the risk of additional inflationary measures. Most recently, the Fiscal Responsibility Act could modestly reduce inflationary pressures through deficit reduction largely deriving from the Act's spending caps. Thank you very much and I look forward to addressing your questions.

Chairman WILLIAMS. Thank you, Ms. Saldana Lee, for her 5 minute opening remarks.

Statement of Silvia Saldana Lee

Ms. SALDANA LEE. Thank you, Chairman Williams, Ranking Member Vela´zquez, and the Committee Members. I appreciate the invite of being here and I pray that my testimony will be beneficial to the objective of this meeting. As Chairman Williams mentioned, my name is Sylvia Lee. I'm a graduate of Texas A and M University Kingsville with a Bachelor's in Finance.

I have been a Texas banker for 32 years with the last 23 years at First Committee Bank in Corpus Christi where I am the Chief Lending Officer. Our bank has 175 employees and is a somewhat unique factor about First Community Bank is that 73 percent of our employees are shareholders via our Employee Stock Ownership Program. Our Community Bank was founded in 1983 and now has eleven branches with 657,000,000 in assets and growing daily. We have a loan portfolio of 458,000,000 consisting of residential and commercial real estate and of course, small business loans, which are the subject of today's hearing.

As a preparatory point, I do want to mention that almost all our Paycheck Protection Program loans that we funded have been paid out at our institution. They consisted of 845 loans in an aggregate amount of 107,000,000. And I can tell you personally that these loans contribute immensely to the ability of our local customers to continue as growing concerns during the pandemic. In my view, lending to small businesses and thereby allowing them to add new customers, purchase property, buy equipment and hire more employees is frankly the most important community service we provide. Federal Reserve data confirmed that small businesses in search of a loan look first to their Community Bank.

With respect to today's hearing topic, namely the impact of inflation on small businesses, the answer is simple and is applicable to small and large businesses and individuals. It is hardship for all, but for small businesses it can often be worse in that they start with smaller margins to absorb adverse outside factors. Everyone is familiar with the severe decline in mortgage origination volume as the Fed's anti-inflation strategy has driven up interest rates nearing the 8 percent range. What is not widely appreciated, however, is that the housing industry is composed almost exclusively of small business contractors.

At our bank, for example, we developed a great market niche in the home construction business, but new credit applications have slowed significantly due to less buyer demand. Recently, a longtime bank customer who owns a small business had an increase in his monthly loan payment of approximately $1,000 due to increased interest rate. The loan has an annual adjustment and repriced. In May 2023, the business owner commented that he would price his goods out of the market to absorb the increased cost of his inventory and increase rates. He mentioned he has increased his prices 10 percent, but would have to raise them 40 percent in order to absorb all those costs. He mentioned that he feels our government does not want small businesses to succeed and wants only large companies in business. It is an unfortunate perspective.

Underwriting small business loans relies primarily on debt coverage ratio, which is monthly debt service in relation to historical net income. With what has been a doubling of interest rates in just the last twelve months, the equation is fairly straightforward in that we are now seeing the cash flow available for debt service drop dramatically for every type of business. This would be especially true for a small startup business, which is probably the most critical local component for a growth economy.

As a bank with a very strong earnings and capital, we are prepared to work with any of our small business borrowers encountering temporary difficulties, and all of us, whether borrowers or lenders, hope that this unprecedented combination of excess fiscal and monetary policy, followed by rapidly rising interest rates will soon come to a pause.

The current market pressure is notwithstanding. Texas is blessed to have a strong economy and very strong banking system. Nevertheless, Texas has not been immune from industry consolidation trends, where the number of FDIC insured banks headquartered in our state has declined from 556 to 387 over the last ten years. An even sadder part of this is that even among the remaining local bank, so many have been forced to abandon important parts of the consumer market, such as home mortgage lending to the larger banks or nonbanks, as the case may be. Fortunately, that has not been the case at First Community Bank. We remain committed to home mortgage, to the home mortgage market, the small business market and as many of the full service banking products as make economic sense. On behalf of the banking industry,

I thank you for your time and the opportunity to appear before you this afternoon.

Chairman WILLIAMS. Thank you very much. And next, I recognize Mr. Zittel for his 5 minute opening remarks.

Statement of Dave Zittel

Mr. ZITTEL. Thank you to the Committee on Small Business and Chairman Roger Williams for inviting me to testify to you today on the impact of inflation on small business like my family farm. My name is David Zittel and my family is owned and operated Amos Zittel and Sons, a fresh market, vegetable and greenhouse farm based in Eden, New York. My brother and cousin and I are currently 4th generation and my son, the fifth generation is now back on the farm. I'm also representing the farming and agricultural community across New York and the country that works hard to produce food and fiber for consumers across the country and globe.

At Amosinol and Suns, we produce a wide variety of fresh vegetables 350 acres in western New York, including lettuce, strawberries, peppers, cabbage, corn, tomatoes, broccoli, eggplant, Brussels sprouts, grape, tomatoes, et cetera. Approximately 95 percent of our produce is sold through our marketing cooperative Eden Valley Growers, which our farm is a proud founding Member of from 1956. This co-op is created to bring growers in the area together to market and sell our produce. In addition, the farm is also consists of greenhouse operations that produce approximately 4 million rooted liner, geraniums and other spring annuals that are marketed through brokers Nationally and retail ready container crops sold to local garden centers. In addition, we grow over 2 million transplants for our field grown vegetables.

The farm employs 40 to 50 individuals year round and approximately 135 employees during the peak season. Because we produce fresh market produce, all the crops must be hand harvested and can be very labor intensive. It also means that our business is directly impacted by market forces and we cannot wait to sell the crop until prices increase. Farmers are price takers, not price makers. As a small family owned business, we feel the direct effects of inflationary pressure to have seen the overall increase in the cost of operating the farm.

While farmers have become more efficient over time and helps overcome the lower commodity pricing, like increasing production per acre, inflation can quickly take away the efficiency gains through the pandemic and even to this day, we continue to feel the impact of inflation. Examples of inflation and rising costs have seen on the farm include tractor equipment parts have increased 15 percent to 30 percent. A delay in timely delivery of these things are also adding to the supply chain issue. The consolidation of agricultural industry, which has decreased available vendors to source, also lends itself to increased prices. The cost of boxes and transportation of our vegetables is up 30 percent, with the cost of the farm of $100,000 this year. Fertilizers and most other inputs are up 30 percent to 50 percent. Cost of feed for dairy farmers is up 25 percent to 40 percent.

All of these things, unfortunately for us, are prices that we receive for our product do not cover and the cost increases since our markets are no longer local but global, resulting in a reduce in profits. Inflation has created a price instability and uncertainty for our farm economy and has made many investment decisions riskier than they would be if inflation remained low or stable. We have an impacted in the last 2 recent historical snowfalls in 2014 and again last November, which resulted in rebuilding greenhouse shops, storage buildings. In both situations we had decent insurance recoveries, but the cost was 3 times. We will be financing another million dollars and the rebuild for the loss from the 72-inch snowfall in November. Held off as long as we could in hopes that interest rates would stabilize or begin to go back down. As we look to the future of our operation, young farmers are so discouraged by challenges that they face in making career in agriculture the expense of land, labor, fuel, energy, machinery, taxes, rules and regulations the list goes on and on.

It is no secret that in New York is a high cost state in the difficult regulations and environment for our family, business and farms. But despite all this, we are so proud that the next generation has decided to carry on the farming tradition. We know that there will remain challenges and need to overcome, including inflation, regulatory requirements and labor challenges. Like to finish with a quote from John F. Kennedy the farmer is the only man in our economy who buys everything at retail, sells everything at wholesale, and pays freight both ways. Thank you.

Chairman WILLIAMS. I now recognize Mr. Bivens for his 5 minute opening remarks.

Statement of Josh Bivens

Mr. BIVENS. Chair Williams, Ranking Member of Vela´zquez and Members of the Committee, thank you for inviting me to testify today. My name is Josh Bivens. I'm the Chief Economist and Research Director of the Economic Policy Institute. EPI is a nonprofit, nonpartisan think tank that uses the tools of economics to identify policies that will boost living standards of low and moderate income families, particularly through their role as workers.

I'd like to make the following points about the subject of this hearing inflation and its effect on small businesses. First, inflation has been a key economic challenge for workers and small businesses over the past 2 years. But inflation is not the only notable economic trend that is emerged in this time. We've also seen by far the best labor market in a generation, particularly for low wage workers. We've also seen extraordinarily fast growth in employment at small businesses and in the aggregate, and extraordinarily fast growth in small business applications. Small business income growth has actually performed better relative to corporate profits since the last business cycle peak than it was doing in the 2 years before the COVID-19 recession. All these salutary trends are the direct result of the policy choice to fight the COVID-19 recession with fiscal relief and recovery at scale.

Second, inflation has not simply been the result of a US Policy mistake. Inflationary pressures have clearly been global, and it is essentially been the inevitable result of massive shocks to the economy and the long lived but steadily dampening ripple effects. The shocks are obvious. The Pandemic, the Russian invasion of Ukraine, and the ripples were mostly about jockeying by different economic actors corporations, workers, small businesses to protect their own real incomes from these shocks. The inflationary pressures, particularly the ripples, could have theoretically been reduced if the economy was allowed to settle into stagnation with really high rates of unemployment for an extended period of time, like we did after the 2008 recession. But inflation wouldn't have been zero even in that scenario and the collateral damage would have been absolutely immense.

Third, the ripple effect stemming from economic actors seeking to insulate their own incomes from price shocks meant that inflation in this time around has mostly been a distributional challenge because one person's income is another person's cost. Higher cost for some has shown up as significant income gains for others that mostly has been the business income of sellers, but particularly corporate profits. A key question is has any small businesses been able to draft in the corporate pricing power wake and charge higher prices themselves to protect their own margins? I would say the first thing to know about this is that the small business sector is incredibly variable and lots of what we call small businesses are actually very rich in privileged enterprises. My guess is this privileged slice of the sector has done quite well to the degree that lots of genuine main street small businesses have been squeezed on the input side but have been unable to pass these costs on. Maybe because their primary customers are big corporations who refuse to pay higher prices to their suppliers. That is more a problem of unbalanced power in markets and monopoly power generating an unlevel playing field. We certainly should address that problem. It is carried long run costs. It is less a problem of inflation per se in terms of the most important input cost labor.

It is important to note that there is no generalized labor shortage anymore relative to pre pandemic trends. Labor supply has essentially fully recovered. There are smart policies we could undertake, particularly large investments, say in Childcare, that would boost labor supply even well above its historic highs. And I think we should absolutely do that. But again, there is no labor shortage today relative to pre COVID trends. Finally, the risk to small businesses from an over aggressive attack on inflation that seeks to slow the economy with contractionary fiscal and monetary policy in the name of tamping down inflation will sacrifice the huge gains from the rapid recovery for no real need. If inflation is already normalizing, and my view is inflation is already normalizing, it is not happening fast enough for any of us.

But I would say one example showing that we do have some time for some patience is if you look at nominal wage growth over the past year. We've seen a sharp deceleration in that growth even as unemployment has remained very low. We had many people a year ago saying that was impossible. We were going to need 6 percent unemployment to get nominal wage growth into a noninflationary place. It is in a noninflationary place today, even with unemployment remaining very low. In short, as challenging as the inflation of the past 2 years has been, it remains the case that many proposed cures could do a lot more damage than normality itself. I look forward to talking more about this issue with the committee. Thank you so much for your time.

Chairman WILLIAMS. Thank you. And we'll now move to the Member questions. Under the 5 minute rule, I recognize myself for 5 minutes. There were many factors that have contributed to inflation. The Pandemic destroyed supply chains, reckless government spending overheated the economy, and businesses are having trouble finding qualified workers to fill open positions. While some of these issues are long, will take some time to get resolved, there are certain things that can be done in the short term that could make an immediate impact on this upward price pressure. And one of these things that the Biden Administration could do to help small business deal with this economic headwind is to end the regulatory assault on the private sector. When businesses are forced to spend more time and resources on compliance, these costs get passed along to the consumer in the form of higher prices or increased fees. So, Mr. Gray, my question to you. Can you discuss the regulatory impact the Biden Administration has had on main street, America, as has inflation, and do you have any suggestions on how Congress could begin to rein in some of the most damaging regulations?

Mr. GRAY. Yes, sir. So I am lucky in that I work with one of the, I think, finer regulatory shops, policy shops in DC. My colleague Dan Gobeck tracks the self reported costs of the accumulation of regulation, and he and his team has been doing this over the years, and we have seen hundreds of billions of dollars in additional regulation. And in the present environment, when a number of the policy approaches that this Congress and policymakers in general have been attempting to expand supply, we later see regulations tacked on that are somewhat in conflict to the notion of supply because they restrict the businesses and workers that may or may not participate in that given activity, and that makes the activity more expensive, thus restricting supply. And so that is a very real challenge at the moment.

Chairman WILLIAMS. Thank you. One of the most harmful aspects of inflation is what the Federal Reserve is being forced to do to get it under control. Interest rates are rising at the fastest pace in decades, and it is making it much more expensive for small business to get loans or service and their debt. We've heard that already today. I have come across my small businesses that have variable term loans we talked about that who are not having to pay a few hundred dollars more each month in interest payments, but it is changing their entire business, even the smallest amount it is eating to their margins and making them unable to remain profitable. So, Ms. Saldana Lee, can you tell us what you're doing on the ground as it relates to small businesses service and their existing debt, as well as the overall loan volume coming through your bank?

Ms. SALDANA LEE. First, the loan volume is not coming through the bank. Our production is very low right now, and most investors have postponed any projects that they had at any one time. And what we're doing is we're actually doing outreach. Our loan officers are reaching out to our borrowers, making sure that they are in a good position, and if they're not, if they're being stressed, if there is anything that we can do to assist them with those stress factors. What we have seen, because we do have a large portfolio of construction loans, our contractors and builders and developers as well, they have limited the amount of inventory that they have on the ground, which is not normal because they just want the inventory to keep rolling because they're selling one house. And they need to have been building a house that would be 40 to 50 percent to 60 percent complete at the time of a sell of a subject house. So that has slowed tremendously. And that end user, the consumer, who is stressing their income as well, their debt to income ratios have increased, making it extremely difficult for them to qualify for a loan.

Chairman WILLIAMS. I've been a car dealer for over 50 years and but also run a calf cow operation. We talked about that at my family ranch, and you've talked about Mr. Zittel, you talked about the cost of fertilizer, inability to find workers, et cetera. So, I've got a little bit of time left. Let me ask you this. Can you tell us how you've been dealing with the persistently high inflation and some of the other economic headwinds that you mentioned and that you're feeling in the economy today?

Mr. ZITTEL. Yes, so 2 specific examples. The winter storm that we went through that knocked down our greenhouses. I think the first round that happened in 2014, we were able to rebuild and take loan money out and be able to handle the inflationary effect with the last November storm. Perfect example of where we're not doing what we should be doing, and that is where we're building infrastructure, but we're not doing the technology tied with the infrastructure that we should be doing right now. So we're basically going at it at a limited fashion, knowing that there are things that are there that we'd like to do but aren't doing.

Chairman WILLIAMS. My time is up. I now recognize the Ranking Member for 5 minutes of questions, Ms. Vela´zquez.

Ms. VELA´ZQUEZ. Thank you, Mr. Chairman. Mr. Bivens, inflation is a complex global phenomenon, and you stated that in your remarks. Can you give us an overview of where America stands compared to our peers in terms of inflation rates and recovery?

Mr. BIVENS. Yeah, I would say it is definitely the case that the inflation acceleration of the past 2 years was global. Every single advanced economy in the world experienced an inflation of core inflation relative to pre COVID trends. And I say that acceleration is actually important. Sometimes people just look at the rate of inflation in, like, the US. Versus the EU, and it is higher in the US. But we went into COVID with higher inflation rates in many of these cases. So you have to look at that acceleration. The US was first in seeing some of those outbreaks of core inflation, but we also have peaked first and we are clearly coming down at, again, too slow a pace, but coming down, whereas other countries are not seeing the retreat in core inflation. I think the really important thing here is the inflation experience has been very common. The policy decisions made immediately after the COVID Pandemic recession were very different. And so that is why I think there is such a weak linkage between any specific piece of policy we did in the inflation exchange.

Ms. VELA´ ZQUEZ. How can you explain how policies like the ones that we passed last Congress contributed to that recovery?

Mr. BIVENS. So the US recovery is clearly there is many other countries in the world. It is clearly at the top end in terms of fast recoveries being experienced in the world. We've been much better on that front than many countries. And I think that is just directly the result of we were also on the leading edge of how big we went with fiscal relief and recovery efforts, which I think were correct, given the scale of the problem.

Ms. VELA´ ZQUEZ. What does that recovery mean for small business in particular?

Mr. BIVENS. By the measures I track, small business has participated fully in this recovery. If you look at their share of net employment gains, their share of sort of total income, they look right on track with what they were pre COVID. So it has been a broad based recovery that has not left small business behind in any way.

Ms. VELA´ ZQUEZ. Thank you. Mr Zittel, you mentioned that consolidation in your industry has led to fewer vendors to source goods from in your lifetime of farming. Has this been an ongoing trend?

Mr. ZITTEL. No, I'd say when I got out of college back in the late 80s, there was expansion, more people were getting in, we had more tractor dealerships, we had more fertilizer plants, we had more seed companies. The consolidation has certainly happened over the last 20 or 30 years and I'm not seeing it getting any better going the other way. It seems like it is getting worse.

Ms. VELA´ ZQUEZ. Can you explain how competition in this area can lead to lower prices?

Mr. ZITTEL. So a perfect example would be we've had upwards of 5 or six seed companies and now we're down to 2 or 3 seed companies. You're forced to go to those houses, there is less competition. Some of them don't even carry the varieties you want. So if you want that variety, you've only got a sole house to go to. They name the price, pretty much.

Ms. VELA´ ZQUEZ. Thank you. Mr Bivens, you mentioned housing as a key factor of inflation. Can you discuss what Congress can do to increase housing development, to alleviate our housing shortage and bring prices back down to earth?

Mr. BIVENS. Yeah, I think that is an incredibly important question. I would say to me, the key to getting house prices in check, which is just a huge challenge for household budgets is building more quality housing. We just have underbuilt housing for a generation. We need to build more lots of the blockages to that building actually happen at the state and local level. So the federal has to do policies that complement that. I think some of the big things the Biden administration has done that will help a lot is they sort of plus up federal grants to state and localities that change their zoning and regulatory laws to allow more housing to be built. I think that is a really good thing to do. This could be even supercharged with legislation that allocated actual money to go to states and localities that do more building or do good things on the regulatory and zoning side.

Ms. VELA´ ZQUEZ. Thank you. Mr. Gray, recently we learned that the producer price index has dropped to only 2.3 percent. Do you think this is a positive development for small businesses and may be able to give them more hope for economic conditions to stabilize?

Mr. GRAY. I think to the extent that we can observe improvements in the inflationary environment in general is a good thing for households, businesses, small business in particular, and that may be an indication of that. So I would view that favorably.

Ms. VELA´ ZQUEZ. Thank you. I yield back.

Chairman WILLIAMS. Thank you. Ms. Valezquez. I now recognize Mr. Luektkemeyer from the great state of Missouri for 5 mi utes.

Mr. LUETKEMEYER. Thank you, Mr. Chairman. In this committee last year, we had a number of economists come in and we talked about the causes of inflation, and they all agreed on 4 different chart costs or reasons energy costs, rules and regulations, supply chain, employee problems, and our immense money supply that was poured in the amount of money was poured in the system. So let's start with Mr. Gray. The Fiscal Responsibility Act cut the NEPA requirements down from what would be an average of seven years to approve a project, down to either one for small projects, 2 for larger projects. Can you give us just a quick recap on the importance of that with regards to the cost of the projects and effects on inflation?

Mr. GRAY. Absolutely. I haven't studied the degree to which that particular policy change would move development costs, because I haven't seen the estimate of that but directionally, that is entirely the right way to go if the goal is to expand the supply of energy production and thus lower the price for households and consumers.

Mr. LUETKEMEYER. Ms. Lee, having been in the banking business myself for a few years, I know that the banking business is extremely regulated, and you've been inundated with even more regulations. So I know that when we were my brother and I had a bank and forever loan officer, we had a higher compliance officer.

Is that kind of your experience as well?

Ms. SALDANA LEE. Well, our compliance department has grown, and it continues to grow.

Mr. LUETKEMEYER. Does it make you any money? No, that is a dead investment, a dead cost for you that you've got to overcome.

Ms. SALDANA LEE. That is correct.

Mr. LUETKEMEYER. And it is all due to more rules, more regulations?

Ms. SALDANA LEE. That is correct.

Mr. LUETKEMEYER. And you haven't any fewer rules and regulations over the last few years? You've had more, probably, have you not?

Ms. SALDANA LEE. That is correct.

Mr. LUETKEMEYER. Thank you. Just kind of curious, too. You mentioned the PPP program. I thank you for those comments. I mean, this committee was one of the key folks that oversaw I was served on Financial Service Committee, and our subcommittee there oversaw the PPP program, helped originate it, and then we provide the oversight here. Thank you for your comments on that because it was a very successful program due to the banks getting involved and using your customer law to be able to protect the integrity of that program. So we thank you for that and for thanking your clients.

With regards to inflation, how is it affecting your small businesses that you're financing right now? Are they struggling as a result of that? And you're seeing increased past dues losses, businesses go out of business. What do you see as the effect of inflation on small businesses?

Ms. SALDANA LEE. There is a variety of things. What we're really watching right now is any small loans that have a fixed rate. At this point, we originate 5 one Arms or 3 one. So that means they're fixed for 5 years or 3 years. So they're in that time frame. As they start to readjust those rates, that is where the stress comes in. We had one business owner that absolutely cannot afford the increase in rates and other costs associated with his business, and he is put his business up for sale. And so it is just a timing aspect of what is going to happen in the future with our loan portfolio and past dues and any kind of restructuring. But that is something that we've talked about already in our bank, is that if there is restructuring which don't want to get into banking too deep, but you start restructuring, that means problem loans and then regulatory burdens and a lot of other work that comes along with that.

Mr. LUETKEMEYER. Thank you for that. Mr. Zittel, you are in a very difficult business. As you said a minute ago with your Kennedy quote, you're the only group that can you have no control over your cost, no control over sale your product, and you hope the weather works. I always tell people that farmers are the ultimate gamblers. Las Vegas folks are nothing compared to what farmers are because you truly roll the dice every day. And I thank you for what you do because you feed our country in the world. But you've had a roller coaster effect with your revenues that you're talking about here with regards to the inflation and the Pandemic. And now the roller coaster of all is can you talk a little bit about that, how that is all affected you and what kind of changes you've made to your organization with regards to inflation?

Mr. ZITTEL. Very briefly, the pandemic did not affect us much because we went to work every day. Didn't know a damn bit of difference beyond that. The inflation rate, like we said, we're not doing the things we should be doing because we don't want to leverage our business. And I think regulation wise, our state has been very difficult to work with as far as passing things like overtime rate, mandatory days off and things like that.

Mr. LUETKEMEYER. Your labor costs have gone.

Mr. ZITTEL. Our labor costs, which 50 percent of cost of doing business for a farmer is.

Mr. LUETKEMEYER. Labor, and you have no control over that cost. And you have no control on being able to pass that cost on like most businesses.

Mr. ZITTEL. Exactly.

Mr. LUETKEMEYER. Thank you very much. I yield back now.

Chairman WILLIAMS. I recognize Mr. McGarvey from the great state of Kentucky for 5 minutes.

Mr. MCGARVEY. Thank you, Mr. Chairman. Very much appreciate it. Really glad we're having this conversation today. Obviously, we are all concerned about the root causes of inflation and how we prevent a recession in this country. I think it is important to understand and identify those causes of inflation so that we can best deal with it. Because, again, we can all, I think, agree that reigning in inflation is vital to protecting consumers and small businesses. And it is appropriate to look at those. I think it is appropriate for this committee to understand how the COVID stimulus programs contributed to inflation. But it is easy to Monday morning quarterback this a little bit as well and just reminding everybody how important these programs were during the Pandemic. As the Ranking Member noted, found that the US GDP would have fallen by 11 percent in 2020 without fiscal stimulus, and that is equivalent to 3 times the actual decline we saw. We did much better here than other places in the world during this kind of difficult time between COVID and what was going on in Russia and Ukraine. So in talking about how we combat a recession, how we help these small businesses, looking at these stimulus programs I think is helpful too, in understanding how they were helpful. Mr. Zittel, you're talking about your experience during the Pandemic. And like so many of the great business people in my state of Kentucky, you're one of the millions of small business owners who participated in and benefited from the PPP program. And so just tell us your experience with that and how you used that funding to help your business and the employees in your area.

Mr. ZITTEL. So I would say probably the best example of it is you are correct. It was well needed and a perfect timing. And not just because of the Pandemic, because like I said before, the Pandemic really didn't change our lives a whole lot. We weren't moving any place anyhow. But I think one of the biggest effects is we've been falling behind. Our margins have been dwindling. Our rate of trying to stay ahead of technology and move with that curve to try and make money has fallen behind because we haven't had money to work with. That was a great stimulus package, whether it was pandemic or non pandemic, it was a breath of fresh air. But we continue to see those regulations that keep pushing us down and pushing us down.

I don't know if I'll have an opportunity, but I just want to say it one time I did a calculation logbook 1935. If you do the calculation on labor, it is 50 times higher. If you do the calculation on a couple of the vegetables that I did that take exact the same amount of space as it did in 1935, you're only talking about 15 to 18 times. So labor costs that cost us 50 percent are rampant. So that was a breath of fresh air. But will it be enough for the future? We don't know.

Mr. MCGARVEY. I appreciate that insight and talking more you're speaking more regulatory pressure than the stimulus funding and the impacts there. Going back again to some of the things that were going on during COVID My home state of Kentucky is using $500 million in American Rescue Plan funding for the Cleaner Water Program to invest in water and sewer projects across the state. I can tell you I was in the state legislature at the time. There are Kentuckians who now have clean drinking water for the first time because of this investment in a state like ours, sewer access for homes, this has been a game changer for us in Kentucky. So Mr. Bivens, looking at how this infrastructure has or Dr. Bivens, I should say, looking at how access to clean drinking water we have 89 million in my state that got people Internet for the first time. We remember people going to McDonald's parking lots during the pandemic so that they could go to school or go to work. Can you explain how this investment in infrastructure and local economies will benefit small businesses and the National economy in the long term?

Mr. BIVENS. Yeah, I think it is a lot of the mechanisms you just talked about, like small businesses, like kind of every other actor in the economy, they need good roads to transport their product on. They need good schools to make sure the workers coming out of those schools are productive and provide good value. And then I think one maybe underrated thing that is in the infrastructure bill that was passed in 2022. A very big investment in broadband and especially in a world if we're going to see more remote work to actually expand the pool of people actually available to work in areas that have been underserved by broadband before, I think that could be a huge boon to small businesses. But basically all the mechanisms you talked.

Mr. MCGARVEY. About, the hardest question I'll ask you with 25 seconds left, given what we're all trying to do, help small businesses, help consumers bring down inflation, you're in our shoes. What would you do to help small businesses and consumers and bring down inflation?

Mr. BIVENS. I think the inflation bit is going to be really hard. It is just going to require a little bit of patience and to make sure we don't make any mistakes going forward to help small business generally, to me, that the biggest arrow in the quiver is antitrust policy that levels the playing field between them and the very large corporations.

Mr. MCGARVEY. So well done. I yield back.

Chairman WILLIAMS. Thank you. I now recognize from Pennsylvania Mr. Meuser for 5 minutes.

Mr. MEUSER. Well, thank you very much, Mr. Chairman. Certainly, thank you to our witnesses. It is appreciated. I spent about 25 years in small business. I talk with small businesses every day, visit them regularly, as I should, being on this committee as well as just being a Member of Congress. Since 70 percent of those employed are in my district are employed through small business, you've been dealing with high inflation supply issues, wage disruptions costs, regular costs going up, regulations. So I'd like to start with the regulation costs, which aren't really factored into well, they're factored into the inflation, but they're not factored into necessarily your added bottom line costs on your balance sheet.

Mr. Gray, the Biden Administration, according to your colleague Dan Goldbeck, American Action Forum, found that the Biden administration accumulated approximately $367,000,000,000 $367,000,000,000 in less than 30 months in regulatory costs. Can you share with us the impact that these costs have on small businesses in what is a very fragile economic climate?

Mr. GRAY. Absolutely. So I should stipulate that those costs come from the administration. So those aren't our estimates. Those are the self reported costs and they are significant. And they are significant to small businesses because whereas a one key difference between a large firm and a small firm is just as has been referenced elsewhere is just the capacity to absorb compliance costs. And I know from the small business in my family, there isn't the capacity to go hire compliance officers. And so each time one of these comes down, all it does is come out of out of their pocket.

Mr. MCGARVEY. Sure. All right. Thank you. I have in my district, we have one of the largest reserves for natural gas. Natural gas, of course, half the carbon emissions of other fossil fuels, and yet we see a regular regulatory.

Russian assault on natural gas pipeline distribution and such. Lately, we're seeing where prohibitions on gas stoves, which boggles the mind, right? I mean, gas stoves, you need electricity for other stoves. Where does that electricity come from? Some don't think a little bit past what is right in front of us. But that being said, would more natural gas be beneficial? Mr. Zettel, first of all, where you are in upstate New York, you'd like to mine or gather some of that natural gas? And I know that is hopefully down the road for you, but what would.

Mr. ZITTEL. We actually started in 1973 and started with our first well, which was an abandoned well, and we've got nine wells. But we can only go down to the Medina region, which supplies about 30 percent of the gas for our greenhouses and our greenhouse operation. If we were allowed to deep well, probably one well would do that in all of our houses and probably half the neighbourhood. But we are limited, but we do have gas wells. And yes, we are very short sighted, at least in our state, to say, let's get rid of gas. Let's go all electric. There has been comments on what would have happened in that November storm, and it would have been a lot more than 40 people die in Buffalo from freezing to death if we would have had all electric instead of gas.

Mr. MCGARVEY. Yeah, and I'm just south of you in Pennsylvania, fortunately, where we have been fracking, and it is been a real benefit and godsend to many of our farmers and businesses, and it is bringing in many new competitive, adding competitive advantages for businesses because of the low cost of energy. Let me move on, Ms. Lee. The CFPB Small Business Data Collection Rule-making, where they're asking for, frankly, a bizarre list of personal data on your clients. How are you doing with that?

Ms. SALDANA LEE. Well, I'm very grateful that I don't have to manage that part of the bank. And so, I'm not in compliance. And we have a compliance officer in his department, and they're working through all the details. It is extremely burdensome, and we're going to have to develop programs and systems. And it is a project committee that has been meeting for months now, and they continue to meet until everything gets finalized.

Mr. MCGARVEY. Thank you. I appreciate all of your work for small businesses. Mr. Bevins, how many years' experience do you have in the small business sector?

Mr. BIVENS. My employer is fewer than 50 people, so I work for a small business.

Mr. MCGARVEY. Okay. I yield back.

Chairman WILLIAMS. I now recognize Ms. Gluesenkamp. Camp Perez from Washington, the great state of Washington, for 5 minutes.

Ms. GLUESENKAMP PEREZ. Thank you, Mr. Chairman. Mr. Bevins, in your testimony, you noted that one avenue for looking at inflation is actually as a distributional issue, because what is a cost to one person is profit to another person. In this case, higher costs for consumers have often shown up as higher profits for some corporations. You note that in normal times, corporate profits contribute about 13 percent to prices. But since the second quarter of 2020, they have instead contributed more than a third to the growth or more than twice as much as they normally do. Inflation has given corporations a lot of room to pad profits and increase margins. But that is not all corporations, right? There is a difference between my corporation with eight employees and some of the big guys. So why is there such a difference? Why are our profits diminishing and some others are getting so much higher? Why is there such a difference in gouging and then the rest of us who are just trying to get by? One thing that I hear about all the time when I'm back at home is the impact of consolidation, particularly in AG and in our food supply chain. I hear about the concentration of power in the hands of a few of these distributors. Transporters has resulted in unfair practices and higher prices for us at the grocery store. So what efforts should be made to improve or better enforce some of these antitrust issues? How can you discuss, can you discuss the benefits of enforcing those laws on small businesses, on competition overall?

Mr. BIVENS. Yeah, I'd say a couple of things. Your question about what explains why some firms have really been able to just pass on all costs and then some, whereas other firms have been more constrained. I think there is 2 answers. One is just partly luck. The supply chain snarls meant that some people who had supply on hand as supply chain shut down were just in a great position to charge whatever they needed to. The more sort of profound answer is just there is lots of market power in the corporate sector and very big corporations exert a lot of that power. What is different this time is they have normally exerted it mostly not against their own customers. They've kept inflation has been low for like 25 years. Instead, a lot of that power has been thrown backward against their own workers and against small businesses. This time the shortest route to profitability was by raising prices and lots of them took it. And that is why you saw such a sort of huge contribution of corporate profits to inflation over those past couple of years. And so I think whether we're talking about the long run problem or the short run problem, the answer is we need a more level playing field between various economic actors and the economy, between workers, between corporations and small businesses. And a key policy lever is the one you talked about, which is more robust antitrust enforcement that doesn't only look at product market competition, but also looks at what is happening in the labor market and to suppliers.

Ms. GLUESENKAMP PEREZ. Yeah, like on a very small frame. Remember when everyone was getting their catalytic converters stolen rampant everywhere? There was one point where there was one catalytic converter on the entire West Coast for a year. Make and model of a vehicle, one on the entire West Coast. And I bought it and I paid for it and it never showed up. And turns out the dealerships get to pull first order off of it. And so prices went up for everyone. And what could have been a simple fix instead was a bill because of these inflationary issues that eviscerated people's savings accounts. So appreciate the seriousness and the perspective with which you all are all taking this issue. Thank you to all of our witnesses for being here and thanks for this hearing today. I yield back.

Chairman WILLIAMS. Yields back and now recognize Mr. Stauber from the great state of Minnesota for 5 minutes.

Mr. STAUBER. Thank you, Mr. Chair. And I've said it in this committee before, small businesses are not only the engine of our economy, but they're the innovators. And we're hearing it here today. During the COVID-19

Pandemic, our small businesses were hit incredibly hard. Yet it was small businesses that held this economy and the entire country together. Our small businesses, just like everyday American consumers, are being hit with inflation the hardest, which are being worsened by the Biden administration's policies. Mr. Bevin, my colleague from Pennsylvania. Maybe I'll ask the question just bluntly. Have you ever owned a small business?

Mr. BIVENS. No.

Mr. STAUBER. No? It sounds like it. Mrs. Lee, I have a few questions about the small business loan activity at First Community Bank. What is the current rate on business loan that most small businesses working with your bank would receive today?

Ms. SALDANA LEE. Approximately 10 percent.

Mr. STAUBER. And what ballpark estimate of the interest rate that a small business would have received in January of 2020?

Ms. SALDANA LEE. Oh, goodness. Probably 5 and a quarter.

Mr. STAUBER. Almost double?

Ms. SALDANA LEE. Yes, sir.

Mr. STAUBER. What kind of trends have you seen over the past year or so in small business loan activity? Have you seen an increase in the number of businesses that are unable to keep up with their loans or small businesses?

Ms. SALDANA LEE. Actually, what we've seen is just a decline in applications because they're in a very difficult situation in which their profits are suffering. And as much as they would like to come to the bank to borrow money, they know that that is going to further their problems. And a lot of things are just services in the moment where you don't want to do some short term lending and borrowing for long term capital. And that is really what they're needing.

Mr. STAUBER. You had said to, I think, Mr. Luke Byer about some of the regulators or specialized workers that follow help with your regulations in the bank. How many of those do you employ right now?

Ms. SALDANA LEE. Oh, goodness. When I look around the bank, it is going to be I'm going to say at least 30 are looking at one piece of compliance and that is more in an in depth level. Every person in the bank has to deal with compliance.

Mr. STAUBER. So you have 30 that you've hired specifically for compliance?

Ms. SALDANA LEE. Not specifically for compliance, but it is throughout the bank where among their responsibilities is looking at something, reviewing something, monitoring something. And in my opinion, that is the compliance piece.

Mr. STAUBER. Thank you. Mr. Ziedel, the farming industry is an incredibly labor intensive industry, as you described. Can you once again share some of the challenges you are facing with recruiting and retaining your employees?

Mr. ZITTEL. So recruiting during the Pandemic was difficult just because of the process in applications, because it is Chicago, California, and the consulate in Mexico. So logistically, during the Pandemic, it was tough. Other than that, the federal H 2 A program is the only program to go with, again, the regulations of our state. Because the H 2 A rate, the AW rate that they call it, is based off of your minimum wage rate. That is one of the driving forces. So the higher the minimum wage rate, the higher the AW rate. But as far as retention wise, we've got a great track record. And I'd like to say because we're good employers.

Mr. STAUBER. I just known you and heard you comment here. You're somebody I could work for. I think you're a straight shooter and common sense and a good business owner.

Mr. ZITTEL. Thank you.

Mr. STAUBER. Mr. Gray, as you noted in your testimony, the federal government has poured an excessive amount of money into our economy over the past few years. Do you believe we would be seeing the same level of inflation we are today if Congress and our president did not pass excessive spending packages like the American Rescue Plan and the so-called Inflation Reduction Act?

Mr. GRAY. I do not.

Mr. STAUBER. Where do you think it would be at?

Mr. GRAY. I don't want to overstate the effect, particularly a couple of years later, and I have not done a backwards looking analysis, but I believe we've seen other research that suggested it was a positive contributor to the inflation rate.

Mr. STAUBER. My next question, and I don't have much time how would lowering regulatory burdens and cutting red tape help tame inflation? You got 2 seconds.

Mr. GRAY. Increase supply. Increase.

Mr. STAUBER. There you go. Thank you. Mr. Chair back. Chairman WILLIAMS. Thank you. I now recognize Ms. Davidson, the great state of Kansas for 5 minutes.

Ms. DAVIDS. Thank you, Chairman. And thank you to the Ranking Member to both of you for holding this hearing today, 3 years after the start of the COVID-19 Pandemic, Kansas families, small businesses and workers are still dealing with high costs. Inflation makes it harder for our small businesses to keep their doors open, for our workers to put food on their tables. And I've been particularly focused on making sure that our domestic supply chains meet our country's demand to move goods efficiently. I've been proud to introduce legislation to support our small manufacturers and vote for critical legislation like the bipartisan infrastructure law and the major manufacturing domestic manufacturing bill that we passed in the last session. These things are helping us get our economy back on track. They're helping to create good paying jobs and lowering prices for folks back home in Kansas. But there is clearly a ton of work still left to be done. Mr. Bivens, I'm curious if you could answer my first question here. I know there are some indicators that inflation is slowing, but that it is not declining fast enough to provide real relief to our small businesses. I'm curious if you could share your insights on how the current supply chain disruptions that we're looking at are impacting the elevated prices that people are still seeing.

Mr. BIVENS. So my sense is that the supply chain disruptions, which were a major cause of the initial surge in inflation, are substantially better than they were years ago. The New York Federal Reserve Bank tracks something called the global supply chain pressure index. It was historically high pressure earlier. Now it is getting much more normalized. And so my expectation is that that along with hopefully some reduction in profit margins over the next year, will start to bring down overall inflation a little faster than what we've seen. But yeah, I think it is headed in the right direction. But I agree it is agonizingly slow.

Ms. DAVIDS. Yeah. And I appreciate the insights on supply chain disruptions. Can you talk a little bit about the other factors that are playing into the elevated prices that we're seeing?

Mr. BIVENS. Yeah, so I think profit margins are a big part of it. So basically, you had this enormous rise in profit margins in corporations that drove at one point about 60 percent of the price increases. Since then, they have been coming down, but they've not anywhere near normal. And so normally at this point in a recovery, you'd see quite a dip in profit margin. They would actually provide some really nice disinflation that has not really happened yet. I think it will happen. I think supply chain unsnarling will increase some competition. People will let go some of those very high profit margins because they'll be forced to. I think the other thing that is keeping inflation too high is just a lot of lagged effects that are taking some time to get through the economy. One obvious one, there is a range of service sector industries that are very labor intensive and inflation is mostly driven by wage increases and very early in the recovery there are some sectors like leisure and hospitality that is all real scramble for workers. And you actually really had a labor shortage. I think those are gone. I think the lagged effect of those wage normalization is going to show up in inflation. And then the last one, everyone knows housing costs only hit official measures of inflation with very long lag. We know in the private sector housing costs really have gone down quite a bit in the past year. It has really not shown up much at all in the CPI. It will show up in the next six to eight months. So, I think there is a lot of disinflations in the pipeline coming.

Ms. DAVIDS. That is really helpful. And I might follow up with you about the housing cost lag that you were mentioning. I did want to touch on really quickly that I have been working specifically on trying to figure out ways to help restore some of our manufacturing capacity and of course I want to do more manufacturing in the Kansas Third. But I am curious, speaking of Lags and what the timing might look like on the commitment to reshoring manufacturing, can you share some insights on how you think that might stabilize or impact the price inflections and that sort of thing?

Mr. BIVENS. My hope is we're going to see enough disinflation over just the next six to twelve months, that all that extra capacity that is coming online from things like the bipartisan infrastructure law won't have a huge effect on this episode, but it will have an enormous effect in the future. It basically means we're not going to be in this situation again. If we're hit by a big shock 3 years from now, it is not going to cause anywhere near the inflationary blow up it did this time because our supply chains will be so much more diversified and strong. So, it really is an investment in the future. Even if it is not going to come online quick enough this time to really shove down inflation over the next 3 months. I think it is absolutely worth doing because of the resilience it builds into the economy.

Ms. DAVIDS. Thank you and I'll follow up with some of the other questions I had. Thank you so much. I yield back.

Chairman WILLIAMS. Thank you. And now recognize Mr. Hunt from the great' state of Texas for 5 minutes.

Mr. HUNT. Thank you Mr. Chairman. Really appreciate it. Also want to thank the witnesses for being here as well. Really appreciate your time and efforts today. Yesterday we observed our greatest generation's greatest moment. D-Day brave men risked their lives to free the world from tyranny to ensure that we don't speak German. Today, they waited through waste deep water in the face of machine gunfire into a barrage of machine gunfire in order to free the world from fascism. And more than 57,000 of these men gave their lives 79 years ago. Yesterday, those fearless and courageous soldiers, sailors, marines and airmen wanted those closest to them to prosper in a free society. Not just then, but now and of course for the future. Today, because of many of the policies from this administration, we can hardly say that we've kept our promise to America, the promise of freedom that our greatest generation sacrificed for us, that we observed yesterday. The American people are suffering under this administration. Small businesses, as you have articulated, are feeling the sting of this administration's actions. Inflation has remained at a record high for going on 2 years now. Groceries and essential items have been at all time highs for American families. Bread, eggs and the most basic staples of life are now exorbitantly expensive for American families.

We are feeling this everyday. Fuel costs are at a halt or at all time high heating. Our homes are at an all time high. American films are struggling right now because this administration has waged war on our oil and gas industry. As you have just articulated, sir, your state is sitting on the Marcel Shale and you can't even get the natural resources needed to fill your home and to fuel your farm. These are not real solutions that are being proposed right now. Solutions like we must demand that everybody buys an EV or we have to use solar panels. And by the way, I'm not an anti green guy. I'm just an all hands on debt kind of guy. And we are a country that must have redundancies. The economic and energy priorities of this administration are flat out not sustainable. We passed the so called Inflation Reduction Act, and we know 2 things about this bill. According to our former Vice President Al Gore, the IRA is a quote is a quote climate bill. He said these words and it will cost the US at least $1.2 trillion in green subsidies instead of cutting the continued wasteful spending, this administration is on track as of last week to spend an additional $4 trillion over the course of the next 18 months instead of curbing our spending to pre COVID levels. Because last I checked, COVID is over. And for you, sir, COVID never started. Thank you for all you've done for our country. Small businesses will continue to feel this and so will the consumer.

Under this administration has become harder to start a business and very costly to do so. President Reagan famously said the nine most terrifying words in the English language are, I'm from the government and I'm here to help. We don't want that. We want you to be able to make your own decisions. We want to empower you. The individual the individual small business owner is the very backbone of this country. We must unleash American energy. We must unleash your spirit fire and reign in the influence that we have seen destroy this country for the past 2 years. Now, ma'am, before I did this job, I was actually in the mortgage business. And also, I worked for a home builder in the greater Houston area. One thing that I found to be very interesting is for every $1,000 increase in a home, you basically price out 2900 potential home buyers. When we have inflation, the input goes into the slab, it goes into the frame, it goes into the brick, it goes into the roof, it goes into the doors, it goes into everything of the home. And that then gets pushed down to the consumer.

So, ma'am, my question is for you. What have you seen in this industry and how damaging has inflation been to the industry that I work in and that you work in every single day? And in spite of the strength of the Texas economy, how has this hurt the home builder and the homeowner?

Ms. SALDANA LEE. I'm going to start with the homeowner we have seen our custom home built. They have decreased by half from about a year ago. And we track that because, again, we're very heavy in construction lending. We have the data to support that. And I see it as because of the home mortgage interest rates, families are not being able to build their dream homes. And the other thing that I'd like to add really quickly, we had some builders that were building custom homes and eight households in particular, homeowners in particular. Those 2 builders went out of business during construction. I was able to talk to one of the owners who was extremely disappointed, distraught, because they were going to have to go out and find another builder to finish her house. And this was like a 2 year period.

Mr. HUNT. Okay, time is up. Thank you very much, ma'am, for your time. And thank you, sir, for feeding our country. I yield back.

Chairman WILLIAMS. I now recognize Mr. Mfume from the great state of Maryland for 5 minutes.

Mr. MFUME. Thank you very much, Mr. Chairman. I want to thank you and in her absence, I want to thank the Ranking Member also, and I want to thank our witnesses. One of the interesting things about this committee and all committees is that we don't always agree. And fortunately, we ultimately found our way out of disagreement, back to the facts and back to the reality and back to the science. And I know it has been oftentimes convenient because President Biden is in the White House, to sort of paint him as the great culprit, the great conspirator that has created a situation that we're all definitely trying to survive under. But the fact of the matter is Joe Biden did not create this inflation. And if we really want to talk about inflation and administrations, the inflation last year got up to what, over 6 percent?

Well, in the 1970s, following 2 back to back Republican administrations, Ronald Reagan and his successor, inflation hit 12.6 percent. Now, can you imagine what that would be like today? 12.6 percent? And small businesses were screaming for help. It was so interesting that in 1974, Gerald Ford addressed the joint session of the Congress, and he gave this long, detailed speech about what we as Americans can do to drive down inflation. And people listened politely. And then at the end of the speech, he pulled out a great big button that said W-I-N. And he hung it on his lapel, and it said it stood for Whip Inflation Now. And that he and the First Lady and his family was going to find a way to spend less, and the government probably needed to find a way to spend less. But all Americans have the responsibility to, quote, Whip inflation. Now, Bob Hope, who was a dear friend of the President at the time, went on stage a few weeks later and gave a joke, or told a joke, saying that since that great speech about whipping inflation at 12 percent, whips have gone up by $0.50 in the last week. So if you live long enough, you'll see everything at least twice. I believe that Greenspan, Alan Greenspan, who was his economic advisor at the time, said it was the most unbelievable demonstration of stupidity that he had ever seen or heard.

So there is enough blame to go around to everybody. And I know someone mentioned, I think it was the gentleman from the great state of Texas earlier, Ronald Reagan. Well, I knew Ronald Reagan. I served with Ronald Reagan. And Ronald Reagan said about inflation that it is not the fault of any particular administration. It is the fault of policies that can carry over from administration to administration. So I just want us all to take a little bit of a deep breath and remember that we're seeing now what we saw then only twice as devastating without as we saw then a Democrat in the White House. So it is really not about parties. It is more about policies, practices, principles. Trying to figure out what works doesn't work and throwing stuff up against the wall and realizing that none of us really have an answer.

But there is a good idea here, there is a good idea they're there, and then we try to find a way to make it all work. So I just have one question of you, Mr. Bivens. I want to go back to the fact that inflation is slowing, but it is not reversing. However, I think that there are some other things that are keeping prices elevated that maybe we should talk about for a moment. You'd mentioned price margins in respect to the gentlewoman's question a moment ago, but wouldn't labor market have something to do with that? Wouldn't employment levels have something to do with that? And wouldn't the monopoly power and pressure downward on really small businesses that operate on the real main street, wouldn't those also be things that sort of drive this uncontrollable beast that we call inflation?

Mr. BIVENS. Yeah, I think all those influences go into the mix of what generates the inflation rate. And so one of the reasons why I'm relatively encouraged by what I'm seeing in very recent data and inflation and think like we some patients will will help us a lot is that we have not seen inflation lock in and become embedded across every sector of the economy like you brought up the 1970s. One reason why that inflation was so incredibly tough to fight was like every sector, workers, rank and file workers, small businesses, corporate profits all saw really rapid gains in their income growth year after year as they all tried to pass on price increases to each other. That dynamic really hasn't happened this time. There is one sector corporate profits that have really increased their share of the total. Everyone else's income is kind of lagging behind and actually being an anchor on inflation and trying to bring it back down.

Mr. MFUME. Thank you very much. That is the thing we don't talk about that much, the corporate side of all this. Well, this gentleman from Maryland yields back. Mr. Speaker, thank you for the opportunity.

Chairman WILLIAMS. Okay, thank you. And I recognize Mr. Phillips from the great state of Minnesota for 5 minutes.

Mr. PHILLIPS. Thank you, Mr. Chairman. Let me start with you, Mr. Gray. You made some comments, and I concur that deficit spending is accretive to inflation. I think it is basic economics. I just looked at core inflation rates around the world. The most recent update I see, the US is about 5.5 percent. Some countries doing a little bit better than us, but we got Germany at 5.8 percent, Italy at 6.9, Denmark, 6.1, Greece, 6.1, Spain, 6.1, Paraguay, 6.2. France, 6.3, Norway, 6.3. Ireland 6.4. European Union 6.45.

Australia, 6.6. Netherlands, 6.6. Honduras, 6.6. Peru, 6.7. United Kingdom, 6.8, Belgium, 6.8, New Zealand, 7.3. I can keep going. Sweden, 7.6. Chile, 8.7. Estonia, 10.8. Poland, 12.2. Pakistan, 20. Egypt, 38. Argentina, 105. Not so bad, comparatively. Is that a fair statement? Compared to developed countries around the world? Compared to those large numbers, our smaller numbers are better. Okay. And by the way, I'm the first to admit I'm really tired of both parties being very poor fiscal managers of our economy. One party talks about doing it a little bit more than the other, neither are doing it. Both deserve blame. What president in our country's history added more to our federal debt than any other in a 4 year term? I don't have that off the top of my head, but I have a pretty good guess. Who do you think? I would imagine it is probably not the current one, but perhaps the last one. That is correct. Donald Trump added $7 trillion. So all I'm getting at here is I'm tired of this nonsense about who. But we're all responsible for it, every single one of us, both parties. And I simply want to focus more on solutions because that is what we're here for.

So to all of your witnesses, thank you. To our Chairman and Ranking Member, thank you. But in terms of culture, man, I just am tired of this throwing stones, because we're both responsible. With that said, I do want to talk about solutions. Some of you have mentioned some before. I've been a small business owner my entire life. I know how darn tough it is during the best of times, let alone during inflationary times. I also, as a banker, Ms. Lee, I can imagine trying to find that intersection between raising rates to cool the economy and reduce inflation with ensuring that we have capital access to small businesses as a challenge. Just share with me what you think is the most important thing that we policymakers can do now in a thoughtful manner to actually make life easier for small business owners as it relates to inflation regulation or anything else. Why don't we. Start with you, Mr. Bivens.

Mr. BIVENS. I would say for small business owners, the most important thing is enhanced antitrust agenda level.

Mr. PHILLIPS. You talk about that a little bit. You mentioned that earlier. Be a little more specific.

Mr. BIVENS. A couple of things. I mean, one, I think we often think about antitrust as a make sure big companies are not charging their own customers really high prices because of their privileged market position. We also need to look at how they treat their suppliers. A lot of the stories about small businesses being squeezed are my input. Prices are rising. I have no control over that. Then when I try to sell my stuff, often to a big corporate retailer, they just tell me no. And they do not give me any sort of extra price boost at all. I think that is a real problem and that is an asymmetry of bargaining power that is going to hurt them even during non inflationary times. But it is becoming really acute now.

Mr. PHILLIPS. I appreciate that. Okay. Antitrust. Got that. All right. Ms. Lee, what can we do expeditiously to help small businesses?

Ms. SALDANA LEE. In my opinion, every Congresswoman, every congressman needs to sit and just be in that small business owner's shoes. Get educated, get in depth into the real cost of each particular different type of industry, different type of business. Because that is one of the best things about banking. We call them deals. No deal is the same, every deal is different and every customer is different. And that is what I feel would be beneficial because it would come back to getting educated and then forming the policies that need to be formed.

Mr. PHILLIPS. Thank you. In fact, I do a series called on the Job with Dean. I spend 2 to 3 hours a shift at small businesses. I've done about 30 of them in my district. Most educational, insightful, enlightening thing. I wish every Member of our Committee would do the same in his or her districts. Why don't we move to you, Mr. Zittle? I'm sorry. I'm sorry, Mr. Gray. Yeah, sorry. Just trying to throw you off a little bit.

Mr. GRAY. I would just say do no harm. And this Congress has paid good attention and discussed opportunities to increase supply across a number of industries, and I would continue those.

Mr. PHILLIPS. Okay. And Mr. Zittel?

Mr. ZITTEL. Consistency and policy making, it doesn't matter whether it is state line or country or in the world. You can't sell coal to China. We live under the same sky and then want to be all electric. Same thing with state to state. Policy making has to have a concept and they got to know what they're talking about.

Mr. PHILLIPS. Any specific policy relative to your business that would be most helpful? You mentioned natural gas, under——

Mr. ZITTEL. Anything labor for

US. Mr. PHILLIPS. Labor——

Mr. ZITTEL. Our state and labor.

Mr. PHILLIPS. Maybe immigration reform to help increase the supply of labor. What do you think of that?

Mr. ZITTEL. No, we're good.

Mr. PHILLIPS. Oh, you're good?

Mr. ZITTEL. Yeah, they work out just fine. It is our state labor.

Mr. PHILLIPS. Okay, thank you. I yield back.

Chairman WILLIAMS. Next, I recognize Mr. Alford from the great state of Missouri for 5 minutes.

Mr. ALFORD. Thank you, Mr. Chairman. I appreciate that. Ranking Member small businesses contribute greatly to the American economy, the fabric of our society, our way of life. But rampant inflation is contributing to the downfall of a lot of small businesses. It is a matter really important to me in our district. Our district is very rural, 24 counties. We have 95,000 farms in the state of Missouri. A lot of these are family owned. We're losing a lot of farms. 1000 a month in America. This is serious business. Farmers are small business owners as well. And everyday small business owners have to deal with the crushing effects of inflation, higher input costs, increased labor costs.

65 percent of small businesses say they are likely or very likely that they will permanently close if inflation continues at its current pace. Economist Larry Summers, who served in the Obama administration, said the risk of this inflation is sizable and that he believes we will tip into a recession. Biden Harris administration has decided to focus on woke policies. Instead of tackling inflation, they've also decided to increase, not decrease, regulations, adding to the cost of doing business. Well, folks, it is time that we and the Small Business Committee and the House of Representatives get down to the business, to once again allowing the greatness of our small businesses to be unleashed and tame the Biden inflation.

My constituents are focused on 3 big things food, fuel and fertilizer. The F 150 is a model of a truck. It shouldn't be what it costs to fill it up. But unfortunately, our farmers are dealing with these higher input costs, driving them some out of business. President Biden has targeted the fossil fuel industry, but he has squarely put the crosshairs on the backs of the American people. And it is time for this to end. Andrew bettering chairs. The Missouri Farm Bureau young farmers and ranchers program. He is very concerned about these input costs. He says, I think we're just in a situation where you have to hold tight and hope for the best. Hopefully there is light at the end of the tunnel. Well, hopefully there is. And Mr. Zittel, I want to start with you. Do you see light at the end of the tunnel? And what can we tell young farmers like Andrew?

Mr. ZITTEL. Same thing I tell my son, be patient. Same thing Andrew is saying. We've weathered the test of time. We've been around 100 plus years. You get creative. It will never be easy, I don't believe I always had the dream that it would happen in my lifetime, but I don't think I'm going to last that long. I believe the American farmer will become more appreciated and better compensated in the future because we're going to lose enough of them where they're going to become a rare enough commodity that pe ple will start to understand what they're putting in their mouth.

Mr. ALFORD. We better start realizing that quickly. Our food security is our National security, as you well know. Mr. Zittel, Mr. Gray, inflation is a burden for all Americans. It is a tax on all Americans. I don't care how much money you make, what your skin color is or what pronoun you go by. It is a tax. The negative effects of inflation are really hard felt in rural communities. As we've talked about, incomes grew slower there while expenses grew faster. It has put rural small businesses in a tough spot. Mr. Gray, how are currently administration policies making it more challenging for rural small businesses to navigate the impacts of inflation?

Mr. GRAY. I would first speak to the current inflationary environment as I think we would all agree is complex. I would identify, however, some policy errors that were made recently that exacerbated it. It certainly not the only cause and as the Members of the Committee have already addressed, the regulatory environment is a challenge for commerce. And I think the combination of those 2 elements are antithetical to our understanding of price discovery which is the intersection of supply and demand. And these policies sort of push in the wrong direction.

Mr. ALFORD. I can't help but think have we had a different president and a different administration? This would not be happening. The war on fossil fuels would not be happening. We would be energy dominant and not energy dependent as we are going on our hands and knees and begging other countries, taking oil out of our strategic oil supply, putting it at risk on a National security level. And I can't help but think that fertilizer prices which are dependent upon natural gas prices, that's what makes fertilizer. We only have 7 percent of the world's fertilizer is made in the United States of America because the overregulation of EPA and other government agencies that see fit to try to shut down businesses so we can't have an active, growing economy, I think that is reprehensible. And I think we here on the Small Business Committee are going to make every step we can to get people back into the business of doing business. Thank you, Mr. Chairman. I yield.

Chairman WILLIAMS. Thank you. I now recognize Ms. Scholten from the great state of Michigan for 5 minutes.

Ms. SCHOLTEN. Thank you so much Mr. Chair and thank you so much to the witnesses for taking time out of your busy lives here today. I want to start by saying that inflation has been a deeply concerning issue for individuals in my district and I am so grateful that we're having this hearing today.

As my colleague Representative Phillips said, this is an issue that has been blown up by both parties. We need to put the politics aside and focus on solutions which is what I hope we can do here today. I know that I came to Congress because I was concerned about working families like mine and the rising costs. So many families in West Michigan work hard, pay their bills and still struggle to make ends meet. Prices across the board are too high and wages are too low. Inflation is slowing which is encouraging. However, it isn't reversing. American families and small businesses are still suffering. Mr. Bivens, in your testimony you spoke about how inflation is the inevitable result of massive shocks to the economy and the long lived but steadily dampening ripple effects. You go on to list the Pandemic and the Russian invasion of Ukraine as some of those shocks but what is keeping prices elevated now that the ripple effects of these shocks have subsided?

Mr. BIVENS. So I would argue they have not fully subsided. I think they're really long lived and there's also big lags between when they actually subside and when they show up in lower inflation. And so I gave the example to your colleague earlier it is widely recognized that what is actually happening in housing markets is only reflected in official measures of inflation with up to a year lag. I think we've only seen in the past month or 2 a deceleration in the housing component of the CPI. I think that's really reliably going to continue over the next year because we know in the private sector the real time data those costs have been moderating a lot. The same story holds with a bunch of very labor intensive sectors in the service industry where prices are really a function of what's happening to wages. Wage growth was through the roof in the very beginning of the recovery. Everyone remembers the restaurant scrambled to rehire 12 percent wage increases. That's an old story and it's just taking time for those to filter through. And then the last thing is profit margins are not as high as they were at their absolute historic peak at the beginning of 2022 but they've only come down a little bit. I think if they normalize to like 2019 levels over the next year that puts a lot of disinflation on the table as well. So I would argue the ripple effects they're still out there but they're going to predictably dampen unless some, god forbid, huge shock hits again.

Ms. SCHOLTEN. So you think it is the ripple effects that are still contributing?

Mr. BIVENS. Yes.

Ms. SCHOLTEN. I wonder if you could talk my colleague Mr. Phillips listed off a number of inflationary rates of other countries and developed nations. I wonder if you can dig into that a little bit and talk about how the United States compares to other similarly situated countries.

Mr. BIVENS. Yeah, when I see that data the first thing I think is it's very clear evidence that there is just not some US specific policy mistake that caused our inflation. It was literally every single advanced economy in the world saw a pronounced acceleration in inflation. Ours came a little sooner than some others but it also peaked sooner and it's on its way down whereas in many other countries it is not. And if you look across the different policy choices those countries made, they're all over the table like some did very aggressive fiscal relief and recovery like we did, which I think was appropriate. Some really didn't at all, but still got the inflation. And so what I take from that data is that the US is kind of in the middle of the pack generally as to what happened with its inflation experience. It's better on the recovery front, and it really means that there is no one dumb US specific mistake that led to this. It was a global pandemic and global war that led to most of the inflation we've seen.

Ms. SCHOLTEN. Thank you. Because I only have a minute left, I want to stick with you. In a little bit of a follow up, we talk about how inflation needs bipartisan solutions. When you think about the best case scenarios for recovery, can you speak to whether we are on track to achieve this recovery scenario and what specifically in terms of policies, especially those policies we can actually achieve in a bipartisan manner in this Congress we can help do as legislators.

Mr. BIVENS. So I think at the moment we're actually on a pretty decent track. Everyone wishes inflation would come down much more quickly, but I don't wish that at the cost of having unemployment rise a lot. And so I don't want the Fed to continue super aggressive rate hikes. I think at the moment the soft landing is in reach. That is, we have inflation come down steadily. Normalize unemployment never really goes up. I think in terms of, like, bipartisan things that can happen, I think they're mostly on the sort of infrastructure spending front. There are still some other things we could do. And I would also include a big investment in childcare that boosts labor supply. And actually I think that's not going to take effect in the next six months, but it really could make us much better prepared for the next big shock that comes our way.

Ms. SCHOLTEN. Thank you. Yield back the remainder of my seconds.

Chairman WILLIAMS. And now recognize Mr. Bean from the great state of Florida for 5 minutes.

Mr. BEAN. A very good afternoon, Mr. Chairman. Thank you so much. And good afternoon, panelists. I'm a rookie in more ways than one, Mr. Chairman, as you know, and everything happens at once. Running from committee to committee. Mr. Who's our banker? Our banker is Miss Lee. But what are we seeing out there? And I was a banker for 13 years. What are we seeing? Are we change because inflation I know it's kicking everybody's tail. What are we doing? Are we changing lending standards? Are we looking at different things? What's changed in banking now that inflation is just kicking everybody's tail?

Ms. SALDANA LEE. Okay, before I answer, can I ask you a question?

Mr. BEAN. Sure, go right ahead. You're recognized

Ms. SALDANA LEE. Why are you not a banker anymore?

Mr. BEAN. I got this Congress gig going on right now, but you never know. You never know if it doesn't work out.

Ms. SALDANA LEE. I thought you were going to say compliance.

Mr. BEAN. No. You never know, though. You never know. But it's certainly a rewarding career of helping businesses and putting people in houses and businesses and whatnot. I know there's great satisfaction. But is it hard now? Is it gotten difficult?

Ms. SALDANA LEE. It's gotten extremely difficult. And I mentioned earlier that I think that the thing that's most difficult is a small business that's already suffering, and they are needing capital to continue to meet some of those increased prices. But they don't want to get into debt further than they might already be or just get debt if they don't have any already. There's a lot of short-term things that the bank is assisting them with, and that has helped tremendously. But it's almost like the paycheck to paycheck for a consumer. That's the way it is for business. But we're just going to continue to help however we can.

Mr. BEAN. Good Deal. Are you finding this is a toss-up question? Is hiring people we've heard that as a recurring theme. Are you all seeing that as well? Getting people to work for you everywhere?

Ms. SALDANA LEE. Everywhere.

Mr. BEAN. You're seeing that, too? Anybody else? Mr. Gray. Jump in.

Mr. GRAY. I don't have any direct reports myself, but I know elsewhere in my organization it's been a struggle to find folks

Mr. BEAN. Very good.

Mr. ZITTEL. People are always surprised when I say this not an issue. But we don't have Americans that want to be farmers either. So, we're depending on the H 2 A program. Good workers, reliable workers, happy to be with us, always come back. So far, so good.

Mr. BEAN. And with the remaining time, does anybody have anything to say that wasn't asked of you? Ms. Lee?

Ms. SALDANA LEE. I can't think of anything off the top of my head. Some of the points that I really wanted to make actually questions were posed and I was able to field those questions.

Mr. BEAN. Very good. Mr. Gray. Anything? Any final thoughts?

Mr. GRAY. Just the observations from the Ranking Member at the beginning are well taken, and I think we would all agree that the response to the inflation is painful and because the Federal Reserve, our primary institution for controlling and moderating price stability, has some very blunt tools. And unfortunately, we are in a position where they are having to deploy them. And the issue is a credit crunch.

Mr. BEAN. Got you. Mr. David?

Mr. ZITTEL. I think the American farmer does what he does because he loves it. It's not ever going to be a get rich scheme. I always tell people I passed 3 very responsible human beings on to the rest of the world and only one of them became a farmer. But I hope more of them become farmers because that's where you get work ethic from. So don't kill the American dream of being a farmer.

Mr. BEAN. Amen. Amen. Mr. Chairman, I yield back.

Chairman WILLIAMS. Thank you very much. I now recognize Mr. Thanedar from the great state of Michigan for 5 minutes.

Mr. THANEDAR. Thank you, Mr. Chair, and I thank all of the witnesses here. This has been a good discussion. I'm a small business owner. I'm a serial entrepreneur, started many small businesses. And Mr. Bivens, I struggled making payroll, hiring, acquiring new customers. Running a small business is tough, even though small businesses create 70 percent of the jobs. Now looking back in this pandemic and in current situation, it somehow seems to me that larger corporations are continue to do well. They continue to command higher prices, but the small businesses continue to struggle. They are closing down. They have felt real pain of the current economic situation. Why is that? Why is the larger corporations able to be able to pad their profits and look robust and healthy as ever? Why is that? Help, help me understand if you can.

Mr. BIVENS. Yeah, I think the simple answer to it is just like different degrees of market power. A lot of the stories on the panel, which I think are totally true, is you've got small businesses and they look on the input side and they see costs rising a lot and then somehow, they're not able to sell their output for much higher prices. And on the one hand that should be a puzzle. There's inflation. I thought all prices were rising. Why aren't they just getting it back on the output side? And it's often the case that because some of their customers tend to be really big corporate retailers who have the ability to say no, don't care about what's happening to your input costs. I'm holding the line on prices and I'm able to just because I'm a big corporation and I've got market power that you don't. And so that's why I think, like inflation or not, long run, short run, one key issue is just to relive level that playing field and actually do more robust antitrust enforcement so that the pain is actually shared more. Equitably across society when you've got these shocks and it just leads to more efficient outcomes when you've got more competition in markets as well.

Mr. THANEDAR. Yeah. Thank you. Thank you so much. And Mr. Gray, I represent Detroit, State of Michigan. Many of the residents in my district average typical annual household income could be as low as $25,000, maybe as high as $45,000. So, people are struggling and they haven't seen, many of these families haven't seen the benefit of the wage increases depending on the type of work that they do. But they are experiencing the same inflation as everybody else, the same cost increases, the cost of grocery, the fuel, everything else going up. Now, Federal Reserve at least looks like indicating that they would want to pause the interest rate hikes. Now, given the current inflation situation, what would that do to the inflation? And do you think that the Fed is gone far enough or they need to continue to go further?

Mr. GRAY. Thank you for the question and your observation is absolutely correct. And this is true of every recovery, is it not? Too often, those at the lowest end of the income distribution recover last. However, I do think in the current recovery, we've actually seen something of a break from that tradition. And we have seen, particularly in this very tight labor market, is unemployment rates across all demographic groups are really bouncing off historic lows. And I view that positively within the context, though, of an inflationary environment. However, in terms of the outlook on the Federal Reserve, I think there's an argument for a pause. We have seen rapid increase in the tightening of monetary policy. So, there's an argument for that at present.

Mr. THANEDAR. Okay. With 30 seconds remaining, do you believe that the Fed policy has helped us avoid a recession and likely to end up into a soft landing?

Mr. GRAY. I believe that's the hope. We're not there yet, and so I simply don't know if that's yet achievable. I am hopeful, and so far, we haven't landed hard.

Mr. THANEDAR. Mr. Gray, thank you. And, Mr. Chair, I'll yield back.

Chairman WILLIAMS. Thank you very much. And I would like to thank our witnesses today. We've had almost 2 hours of a hearing. It's been great for your testimony, and I hope that when you go back, you realize that everything in Washington is not one side or another. I think you see on this committee, we agree to a lot of things, which is important because we need to agree on main street, America and so forth. So, I appreciate you being here. I appreciate all my colleagues being here today. And without objection,

Members have 5 legislative days to submit additional materials and written questions for the witnesses to the Chair, which will be forwarded to the witnesses. I ask the witnesses to please respond promptly if that happens. And if there's no further business, without objection, the committee is adjourned. Thank you.

[Whereupon, at 3:50 p.m., the committee was adjourned.]

Appendix

Testimony on: Prices on the Rise: Examining the Effects of Inflation on Small Businesses
Gordon Gray American Action Forum#
United States House of Representatives Committee on Small Business
June 7, 2023

Chairman Williams, Ranking Member Velázquez, and members of the Committee, thank you for the privilege of appearing today to discuss inflation and its effects on small business. I hope to make the following main points:

- The United States is experiencing persistent inflation that is taxing America's families and businesses.
- Policy choices have contributed to the recent, rapid acceleration in price levels.
- Federal policy should be oriented around reducing inflationary pressures – and the record has been mixed at best.

Let me discuss these in turn.

The Inflationary Environment

According to the U.S. Census Bureau, the median age in the United States is about 39, which means that a bit more than half of the country has never experienced inflation like what the United States has seen over the last two

The views expressed here are my own and not those of the American Action Forum.

years. Not since 1980 has the Consumer Price Index (CPI) grown as rapidly as was observed in June of 2022 when yearly inflation topped 8.9 percent.

Stripping out more volatile food and energy price components to isolate core price growth reveals a similar story of rapid, historically aberrant inflation. Notably, one can observe a significant divergence between the two indices around the time of the Russian invasion of Ukraine that significantly disrupted energy markets. It is clear that event moved food and energy prices, but the fundamental story of U.S. price growth is not about the Russian invasion, but the laws of supply and demand.

These laws are in force, and they are taxing small businesses and the households that support them. Over the last two years, yearly price inflation has averaged 2 percentage points higher than yearly wage growth. Wage growth has been substantially elevated over the same period but has nevertheless failed to keep pace with price growth. Put another way, small business and households are falling behind. While inflation is down off of the recent peak, it remains stubbornly elevated at well above the average of recent decades, and more than twice the target rate set by the Federal Reserve.

Thus, even though the U.S. inflation outlook is improved, enduring inflation nevertheless is a significant tax on household finance that will diminish the U.S. standard of living. At the current rate of 5 percent, a family with the median income of $70,784 is paying over $3,500 in price growth.[1] Relative to stable price growth, this is a $2,000 tax right out of household budgets. Food, energy, and shelter prices – which tend to be more volatile but nevertheless represent about half of the average household budget – have been even more elevated, and serves as a uniquely regressive tax.[2]

Recent Macroeconomic History

Prior to the onset of the COVID-19 pandemic, there had been a meaningful improvement in the persistence of healthy economic growth over the prior three years. Gross domestic product (GDP) growth, measured as the growth from the same quarter in the previous year, accelerated steadily from a low of 1.4 percent in the 2nd quarter of 2016 to a pre- pandemic peak of 3.3 percent in the 2nd quarter of 2018. Notably, throughout this period, GDP growth remained above the 1.9 percent growth rate that prevailed throughout the 14 years since the Great Recession.

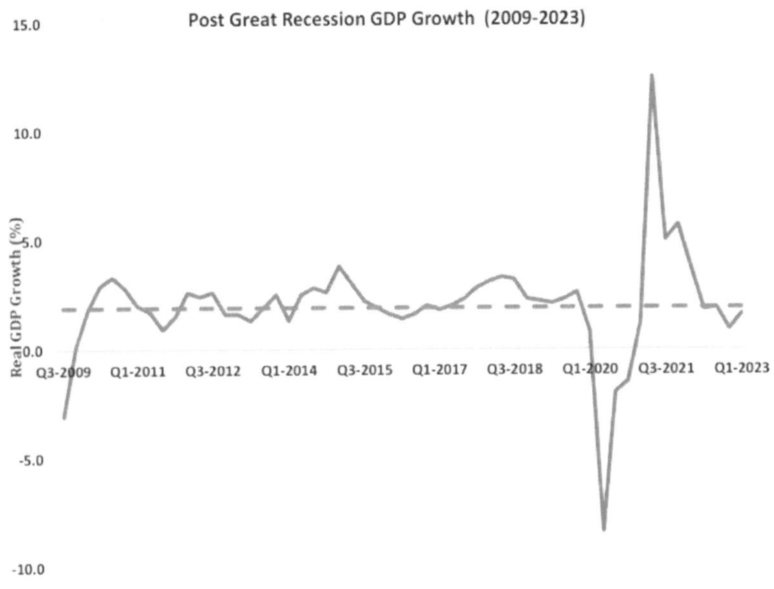

---

[1] https://www.census.gov/library/publications/2022/demo/p60-276.html.

[2] https://oversight.house.gov/hearing/inflation-a-preventable-crisis/dhe-testimony-house-oversight-final-3-9-23- holtz-eakin/.

In March of 2020, the COVID-19 pandemic precipitated a historic shuttering of the economy. The broadest measure of economic wellbeing – real quarterly GDP growth – reflected the devastation. The Bureau of Economic Analysis (BEA) estimated that that the economy contracted 8.4 percent between the 2nd quarter of 2019 and the 2nd quarter of 2020 – the single largest drop in real GDP since the Depression-era.

The public policy response was robust, with the combined monetary, fiscal, and administrative actions estimated to be on the order of $11 trillion.[3] The most conspicuous of these actions was the series of bipartisan measures that were enacted in 2020. Through a combination of public policy, effective vaccines, and more than a fair amount of grit from the American public, the nation and the economy recovered rapidly, such that the economy as measured from the 2nd quarter of 2020 to the 2nd quarter of 2021 had expanded by 12.5 percent. The pace of growth has somewhat tempered in real terms since.

A somewhat similar story can be told of the U.S. labor market. U.S. unemployment gradually moderated over the last decade, before finally bouncing near historic lows. In February of 2020, the regular unemployment rate stood at 3.5 percent. Just one month later unemployment had shot up to 14.7 percent, the highest rate and largest monthly increase in dataset going back to 1948.[4]

But robust policy actions by Congress and the Federal Reserve combined with an improved public health outlook provided for a rapid recovery in the labor market from the depths of the pandemic. Yet somewhat differently than the pace of real GDP, the labor market remains quite tight such that as recently as last month the unemployment rate remained at lows not seen since the 1960s.

A more nuanced economic history is borne out by the evolution of the pace of nominal average hourly earnings.

Here, we see a somewhat similar trajectory to other major economic indicators over the last decade, reflecting slow building wage growth. Unlike employment, however, earnings growth did not crater but rather have cycled between high and very high rates of growth. This is a feature of a very tight labor market. In the presence of historically high inflation, it reflects an economy running hot.

---

[3] https://www.covidmoneytracker.org/.

[4] https://www.bls.gov/opub/ted/2020/unemployment-rate-rises-to-record-high-14-point-7-percent-in-april-2020.htm.

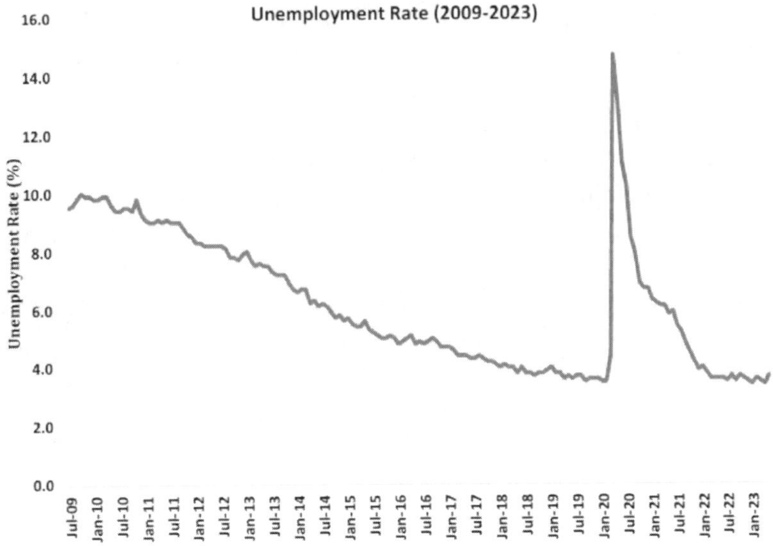
Unemployment Rate (2009-2023)
Unemployment Rate (%)
16.0
14.0
12.0
10.0
8.0
6.0
4.0
2.0
0.0
Jul-09
Jan-10
Jul-10
Jan-11
Jul-11
Jan-12
Jul-12
Jan-13
Jul-13
Jan-14
Jul-14
Jan-15
Jul-15
Jan-16
Jul-16
Jan-17
Jul-17
Jan-18
Jul-18
Jan-19
Jul-19
Jan-20
Jul-20
Jan-21
Jul-21
Jan-22
Jul-22
Jan-23

Average Hourly Earnings Growth (2009-2023)
YoY Percent Change, 6-Month MA
8.0
7.0
6.0
5.0
4.0
3.0
2.0
1.0
0.0
Jul-2009
Jan-2010
Jul-2010
Jan-2011
Jul-2011
Jan-2012
Jul-2012
Jan-2013
Jul-2013
Jan-2014
Jul-2014
Jan-2015
Jul-2015
Jan-2016
Jul-2016
Jan-2017
Jul-2017
Jan-2018
Jul-2018
Jan-2019
Jul-2019
Jan-2020
Jul-2020
Jan-2021
Jul-2021
Jan-2022
Jul-2022
Jan-2023
Average Hourly Earnings
Average Hourly Earnings (production and non supervisory)

Rising Inflation and Policy Design

On the fundamental questions as to whether the current inflationary cycle is a function of excess demand or insufficient supply, the answer, of course, is "yes." Unquestionably, the pandemic imposed somewhat unique challenges on the economy. It was the deliberate policy of the United States to essentially shutter commerce for a significant period of time. The disruptions rippled through every institution in the United States, from government, to schools, to businesses and households.

The U.S. policy response in 2020 was rapid, appropriately sized, and included policies that were well-tailored to the challenge – the Paycheck Protection Program loans are a conspicuous example. The first pandemic-era response, the Families First Coronavirus Response Act (H.R. 6201) was signed into law on March 18th and offered over $300 billion in emergency support for paid family and sick leave for workers and employers. This law was followed soon after by the enactment of the CARES Act, which provided more than $2 trillion in relief and support to households, government agencies, and businesses. Follow- on legislation enacted on a bipartisan basis throughout the year variously extended certain programs to maintain federal support for families and business and ensure government functioning. The last such legislation was the Consolidated Appropriations Act of 2021, which featured about $900 billion in additional relief and support largely modeled on policies in the CARES Act. At the time, inflation as measured by the CPI was 1.4 percent year-on-year and real GDP grew 3.9 percent on an annualized basis in the 4th quarter of 2020.[5]

Subsequent policy changes marked a break from the bipartisan tradition that largely characterized the congressional response to the pandemic. On March 19, President Biden signed into law the American Rescue Plan Act, which injected on the order of $1.9 trillion into the economy. Setting aside the policies within the Act, which were somewhat inconsistent in design with past coronavirus-response measures, the Act was quite simply too big.

According to the Congressional Budget Office (CBO), the gap between the capacity of the U.S. economy to grow and actual economic performance – known as the output gap – was about $380 billion for the rest of the year.[6] At the time, the U.S. economy was growing at 6.3 percent annualized. The upshot

---

[5] https://www.bls.gov/news.release/archives/cpi_01132021.htm; https://www.bea.gov/itable/national-gdp-and- personal-income.

[6] https://www.cbo.gov/system/files/2021-02/51135-2021-02-economicprojections.xlsx.

is that Congress and the administration gave a massive injection of fiscal stimulus at a time when it needed it least – within two months inflation had nearly doubled before doubling again in the subsequent months. It is important to note that while other global economies faced rapid inflation – the United States was a conspicuous frontrunner subsequent to the enactment of the American Rescue Plan. That excessive stimulus uniquely contributed to U.S. inflation has been found in research published by Federal Reserve banks.[7]

Unquestionably there are global forces at work that can and ultimately do swamp the effects of temporary legislation. There is a temptation to identify a single cause of America's inflation challenge. The reality is that it is a challenge with myriad interactions and lags. Economies around the world have been grappling with the same challenges that confronted the United States. Many of these challenges are beyond the direct control of policymakers. Accordingly, while I want to emphasize that no single policy change is responsible for the current inflation challenge, to the extent legislation is within the direct control of policymakers, the American Rescue Plan stands out as a significant policy error.

And it was a foreseeable error. As noted, the output gap was about $380 billion at the time. According to the nonpartisan Committee for a Responsible Federal Budget, the American Rescue Plan was plainly excessive, and was sufficient to close the output gap "two to three times over."[8] The analysis, which assessed the tradeoffs in such a policy identified the risks of inflation and noted that CBO may have overestimated the relevant output gap. If nonpartisan analysis was an insufficient deterrent, Congress could have availed itself of the warnings from key members of President Obama's economic team and other well-known "doves" that the ARP was excessively large.[9]

[7] https://www.frbsf.org/economic-research/publications/economic-letter/2022/march/why-is-us-inflation-higher-than-in-other-countries/; https://www.federalreserve.gov/econres/notes/feds-notes/fiscal-policy-and-excess-inflation-during-covid-19-a-cross-country-view-20220715.html#:~:text=Our%20back%2Dof%2Dthe%2D,ppt%20in%20the%20United%20Kingdom.

[8] https://www.crfb.org/blogs/how-much-would-american-rescue-plan-overshoot-output-gap.

[9] https://www.crfb.org/blogs/voices-skeptical-size-19-trillion-covid-relief-plan.

Policy Considerations in an Era of High Inflation

The Federal Reserve, as per its dual mandate, is charged with maintaining price stability. The Central Bank's rapid tightening of monetary policy, and eventually improved public comments on the likely course of monetary policy have done and will continue to do most of the work in bringing stubborn inflation under control. This body nevertheless has an important role to play by pulling in the same direction.

Congress has a somewhat uneven record since the enactment of the American Rescue Plan.[10] The Inflation Reduction Act, for instance, was found to have no effect on inflation by CBO and Penn Wharton.[11] Policies such as the CHIPs Act must be balanced against the risk of additional inflationary measures. Most recently, the Fiscal Responsibility Act could modestly reduce inflationary pressures through deficit reduction, largely deriving from the Act's spending caps.[12]

Thank you very much, and I look forward to addressing your questions.

Congressional Testimony Silvia Lee
Executive Vice President & Chief Lending Officer First Community Bank
Corpus Christi, TX before the House Committee on Small Business "Prices on the Rise: Examining the Effects of Inflation on Small Businesses" June 7, 2023

My name is Silvia Lee. I am a graduate of Texas A&M University, Kingsville with a Bachelor of Science in Finance. My first and only jobs have been in the Texas banking industry with the last 23 of those at First Community Bank, Corpus Christi where I am the Chief Lending Officer.

We have 175 employees, and a somewhat unique factor about First Community Bank is that 73 percent of our employees are shareholders of the bank via our Employee Stock Ownership Program (ESOP). This has proven to be an important contributor to building a satisfied and growing customer base.

---

[10] https://www.americanactionforum.org/insight/is-congress-helping-or-hurting-inflation/.

[11] https://budgetmodel.wharton.upenn.edu/issues/2022/8/5/inflation-reduction-act-comparing-cbo-and-pwbm- estimates.

[12] https://www.americanactionforum.org/insight/highlights-of-the-fiscal-responsibility-act/.

Our community bank was founded in 1983 and now has 11 branches and $657 million in assets. We have a loan portfolio of $458 million consisting of residential and commercial real estate and, of course, small business loans which are the subject of today's hearing.

As a prefatory point, I do want to mention that almost all our Paycheck Protection Program (PPP) loans have been paid out at our institution. They consisted of 845 loans in an aggregate amount of $107 million and I can tell you personally, that these loans contributed immensely to the ability of our local customers to continue as going concerns during the pandemic.

In my view, lending to small businesses and thereby allowing them to add new customers, purchase property, buy equipment, and hire more employees is frankly the most important community service we provide. Federal Reserve data confirm that small businesses in search of a loan look first to their community bank. The Fed's annual surveys in the small business sector confirm our experience that almost 70 percent of small businesses apply for this type of credit at an FDIC-insured bank.[13]

With respect to today's hearing topic, namely the impact of inflation on small businesses, the answer is simple and is applicable to small and large businesses, individuals, institutions, government entities and any other category I may have omitted. It's a hardship for all but for small businesses it can often be worse in that they start with smaller margins to absorb adverse outside factors.

Everyone is familiar with the severe decline in mortgage origination volume (40-60 percent) as the Fed's anti-inflation strategy has driven up interest rates nearing the eight percent range. What is not widely appreciated, however, is that the housing industry is composed almost exclusively of small business contractors.

At our bank, for example, we developed a great market niche in the custom-built home construction business but new credit applications have slowed significantly due to less buyer-demand. Even on larger build-out sites and non-housing construction, the rising costs of building materials, not to mention supply-chain delays, has impaired the overall business environment for the small businessmen and women who provide the component construction elements: architecture, design, carpentry, electric installation, plumbing, landscaping and the many other services which go into this critical aspect of local economies.

---

[13] Availability of Credit to Small Businesses, Federal Reserve Board (Oct., 2022).

On the retail front, higher interest rates are likewise having a negative impact on rents and, at least in the State of Texas, higher commercial building taxes which are also passed on to the family businesses, including many immigrant families, which constitute a larger number of this vital economic segment.

These retail stores have landlords of course which are also included in our small business customer base and likewise are subject to the same financial pressures. At this point, we have not seen this rise to the level of actual loan defaults in our commercial real estate portfolio, but we also see a slow-down here as well as some business owners increasingly looking at the sale option. In the retail sector, however, many of the difficulties, as is well known, remain focused on just filling employee positions.

As a coastal community, Corpus Christi's hospitality industry remains a positive driver of local employment growth. We are also a lender in this area which includes mid-scale hotels/motels, RV parks and related leisure businesses that are fortunately witnessing full post-COVID recovery.

Recently, a long-time bank customer who owns a small business had an increase in his loan monthly loan payment of approximately $1,000.00 due to increased interest rates. The loan has an annual adjustment and re-priced in May 2023. The business owner commented that he would price his goods and services out-of-the market to absorb the cost of his inventory and increased interest rates. He mentioned that he feels our government does not want small businesses to succeed and wants only large companies in business. It is an unfortunate prospective.

Even in areas where the economy remains strong, however, underwriting small business loans relies primarily on a business' debt coverage ratio, i.e., the new or refinanced monthly debt service in relation to the business' historical net income. With what has been a doubling of interest rates in just the last twelve months, the equation is fairly straightforward in that we are now seeing the cash-flow available for debt service ratios drop dramatically for every type of business. This would be especially true for a start-up small business which is probably the most critical local component for a growth economy.

As a bank with very strong earnings and capital, we are prepared to work with any of our small business borrowers encountering temporary difficulties and all of us, whether borrowers or lenders, hope that this unprecedented combination of excess fiscal and monetary policy followed by rapidly-rising interest rates will soon be coming to a pause.

The current market pressures notwithstanding, Texas is blessed to have a strong economy and very strong banking system. In our area of the state, the macro-economy is driven by oil, gas and hydrogen production and transportation, of course, as we are a port city.

Nevertheless, Texas has not been immune from industry consolidation trends where the number of FDIC-insured banks headquartered in our state has declined from 556 to 387 over the last ten years. An even sadder part of this is that even among the remaining local banks so many have been forced to abandon important parts of the consumer market such as home mortgage lending to the larger banks or nonbanks as the case may be.

That has not been the case at First Community Bank, we remain committed to the home mortgage market, the small business market and as many of the full-service banking products as make economic sense. In this regard, we are very concerned about the massive new regulation on small business data collection just finalized by the CFPB which puts us in the position of having to collect nonfinancial personal information on prospective business borrowers.

Thank you for the opportunity to appear before you this afternoon.

Statement by David G. Zittel to the House Committee on Small Business
"Prices on the Rise: Examining the Effects of Inflation on Small Businesses"
Presented by David G. Zittel Wednesday, June 7, 2023

Thank you to the Committee on Small Business and to Chairman Roger Williams for inviting me to testify before you today on the impacts of inflation on small businesses like family farms. My name is David Zittel, and my family and I own and operate Amos Zittel & Sons, a fresh market vegetable and greenhouse farm based in Eden, New York. My brother, cousin and I are currently the fourth generation to run the farm. My son, the fifth generation is back on the farm as well. I'm also representing the farming and agriculture community across New York and the country that works hard to produce food and fiber for consumers across the country and globe.

At Amos Zittel & Sons, we produce a wide variety of fresh market vegetables on 350 acres in Western New York including lettuce, strawberries, peppers, cabbage, sweet corn, tomatoes, broccoli, eggplant, squash, brussel sprouts and grape tomatoes. Approximately 95% of our produce is sold through our marketing co-op, Eden Valley Growers, which our farm is proud to be a founding member of. This co-op was created to bring growers in the area together to market and sell our produce. In addition, the farm also consists of a greenhouse operation that produces approximately 4 million rooted liners of geraniums, and other spring annuals that are marketed through brokers nationally, and a retail ready container crop sold to local garden centers. In addition, we grow over 2 million transplants for our field grown vegetables.

The farm employs 40-50 individuals year-round and has approximately 135 employees during the peak of the season. Because we produce fresh market produce, all our crops must be hand harvested and can be very labor intensive. It also means that our business is directly impacted by market forces, and we cannot wait to sell a crop until prices increase. Farmers are price takers, not price makers.

As a small, family-owned business, we feel the direct effects of inflationary pressures and have seen an overall increase in the cost of operating the farm. While farmers have become more efficient over time to help overcome low commodity prices, like increasing production per acre, inflation can quickly take away any efficiency gains. Through the pandemic and even to this day, we continue to feel the impacts of inflation.

Examples of inflation and rising costs that we have seen on our farm include tractor and equipment parts, which have increased 15-30%, with a delay in receiving them on a timely basis. Inflation and supply chain issues have also led to consolidation in the agriculture industry which has decreased available vendors to source goods and services and led to increased prices.

The cost of the boxes used to transport our vegetables is up about 30%, which will cost the farm an extra $100,000 this year. Fertilizer and most other input costs are up 30-50% for the farm as well, which impacts our bottom line. The cost of feed for dairy farmers is up 25-40% and transportation costs have contributed to much of our inflationary increases. Unfortunately for us the price we are receiving for our product does not cover these cost increases since our markets.

The largest negative impact to our bottom line is due to increases in labor cost and regulations imposed on us by NYS and Federal governments. Labor costs account for 50% of our business expenses and continues to rise. Not only have we seen yearly increases in the minimum wage rates in New York, which is currently $14.20 per hour, the H-2A guest visa rate is $16.95 per hour, an increase of $1.41 per hour from the 2022 AEWR of $15.66 (a 9% increase). A recently released rule by the DOL will further drive the AEWR up as there is now a rule that requires separate wage rates for various job functions. New York also has an overtime threshold of 60 hours for farm workers, which has increased labor costs and narrowed the hours we can afford to pay. This puts us at a competitive disadvantage compared to other states with lower minimum wages and no overtime requirements. Paired with a short growing season, we must be efficient as possible to ensure that we can stay in business.

Inflation has created price instability and uncertainty in the farm economy that has made many investment decisions riskier than they would be if inflation had remained low and stable. Higher interest rates also continue to impact farms like mine. We work closely with Farm Credit East, an agricultural lender, to assist with continued investment in our farm. However, we have been carefully monitoring interest rates and have held off expanding the farm business because we don't want to overextend our operation given current rates. We were impacted by two recent historical snow falls in 2014 and again last November which resulted in rebuilding greenhouses, a shop and storage buildings. In both situations, we have had decent insurance coverage but the cost to rebuild is 3x. We will be financing an additional $1 million to rebuild the loss from that 72" of snowfall in November, holding off as long as we could, and hoping interest rates would stabilize or begin to go back down.

Having a healthy farm economy is key to ensuring a healthy domestic food system and vital to national security. In New York, we have access to markets that other farmers would envy. Our farm is located near the cities of Buffalo and Rochester, but we are also located within 500 miles of one-third of the U.S. population with New York City, Boston, Philadelphia, Washington, D.C., Pittsburg, and Cleveland, all areas hungry for what we grow. However, if we cannot ensure a viable domestic agriculture industry and control rising production costs, we could see food production continue to shift to other countries because in many cases it is cheaper and easier to produce food in other areas and then transport it to metropolitan areas.

As we look to the future of our operation, young farmers are so discouraged by challenges they face by making a career in agriculture—the expense of land, labor, fuel, energy, machinery, taxes, rules and regulations, the list goes on and on. It is no secret that New York is a high-cost state with a difficult regulatory environment for family businesses and farms. But despite all this, we are so proud that the next generation has decided to carry on our farming tradition.

We know that there will remain challenges that need to be overcome including inflation, regulatory requirements, labor challenges, and others.

The Zittel's' hope that vegetables will always be grown on our land for generations to come, and we look forward to carrying on the farming tradition but also look to Congress to ensure that laws and regulations do not put us out of business. We always say fresh market vegetable farming is the only business that buys all inputs, plants and harvests the crops before we have any idea what our return will be.

If I may quote John F Kennedy:

> "The farmer is the only man in our economy who buys everything at retail, sells everything at wholesale, and pays the freight both ways."

Thank you again for the opportunity to share my family's farm story and how our small business has been impacted by inflationary pressures. I would be glad to take any questions you may have.

David Zittel

Testimony for the Committee on Small Business of the U.S. House of Representatives on "Prices Are On the Rise: Examining the Effects of Inflation on Small Businesses"
Josh Bivens, Ph.D.
Chief Economist and Research Director, Economic Policy Institute, Washington, DC

Chairman Williams, Ranking Member Velázquez, and distinguished Members of the Committee: Thank you for inviting me to testify at this hearing. My name is Josh Bivens and I'm the Chief Economist and Research Director of the Economic Policy Institute (EPI). EPI is a non-profit, non- partisan think tank that uses the tools of economics to identify policies than will boost the living standards of low- and moderate-income families, particularly through their role as workers.

I'd like to make the following points about the subjects of this hearing – inflation and its effects on small businesses.

- Inflation has been a challenge over the past two years, but inflation is not the only notable economic trend that's emerged in this time – we've also seen by far the best labor market in a generation, particularly for low-wage workers. Policy changes that are undertaken in the name of fighting inflation may threaten these labor market gains, and if inflation is poised to moderate on its own even absent these changes, then they would be pure gain for little gain.

- Inflation has not been the result of policy mistakes. Instead, it's been the essentially inevitable result of massive shocks to the economy and the long-lived – but steadily dampening – ripple effects. These shocks were obviously the pandemic and the Russian invasion of Ukraine, and the ripples were mostly about jockeying by different economic actors – corporations, workers, and suppliers – to protect their own real incomes from these shocks.
- All of this means that inflation has mostly been a distributional challenge – because one person's income is another person's cost, the higher costs for some have shown up as significant income gains someplace in the economy. This "someplace" has mostly been the business income of sellers - particularly corporate profits.
    - Have small businesses been able to draft in this corporate pricing power wake and charge higher prices themselves to protect their own margins? It's very hard to generalize, but it is vital to remember that lots of "small businesses" are actually incredibly rich and privileged enterprises. My guess is that these privileged businesses have largely been able to pass input price increases on and then some.
    - To the degree that some genuine Main Street small businesses have been squeezed on the input side but have been unable to pass these costs on – maybe because they are suppliers to big corporations who refuse to pay higher prices to their suppliers – this is not really a problem of inflation per se, it's a problem of monopoly power in markets that's been growing for years. We certainly should address this, particularly with more assertive anti-trust policy.
    - There is no labor shortage relative to pre-pandemic trends – recovery in labor supply is effectively complete.
- But, the risk to small business from an overaggressive attack on inflation that seeks to slow the economy are the same as to workers writ large – it will sacrifice the huge gains from the recovery for no real need if inflation is already normalizing (and it almost surely is).

Below I'll say a bit more on each of these.

Inflation Not the Only Notable Economic Trend of Recent Years

This hearing is predominantly about inflation and its effects on small businesses – and inflation has obviously been a key economic challenge facing working families throughout the recovery from the recession caused by the COVID-19 pandemic. But inflation is not the only notable economic trend in recent years – and it is certainly not the only notable trend highly relevant to small businesses.

In short, this has been a remarkably rapid recovery – particularly when compared to recoveries following the recessions of the early 1990s and 2000s and the recovery from the Great Recession and financial crises of 2008. Over 13 million jobs have been added since January 2021, a rate of around 450,000 jobs per month since President Biden took office.

The pre-recession unemployment rate was reattained in essentially 2 years following the recessionary shock. It took 10 years to reattain the 4.3% unemployment trough after 2007.

Growth in hourly pay – even adjusted for inflation – has been extraordinarily strong for low-wage workers. Between 2019 and 2022 hourly real wages for workers at the 10th percentile rose by 9%. In the first three years following the business cycle peak of 2007, inflation-adjusted wages grew by just 1.1%.

Since the recovery from the COVID-19 recession began in the third quarter of 2020, gross job gains have outpaced gross job losses in the Business Employment Dynamics (BED) data by more than 5 million. A third of these net job gains have been in businesses with less than 50 people – a bit higher than the average share of net job creation that could be accounted for by small businesses in the two years before the pandemic hit. In 2021 and 2022, 10.5 million applications to start new businesses were filed, the highest two years on record. Work from the Federal

Reserve finds that these applications have turned into new establishments and new hiring.[14] (Fed).

All of these salutary economic trends have been supported by Biden administration efforts, including but not limited to the rapid recovery ensured

[14] Decker, Ryan and John Haltiwanger. 2022. Business entry and exit in the COVID-19 pandemic: a preliminary look at official data.

by the American Rescue Plan (ARP). Additional efforts for small businesses have included expanded access to capital through small business lending and investments in support services for small businesses.[15]

Inflation Was Not the Result of a Policy Mistake – It Was the Inevitable Result of Mammoth Global Shocks and Their Long-Lived – But Dampening - Ripples

In early 2021, debate raged about the potential economic effects of the American Rescue Plan (ARP). The ARP, passed in early 2021, was explicitly designed as fiscal stimulus, with large and front-loaded transfers to households as its centerpiece, along with substantial aid to state and local governments.[16]

It is worth remembering the macroeconomic situation at the time of this debate. Of the 22 million jobs lost due to the COVID-19 shock, barely half had been recovered by December 2020, leaving the economy more than ten million jobs below pre-recession levels. This was a larger jobs gap than we had at the trough of the Great Recession and financial crisis of 2008-2009.

Further, the recovery that had begun in May 2020 was flagging. Monthly job gains had been getting smaller and smaller since September of that year, and December 2020—the last month's data informing the meat of the debate over the ARP—saw outright job losses again. Hence, the decision to go for a large fiscal stimulus was very well founded in the evidence.

Some critics of the ARP worried about its potential effect on inflation, as it was argued that the ARP would push gross domestic product (GDP) well over the economy's long-run potential to deliver, hence causing inflation. In this story, a positive "output gap" with actual GDP far exceeding the economy's long-run potential should have appeared in the data. Yet both real GDP and estimates of potential GDP today sit almost exactly where pre-pandemic forecasts predicted they would be in 2023 – and these forecasts included no indication of inflation. If the economy is not trying to produce more than it is capable of relative to pre-pandemic forecasts, it is hard to see where the heat that is generating inflation is coming from.

Reasonable estimates of potential GDP that account for the damage done by the pandemic were also slightly below pre-pandemic trends, but the size of

---

[15] See the fact sheet from the Biden-Harris administration here: https://www.whitehouse.gov/wp-content/uploads/2023/04/Small-Business-Report.pdf.

[16] This section draws on Banerjee, Asha and Josh Bivens. 2023. *Lessons from the Inflation of 2021-202?.* Economic Policy Institute.

the resulting output gap was utterly unremarkable—totally in line with recent past episodes that saw larger and more sustained gaps without generating any inflation at all.

Another piece of evidence against this simple overheating view comes from international data. Inflation—even outside of food and energy prices—has clearly been global. Every single advanced economy has seen inflation accelerate relative to pre-COVID trends, and most of these countries have seen a large acceleration, whether or not they used large stimulus programs. Some have argued that this just means that every single other advanced country replicated the U.S. "mistake" of overheating their economies. But this would suggest that the extent of inflationary acceleration should be correlated with reductions in unemployment—for overheating to take hold, it must run through labor market tightening. Yet across countries, there is no correlation at all between the reduction in unemployment and the acceleration of inflation in recent years.

Finally, key aspects of the labor market show little conventional signs of heat. One of the most reliable empirical relationships in modern business cycles is that low and falling unemployment (i.e., an economy that is "heating up") pushes up the share of corporate-sector income claimed by workers (rather than capital owners). Yet the labor share fell sharply and has remained depressed all through the recent inflationary surge.[17]

Shocks and Ripples

If inflation was not driven by macroeconomic overheating, what's the alternative account?

Extreme sectoral shocks kicked off large—but steadily diminishing—ripple effects. In this "shocks and ripples" account, if shocks relent, then inflation will normalize—even if it will take some time.

The shocks are fairly obvious: The pandemic led to a historically sharp reallocation of spending away from face-to-face services and toward goods consumption and residential investment.

Simultaneously, the pandemic introduced huge snarls in global supply chains that need to function smoothly to meet demand for goods and materials used in residential investment. These extreme shocks to both sectoral demand

[17] See Bivens, Josh. 2023. What Profit-Price Spirals Are Telling Us About Post-Pandemic Inflation. Intereconomics. Volume 58(3), pp. 167-168.

and supply was the spark to inflation in 2021. In 2022, the Russian invasion of Ukraine added another, more familiar shock to energy and food prices.

Proponents of the macroeconomic overheating view often refuse to acknowledge that sectoral shocks that lead to large changes in relative prices (i.e., prices for specific goods and services) can cause overall inflation. Their reasoning is that if, say, gas prices rise by 50 percent in a short period, then this should lead to a near-immediate reduction in demand for other goods and services that forces down their prices, leaving overall inflation unaffected. There's some logic to this, but the time span in which this kind of countervailing demand reduction happens following sectoral price shocks is far longer than they think—measured in years, not months. In short, thinking that sectoral shocks can have profound implications for inflation is not a simple failure to understand macroeconomics. James Tobin, perhaps the greatest macroeconomist of his generation, wrote in 1972 that:

> "dispersion is inflationary … the rate of wage inflation will depend not only on the overall dispersion of excess demands and supplies across markets but also on the particular markets where the excess supplies and demands happen to fall. An unlucky random drawing might put the excess demands in highly responsive markets and the excess supplies in especially unresponsive ones."

Ripples That Were Surprising—But Likely to Decline Without High Interest Rates

These sectoral shocks led to more persistent effects on inflation than many anticipated in part because of a key ripple effect—nominal wage growth accelerated noticeably in late 2021 and early 2022. This nominal wage acceleration did not provide the initial impetus to inflation—the pandemic and war shocks did that. Further, while nominal wage growth accelerated relative to pre-pandemic levels, it remained slower than overall inflation and so actually muffled rather than amplified the inflationary shock.

Essentially, the pandemic and war shocks to prices sent economic actors—firms, workers, and consumers—scrambling to protect their own real incomes from higher costs. As nonlabor costs rose due to pandemic and war shocks and pushed up prices, workers tried to protect their real (inflation-adjusted) incomes by demanding higher nominal wages. Firms in turn tried to keep their own profit margins intact or even to opportunistically raise them.

This cascade of higher nominal wage demands and profit margin hikes intensified the inflationary effect of the initial shocks and made them more persistent.

Nominal wage acceleration did keep inflation higher than it would have been had wage growth not budged from its pre-pandemic pace. But even if nominal wage growth had not quickened at all, we still would have had a burst of inflation over the past two years. The reduced inflation that could have been "bought" by keeping unemployment higher and nominal wage growth lower in 2021 and 2022 would have been relatively small—and the price of this slightly slower inflation would have been even larger declines in real wages for working families than we have seen. In short, given the incredibly binding constraints put on the range of economic choices by the pandemic distortions and the Russian invasion of Ukraine, choosing to tolerate some inflation as the price of engineering a remarkably fast recovery was the right thing to do.

Inflation Has Been Mostly a Distributional Challenge – Sellers Have Done Well

There are times when inflation really can be driven by most incomes in society rising at mostly the same pace. In this case, inflation is distributionally neutral, but there's also no "real" cost. For example, if inflation accelerates from 0% to 4%, but nominal wage growth accelerates from 2% to 6%, real wages haven't been harmed (they grow at 2% in either case). The inflation we have seen since 2021 has not been distributionally neutral. Prices and incomes for low-wage workers, middle-wage workers, high-wage workers, and profits have not moved in lockstep but have seen very different rates of growth.

Most striking is the role of corporate profits in starting and sustaining inflation since 2021. Figure A below shows one measure of profit "mark-ups" in the non-financial corporate (NFC) sector of the U.S. economy. We look at this sector because it has rich and timely data coverage. Mark-ups are essentially profits earned per unit of output divided by labor and non- labor costs.

When these profit markups rise, the result is increasing prices for consumers (inflation). The very large spike in the beginning quarters of the COVID-19 recovery is clear. Since then, mark- ups have come down a little, but remain extremely elevated relative to historic norms. Many (including me) had hoped these high mark-ups would relent sooner and provide more relief from too-high inflation by now, but it has not yet happened in a serious way.

Figure A

Profit markups spiked during COVID-19 economic recovery

Profits per unit of output divided by unit labor and unit nonlabor costs in the NFC, 2017–2022

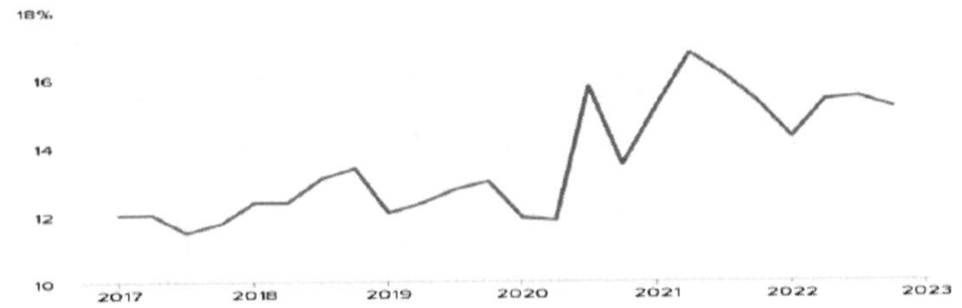

Source: Bureau of Economic Analysis (BEA) National Income and Product Accounts (NIPA) data, Table 1.15.

Economic Policy Institute

Figure B

Corporate profits contributed disproportionately to price growth in the COVID-19 economic recovery

Share of NFC price growth accounted for by unit labor costs, non-labor costs, and profits, 2020q2–2022q4 and shares of each between 2007–2019

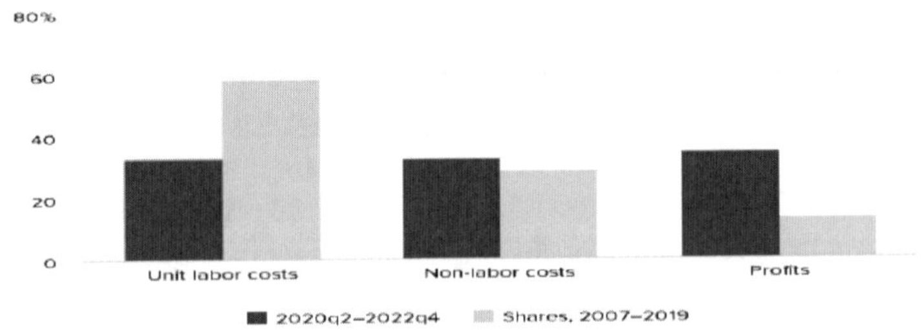

Source: Bureau of Economic Analysis (BEA) National Income and Product Accounts (NIPA) data, Table 1.15.

Economic Policy Institute

Figure B shows the contribution of profits, labor costs, and nonlabor costs to growth in NFC prices between the beginning of the COVID-19 recovery (the second quarter of 2020) and the end of 2022. Measuring since the last business cycle peak (the fourth quarter of 2019) does not change this story radically.

In normal times, corporate profits contribute about 13% to prices. Between the second quarter of 2020 and the end of 2022, they have instead contributed more than a third of price growth, or more than twice as much as they normally do. This contribution was larger in previous quarters, which means the slight decline in mark-ups shown in Figure A has put a small bit of welcome downward pressure on inflation in recent quarters. But there remains a long way to go before profits are back to normal, and this profit normalization drive even more disinflation.

Have Small Businesses Also Been Able to Increase Their Profit Margins Due to Pandemic and War Distortions?

Much of the income earned by small businesses is classified as "proprietors' income" in by the National Income and Product Accounts (NIPAs) – the statistical backbone of the U.S. economy. Before looking at aggregate trends in this measure, it is vital to note that many firms that get classified as small businesses or included in proprietors' income are actually extraordinarily privileged and rich enterprises.

For example, as Smith, Yagan, Zidar and Zwick (2020) note – "*More than 69 percent of the top 1 percent of income earners - and more than 84 percent of the top 0.1 percent of income earners accrued some pass-through business income in 2014, the most recent year for which complete data are available.*"[18] Pass-through income is essentially all business income earned by entities that are not traditional C-corporations (ie, corporations that pay federal taxes at the enterprise level). Further, these same authors estimate that half of the post-1979 doubling of the share of total national income claimed by the top 1 percent can be accounted for by rising pass-through business income. In short, small businesses are an even more-varied and unequal set of economic actors than any other in the U.S. economy.

In the aggregate, proprietors' income has lagged overall domestic income growth since the last business cycle peak in the last quarter of 2019 – growing at a 4.6% annualized rate in nominal terms compared to over 5.6% for overall domestic income. But, proprietors' income growth lagged even worse in the last 2 years before pandemic – growing at just an annualized rate of 3.2% between 2017 and 2019, compared to 4.5% growth in overall domestic income. In short, there is little evidence that any economic development – inflation or anything else – has severely affected the relative performance of the sector that small business incomes appear in since 2020.

---

[18] Smith, Matthew, Danny Yagan, Owen Zidar, and Eric Zwick. 2019. *Capitalists in the Twenty-First Century*. Quarterly Journal of Economics. Volume 134(4), pp. 1675-1745.

Many genuine small businesses surely find themselves facing rising input cost pressures. The huge increases in corporate prices, however, should have given many of these smaller businesses some elbow room to raise their own prices to deal with some of these more expensive input costs. In cases where small businesses work as suppliers for larger corporations, and these corporations have held the line on what they will pay their suppliers, this is obviously a huge source of pressure for the smaller businesses – but its root cause is the asymmetry in market power, not inflation per se. This asymmetry in market power that allows "lead firms" to pressure their own suppliers and starve them of opportunities is a real problem in the U.S. economy in recent decades.[19] It should be met primarily with enhanced anti-trust efforts that put market power in labor markets and supplier markets on the same footing as power in product markets. The Biden administration's Federal Trade Commission (FTC) and the Anti-Trust division of the Department of Justice have made admirable steps in this regard.

There Is No Labor Shortage

There has been a consistent complaint by business over the course of the recovery over labor shortages. For short periods in some sectors since the recovery from the COVID-19 recession began, there did indeed seem to be some labor shortages which were relatively quickly alleviated by raising wages. But by now, there is no evidence at all of any economy-wide labor shortage relative to pre-pandemic trends. The level of employment and the labor force participation rate are higher than what the CBO projected in February 2021, before the American Rescue Plan took effect. Further, these are both higher than what the CBO projected in early 2020, before the Covid pandemic.

The number of prime-age adults (those between 25 and 54) working is not only higher than 2019 levels, it is the highest it has been since 2001. Black workers, in particular, have had historically high levels of employment in the recovery, a testament to the broad nature of this recovery. In recent months, for the first time in recorded history, the overall employment to population ratio for the Black population exceeded that of the white population. Much of

---

[19] See Wilmers, Nathan. 2018. Wage Stagnation and Buyer Power: How Buyer-Supplier Relationships Affect U.S. Workers' Wages, 1978-2014. American Sociological Review. Volume 83(2). Pp 213-242.

this crossover was driven by differential aging trends (the white population is getting older faster and relatively more of them are crossing over retirement), but much of it is the natural tightening of racial gaps in employment that occur when the labor market is in good health.[20]

There is work that we could certainly to do to expand labor supply even further and beat past trends by supporting workers and by extension small businesses. The most obvious plank of a progressive labor supply policy that would yield big results would be a robust public investment in child care. By making high-quality childcare more affordable, we would reliably boost the labor supply of young parents – particularly women.[21]

Risks to Robust Recovery – And Small Businesses – From Attacking Inflation with the Wrong Policy Tools

If one sees inflation as ipso facto evidence that the economy has a macroeconomic excess of demand over productive capacity, and one sees this productive capacity as relatively fixed in the short-run, the obvious policy corollary is to tamp down demand – either through contractionary fiscal or monetary policy. But if one instead sees the inflation over the past 2 years as a set of long-lived ripples stemming large pandemic and war shocks, then one would expect inflation to normalize even without sharply contractionary policy.

In recent months there has been a sharp decline in the pace of nominal wage growth even as unemployment has remained low. Further, home price declines from early and mid-2022 are just now showing up in official inflation data. In short, there is substantial reason to expect a normalization of inflation in the coming months even if we manage to keep the unemployment rate very low.

This scenario where inflation normalizes without a recession – the "soft landing" – is by far the best one for small businesses and nearly every other actor in the U.S. economy. The necessary condition for success in business – whether small or large – is a steady stream of customers.

These customers will dry up if contractionary policy takes hold.

---

[20] See Bivens, Josh. 2021. *The Promise and Limits of High-Pressure Labor Markets for Narrowing Racial Gaps*. Economic Policy Institute.

[21] See Bivens, Josh, Emma Garcia, Elise Gould, Elaine Weiss, and Valerie Wilson. 2016. *It's Time for an Ambitious Investment in the Nation's Children*. Economic Policy Institute.

Inflation has been key challenge to the U.S. economy and its small businesses in recent years, but it remains the case that many proposed cures for this inflation would do more harm than the malady itself. Further, given the many promising signs on disinflation coming down the pike, risking a recession now by calling for ever more-contractionary monetary and fiscal policy would be akin to snatching defeat from the jaws of victory.

Chapter 5

Bidenomics: A Perfect Storm of Spending, Debt, and Inflation*

Committee on Oversight and Accountability

Tuesday, September 19, 2023
Washington, D.C.

The Subcommittee met, pursuant to notice, at 2:06 p.m., in room 2247, Rayburn House Office Building, Hon. Pat Fallon, Chairman of the Subcommittee, presiding.

Present: Representatives Fallon, Boebert, Edwards, Langworthy, Bush, Brown, Stansbury, and Norton.

Mr. FALLON. The hearing of the Subcommittee on Economic Growth, Energy Policy, and Regulatory Affairs will come to order. I want to welcome everybody here.

Without objection, the Chair may declare a recess at any time. I recognize myself for the purpose of making an opening statement.

Today's hearing is an opportunity to discuss an issue every household in America is familiar with, with a clear failure of Bidenomics and the crisis caused by this current Administration's reckless spending. Joe Biden likes to say that Bidenomics is just another way of saying restoring the American Dream. I beg to differ. But just last week, the Consumer Price Index showed prices have risen 17.4 percent since Mr. Biden took office. That means that 26 months of consumers watching their paychecks disappear before their very

---

* This is an edited, reformatted and augmented version of Hearing Before the Subcommittee on Economic Growth, Energy Policy, And Regulatory Affairs of the Committee on Oversight and Accountability, House of Representatives, Serial No. 118–67, dated September 19, 2023.

In: Inflation: Background, Causes and Current Policies
Editor: Julie Taylor Lowe
ISBN: 979-8-89530-696-3

eyes due to the rising costs of living. Worse yet, mortgage rates have nearly doubled since Joe Biden took office, making it much harder for Americans to buy a new home, and that is clearly not the American Dream.

Joe Biden likes to say Bidenomics is about building from the middle out and the bottom up. That is a clever slogan, but it does not reflect reality. In fact, let me say this, those hurt most by these rising prices are low-income households and seniors that are relying on Social Security for their monthly retirement.

Wage growth has fallen behind the pace of inflation in 20 of the past 22 months, and most Americans are now unable to pay for the surprising expense of, you know, if there is something that cost $400, suddenly they are struggling to pay that bill, something that was unforeseen, and that is not building from the middle out or from the bottom up. Joe Biden likes to remind us he promised not to raise taxes on anyone earning less than $400,000 a year, but as of June 2023, the average worker was paying an inflation tax, kind of an invisible tax because what inflation is, is a tax on everything that we need and have to buy. That 13.5 percent is effectively like a second Federal income tax, particularly for low-income earners. The truth is Bidenomics has been an abject disaster, and I think most of the American people know that.

A recent poll found that 80 percent—let me say that again—80 percent of Americans credit Joe Biden's policies for the current state of the economy, and 70 percent agreed that their incomes were not keeping pace with inflation. And if you see any poll in the last year-and-a-half, 2 years, you have seen that the Biden Administration scores, of all the major topics that we discuss, they score the worst on the economy.

Our current economic track is nothing short of unsustainable, yet the Biden Administration really does not seem to be concerned. In fact, Joe Biden considers the current environment a huge success, and he said that often on the campaign trail, proudly taking credit for every failed business that could not stay afloat under his crushing regulatory regime, or parents that are forced to pay bills with a credit card and then going into debt because their wages were not keeping up with inflation.

According to Joe Biden, we are supposed to believe that we are actually better off today than we were when he took office, but the facts tell a very different story. The pain households are experiencing can be tied directly back to the disastrous policies posed by this Administration, which was so much reckless spending into the trillions of dollars. Now we are about to cap over $33 trillion in debt that our grandchildren and their grandchildren will have to pay.

In the early days of COVID, emergency spending did make some sense. It clearly did. I was not in Congress at that time. I believe my colleague, my Ranking Member, was not either, but the country was thrown into a tailspin, and we had to ensure that our economy did not capsize. However, this Administration plowed forward, maintaining these "wartime" spending levels long after the spending was necessary and really long after the pandemic was a national emergency any longer. It has been said "never let a good crisis go to waste," and they did not. From the American Rescue Plan to the Inflation Reduction Act, the Administration has wasted no time throwing mindboggling numbers at varying crises at their choosing with seemingly no regard for the consequences. The Biden Administration apparently does not care if a gallon of milk cost six bucks—I know I do—or how much gasoline costs or an airline ticket, so long as it forces everyone to purchase an electric vehicle that costs more than the yearly median household income.

Decades ago, Republicans banded together with the Contract with America to bring about some of the most impactful economic reforms seen in generations. By combining a series of targeted, fiscally conservative policies into one unified agenda, House Republicans paved the way for Americans everywhere to prosper. We have already seen the blueprint for what works, so we do not need to reinvent the wheel. We should go ahead and achieve that kind of success again, or at least that should be our goal. We have also seen the blueprint for what does not work, and thanks to Bidenomics, we have an ugly reminder of what anti-growth policies bring.

I want to thank our witnesses, all four of you all, for being here today, and I look forward to a thoughtful discussion. The Chair now recognizes Ranking Member Bush for the purpose of making an opening statement.

Ms. BUSH. Thank you, Mr. Chairman. St. Louis and I are here today to discuss the real economic situation of the people of this country. From gas prices to food, the cost of living is rising. New Census data indicates that real incomes fell significantly in 2022 as inflation reduced the size of our constituents' paychecks. We know there are investments that the Federal Government can make to reduce poverty.

The Republican Party's inability to govern has us rapidly moving toward a total government shutdown. This will disrupt important benefits and services for all of our constituents, such as food and cash assistance. Too many people across this country are struggling to make ends meet. A government shutdown would affect more than 42 million people who receive SNAP benefits, nearly 3 million people who receive TANF benefits, and over 6 million participants who receive WIC benefits. Congress pulled together in a crisis to provide COVID relief, this emergency relief that people needed.

My vision of a progressive economy led by the Biden Administration must include Medicare for All. It must include raising the Federal minimum wage, ensuring housing affordability, reinstating the child tax credit, and canceling student debt. That is my vision. During the pandemic, we made direct payments to families through the child tax credit and provided student debt relief by freezing interest and payments. We still need to do more now. These two concrete examples show Congress can ease the effects of economic hardship and boost the economy overall. When it was in place, the child tax credit lifted nearly 4 million children from poverty, causing child poverty to hit a historic low of 5.2 percent. The expanded child tax credit slashed child poverty, infused local economies with billions of dollars, and reduced food insecurity by nearly one-third. In Missouri alone, the child tax credit lifted 73,000 children out of poverty. Without the child tax credit, child poverty in the United States has more than doubled in just 1 year. Since its expiration, nearly 3.7 million children have fallen back into poverty, including the impacted children of Missouri.

Millions of people in this country are buried in burdensome debt to make ends meet—medical, credit card, and student debt. Student debt payments will resume soon after numerous payment policies extended by the Biden Administration. Though that temporary relief has helped many, we need much more, and we must cancel student debt. The Federal student loan portfolio currently totals more than $2 trillion owed by over 40 million borrowers. Black people carry the heaviest debt burden, meaning student debt. Say it again. Student debt relief is a racial and economic justice issue. As lawmakers, we must ensure education leads to prosperity, education leads to opportunity rather than inescapable debt.

While my Republican colleagues are slashing programs to help keep kids out of poverty and fighting against student debt relief every step of the way, we have an over $880 billion defense package moving forward. The money is there. The question is how we as elected officials choose to invest in our communities. The money is there. We can deliver for our constituents to help them out to not only survive, but to prosper.

Republicans are trying to distract us from the internal dysfunction which is steering our Nation toward a government shutdown. The question is, do we choose to invest in defense contractors or reduce poverty for millions of people? Thank you, and I yield back.

Mr. FALLON. We have with us today an expert panel of witnesses who each bring valuable experiences and policy insights that will be beneficial to our discussion. First, we have Carrie Sheffield, who is a senior policy analyst for the Independent Women's Forum. She previously managed Municipal Credit Risk at Goldman Sachs and rated healthcare bonds at Moody's Investor Service. We also have E.J.—it is Antoni, right? OK. I get nervous when I see vowels. My mother's maiden name is Genovese. I want to get it right. OK.

Mr. Antoni serves as a research fellow for the Heritage Foundation's Grover H. Hermann Center for the Federal Budget and a senior fellow at the Committee to Unleash Prosperity. He focuses his work primarily on fiscal and monetary policy. Casey Mulligan serves as a professor of economics at the University of Chicago and previously served as the chief economist for the Council of Economic Advisers under the Trump Administration. And finally, we have Bobby, is it Kogan? OK. Bobby Kogan, who serves as a senior policy director of Federal Budget Policy at the Center for American Progress. I am a Member of Congress from Texas, but I grew up in Massachusetts. So, I will quote a Boston term, "you are all wicked smart." Thank you again for being here.

Pursuant to Committee Rule 9(g), the witnesses will please stand and raise their right hands.

Do you solemnly swear or affirm that your testimony you are about to give is the whole truth and nothing but the truth, so help you God?

[A chorus of ayes.]

Mr. FALLON. Let the record show that the witnesses answered in the affirmative. Please sit.

We appreciate you being here and look forward to your testimony. Let me remind the witnesses that we have read your written statements and they will appear in the full hearing record. Please limit your statements to 5 minutes.

As a reminder, please press the button on the microphone in front of you—I believe it says "talk"—so that the Members will be able to hear you. When you do speak, the light in front of you will be turning green for 4 minutes, 1 minute will be yellow and then will be red, and that is when your 5 minutes are up, and if you are at that red, if you can just wrap it up, that would be great.

I now recognize Ms. Sheffield for her opening statement.

Statement of Carrie Sheffield Senior Policy Analyst Independent Women's Forum

Ms. SHEFFIELD. Thank you, Chairman Fallon, Ranking Member Bush, and Members of the Committee. Thank you for inviting me here today. As has been said, my name is Carrie Sheffield, and I am a senior policy analyst at the Center for Economic Opportunity at Independent Women's Forum. We are a nonprofit organization committed to increasing the number of women who value free markets and personal liberty. We advance policies that enhance people's freedom, opportunities, and well-being. My work focuses on expanding economic opportunities for women.

We are here to discuss "Bidenomics: A Perfect Storm of Spending, Debt, and Inflation," and indeed this storm is already hammering suffering communities and homes nationwide. Evidence shows that President Biden's signature legislative packages, such as the American Rescue Plan and the Inflation Reduction Act, contributed to persistent inflation and are failing to bring it back down more sustainably. This increased government spending triggered more inflation, eroding wages and increased government spending and buying power. The White House has talked about an uptick in nominal wages, but as research from the Federal Reserve Bank of St. Louis shows, real wages have not recovered to pre-pandemic levels even as they are starting to rise nominally.

Families are stretching their dollars further each day since their paychecks and retirement funds are worth far less than they were when President Biden took office. CNBC reported this year that an alarming 54 percent of the American public reported using savings to pay for everyday expenses, such as groceries and rent. Savings are down as is economic confidence.

The recent, multi-trillion dollar increases in government spending erode the value of the dollar through inflation because the money is expanding demand and driving prices up. CBO projects the Federal budget deficit in 2023 is $34 billion, more than the deficit recorded last year. That increase would be larger if not for a shift in the timing of certain payments and the spending cuts that were forced by House Republican leadership this past April in a sustainable manner.

Fraudulent actors may have stolen some $1 out of every $7 in pandemic unemployment, totaling as much as $135 billion, according to a new GAO report. That means that scammers made off with between 11 and 15 percent of the increased jobless benefits that Congress approved on a bipartisan basis early in the coronavirus crisis. This tragic waste of taxpayer money is stealing from American families, who are now more than $1 trillion in credit card debt, a historic high hit last month. That is Bidenomics in action. Regarding America's ticking debt bomb, The Wall Street Journal notes that the Congressional Budget Office regularly updates its long-term budget forecasts and says that U.S. debt held by the public will surpass gross domestic product this fiscal year, and that interest on the debt will equal about three-quarters of discretionary non-defense spending. By 2031, it will be as large. Medicare, Social Security and, of course, interest are legally non-negotiable. Military spending is not really optional either. It is no wonder that the Federal Government is described as an insurance company with an army.

These unsustainable public debt interest payments will crowd out important public expenditures for other discretionary needs. Congress must act now to cut spending in order to rein in these unsustainable debt and interest levels. Increased upward pressure on U.S. interest rates we are experiencing now will add additional pressure to businesses and the real estate market, which has experienced a significant constriction under Bidenomics.

The civilian labor force participation rate remains below pre-pandemic levels under Bidenomics. It is currently at 62.8 percent in August 2023, compared to 63.3 percent in February 2020. The Consumer Price Index stood at 3.67 percent on August 1, which is a steep drop below the inflation of 9.1 percent last summer, but it is still above the Federal Reserve's 2 percent target. And more importantly, a sharper measure of inflation is the Median Consumer Price Index, or median CPI. That measure was 5.72 percent at August 1, 2023, significantly higher than the standard CPI. That is why the headlines are, even though they sound rosier, the median CPI shows that families are actually still suffering significantly because of Bidenomics and inflation.

While Bidenomics may define inflation as a high-class problem, as Ron Klain, the former chief of staff for Joe Biden said in the White House, most Americans disagree. The median CPI helps explain why in his recent CNN poll, 66 percent of Americans disapprove of how Biden has handled the economy with 76 percent describing the economy as in poor shape. Congress can act to help slow the ill effects of Bidenmomics through a return to the economic principles that built America's extraordinary economic engine: fiscal prudence, competition, and regulation that enhances rather than undermines fair competition and growth. Thank you very much.

Mr. FALLON. Thank you. The Chair now recognizes Mr. Antoni for his opening remarks.

Statement of E.J. Antoni Research Fellow Grover M. Hermann Center for the Federal Budget Heritage Foundation Senior Fellow Committee to Unleash Prosperity

Mr. ANTONI. Chairman Fallon, Ranking Member Bush, Members of the Subcommittee, thank you for the invitation to discuss with you today the impact of Federal spending, debt, and inflation on the American people and various aspects of our economy as well. I am a public finance economist at the Heritage Foundation, where I research fiscal and monetary policy, with a particular focus on the Federal Reserve, and I am also a fellow at the Committee to Unleash Prosperity.

The last 3 years of public policy have been characterized, most notably, by excessive government spending, inflation, and anemic economic growth. Despite periods of near-record high Federal revenues by multiple measurements, we have seen deficits of $2.7 trillion, $1.4 trillion, and $1.6 trillion in fiscal years 2021, 2022, and 2023, respectively, with the last month of 2023 being estimated, and with the deficit for Fiscal Year 2024 projected to be $1.9 trillion, yet another increase.

Massive borrowing by the Treasury and monetary financing of deficits by the Federal Reserve created 40-year high inflation and imposed a hidden but heavy tax on the American people. Inflation transfers wealth from the people to the government, and, frankly, there is no better definition of a tax than that. It is worth pausing for a moment, as well, to emphasize that it is the government and only the government which can create inflation because it is only the government that has control over the money supply.

A lot of scapegoats are thrown around for inflation, such as greedy businesses or spendthrift consumers or grasping unions trying to get higher wages, whatever the case may be. These are all tropes that were dragged out in the 1970's, and they are just as untrue today as they were then. As just one example, prices paid by businesses have actually increased faster under President Joe Biden than prices paid by consumers. If businesses are being greedy, they are certainly doing it wrong.

Prices, on average, for consumers have increased 16.6 percent since President Joe Biden took office, and wages have not kept up. Meaning inflation adjusted weekly earnings are down 4.7 percent for the typical American family with two parents working and earning that average weekly pay. This has been a loss in annual purchasing power of over $5,100. Shockingly, the average American worker now loses more through the hidden tax of inflation on his hourly wages than he pays in Federal income tax. Similarly, house- hold net worth has increased about $23 trillion during Mr. Biden's tenure, but nearly all of that is just inflation. Almost all the household net worth generated over the last 2 1/2 years has effectively been transferred to the government through inflation. And while headline inflation has come down since June 2022, things are not improving for many Americans. Inflation has actually reaccelerated in the last 2 months, and the monthly change in real earnings was negative in both July and August. In terms of annual change, things have been even worse under Mr. Biden.

Annual weekly earnings growth has lagged inflation for all but the first 2 months and the last 3 months of Mr. Biden's presidency to date. The 26 months in between are record for consecutive annual declines in real earnings growth. As interest rates rise in the wake of 40-year high inflation, borrowing costs have risen for businesses, consumers, and the Treasury, creating an unsustainable problem for the United States Treasury and the current trajectory of both the deficit and the debt.

In terms of the American family, I estimate that for the typical American family, they are paying an additional $1,800 a year now in higher financing costs compared to January 2021. Coupled with the decline in real earnings, this leaves a family roughly $7,000 poor than when Biden took office. However, it should be emphasized that many Americans are even worse off than that. For those trying to buy a home today, the monthly mortgage payment on a median priced home has risen over $1,000 during that time, and so, it costs a family about $13,000 more per year every year over the life of a 30-year mortgage.

These are just a few examples of how Bidenomics, excessive government spending, borrowing, and creation of money has inflicted a tremendous amount of financial pain on the American people.

Mr. FALLON. Thank you. The Chair now recognizes Professor Mulligan for his opening statement.

Statement of Casey Mulligan Professor of Economics University of Chicago

Mr. MULLIGAN. Chairman Fallon, Ranking Member Bush, and Members of the Subcommittee, thank you for the opportunity to discuss with you today how Federal policy is affecting the economy, workers, and consumers.

Under the Biden Administration's policy agenda, high inflation has emerged as a hidden and bothersome tax. Regulatory costs add another layer of hidden taxation, especially burdening small businesses and low-income households. The labor market has been affected by this agenda with real wages falling below pre-pandemic trends. According to the CBO, the Federal debt held by the public is already 98 percent of a year's GDP and would almost double to 181 percent by 2053 under current law. This is driven by Federal spending.

Government spending has to be paid for either with taxes narrowly defined, such as income taxes, or taxes in the future, or the inflation tax. For example, the recent inflation surge translated to a $2.2 trillion unanticipated tax on debt holders administered in less than 3 years as the purchasing power of their assets was eroded. A recent econometric study concludes that the recent and previously unanticipated fiscal expansion in the U.S. and other OECD countries is likely a key driver of inflation in 2020 through 2022. Even without new tax legislation, inflation increases marginal tax rates on businesses and personal incomes, deterring business investment and reducing real wages.

Beyond taxes, many regulations make workers less productive and, thereby, reduce the wages that they can earn. Others make consumer products, such as prescription drugs, automobiles, and internet service, more expensive. The rules finalized by the Biden Administration through the end of 2020 impose costs of nearly $10,000 per household. That is new. Of course, we had regulations before that, which is a $1,300 more than the new regulations that the Obama Administration had created during the comparable timeframe. If the 2021–2022 regulatory pace accelerates as it did in the Obama years, costs would near $60,000 per household after 8 years of rulemaking.

President Trump's pace was in the opposite direction, saving the average household $80,000 compared to what the Biden Administration is doing. The $80,000 in regulatory costs far exceeds, for example, the revenue provisions of the Build Back Better Act, which would have cost only—only in Washington could I use that phrase—$14,000 per household if it had passed.

For the purposes of understanding economic consequences, the Biden agenda fits into two categories. One category would be redistributive policies that reduce employment, and the second category would be policies that reduce productivity and real wages. Redistributive policies distort the economy twice. First, as the revenue is raised, households and businesses change their behavior to aleviate the burden. Often this involves less investment in business capital, less investment in human capital, and less work. Other times investment in work are redirected to less productive uses.

Second, economic distortions are created as the revenue is dispersed, particularly regarding safety net programs. Households and businesses change their behavior to become eligible for the program or increase the benefit received. A good projection of the combined effect of the Biden spending regulatory and tax agenda is to reduce labor income, the income that workers get, by 5 to 6.5 percent. Unsurprisingly, the labor market is, in fact, falling short. Real employee compensation per adult was already 3.3 percent below the pre-pandemic trend as of the end of 2022.

Small businesses are especially burdened by taxes and regulations. New Federal regulations are regressive, meaning they proportionately hit lower-income households more than high-income households, especially because many rules, from health insurance to telecommunications to environment, are, in effect, forcing middle-and lower-class families to have champagne taste on a beer budget. Several policy options can reduce tax debt and/or regulatory burdens.

Regarding safety net programs, eligibility and benefit rules could return to, say, what they were in 2008 when we had a safety net, but not as large as it is now. Even though the latest poverty rate is 15 percent below what it was in 2008, the fraction of the population participating in Medicaid has increased more than 70 percent. Poverty goes down, but government program participation up. SNAP participation far exceeds the number of households in poverty. Safety net program integrity has also dramatically eroded. I am not sure there is much left with hundreds of billions of dollars spent that should not have been spent under the law. Federal healthcare programs can be reformed to require less revenue while providing greater value to patients.

More specifics are provided in my written testimony on the Trump Administration's Choice and Competition Report. Thank you.

Mr. FALLON. Thank you. The Chair now recognizes Mr. Kogan for his opening remark.

Statement of Bobby Kogan, Senior Director of Federal Budget Policy Center for American Progress

Mr. KOGAN. Chairman Fallon, Ranking Member Bush, Members of the Subcommittee, thank you for inviting me to testify.

Today, I intend to make two points. First, the investments in the last 3 1/2 years were appropriately sized and led to the strongest economic recovery in my lifetime. And second, the cuts proposed by the House Appropriations Committee Republicans would harm America by underfunding critical programs. In response to a once- in-a-century pandemic, American demand plummeted, leaving the economy at its most vulnerable states since the Great Depression.

[Chart]

Mr. KOGAN. The prime-age employment-to-population ratio, or EPOP, dropped 10 percentage points in 2 months. And even when the economy largely reopened, prime-age EPOP still stood roughly as low as the trough of the Great Recession, but rather than taking 10 years to recover, our economy did so in under 2 years. Our rapid recovery was possible only because of significant investment into the economy and the American people.

The Biden Administration built upon the previous COVID bills to provide relief and ensure the American economy was able to invest in the future. The American Rescue Plan expanded on many of the earlier critical programs. It was intended both to ensure households could weather a difficult economy and to ensure that the economy that we rebuilt would be better and more resilient. Through the Bipartisan Infrastructure Law, the bipartisan CHIPS and Science Act, and the Inflation Reduction Act, the Biden Administration made significant investments in the future. The result has been large progress.

Among G7 nations, the United States has had the strongest pandemic recovery, and, incredibly, U.S. real GDP has roughly returned to where CBO projected it would be before the pandemic even happened, as if COVID and the ensuing recession had never happened. Our historic recovery has also led to the strongest job market in U.S. history. Adjusting for demographics, the employment-to-population ratio is at its highest level in history, and black prime-age EPOP is hovering around its historic high with a historically small gap between black and white prime-age employment.

This strong job market has benefited the American people. Real average hourly earnings of production and nonsupervisory employees have matched their pre-pandemic trend also as if the pandemic had never happened, and gains have been particularly strong among lower-wage workers. Importantly, that has happened because inflation has come down. The United States also has the lowest core harmonized inflation among G7 countries. Further, the path in recent months is encouraging. Core CPI has been trending down since the spring of 2021, with a 3-month annualized average down to 2.4 percent. And even better, the contribution of housing rents to CPI inflation, which rose due to longstanding supply shortages in the U.S. meeting pandemic shifts in demand, is cooling and approaching pre-pandemic levels.

While inflation rose to uncomfortable levels as the economy largely reopened, this was not caused by excessive stimulus. CBO estimates potential GDP, which measures how much the economy can produce without creating excessive inflation, and it believes that GDP ran barely above potential for only one quarter, and that the economy otherwise has run slightly below potential. In other words, our COVID response was appropriately sized. Instead, a global pandemic broke supply chains and caused monumental shifts in demand. It is impossible for inflation to not rise in the presence of supply chain issues and massive shifts in demand, but as supply chain issues subsided and companies shifted their supply and production to match new habits and demand, inflation has come down.

This progress is being threatened now by the work of the House Appropriations Committee Majority. Despite rhetoric to the contrary, non-defense discretionary funding, excluding VA medical care, or NDD Star, shrank as a percent of GDP in the first 2 years of the Biden Administration. Despite this, House Republican appropriators wrote levels $58 billion below the debt limit deal, which would leave NDD Star at its lowest level on record going back more than 60 years. Even worse, the cuts proposed to achieve this low level of funding are extreme. To highlight just three: Title I education grants would be cut by nearly 80 percent, money that ensures our drinking water is safe would be cut by 59 percent, and nutrition assistance for newborns and pregnant moms would also be cut. These cuts would harm the American people. Even worse, they seem to be the asking price for not forcing a government shutdown. Immediately during a government shutdown, some children with cancer would be denied treatment at NIH facilities, and some of our food would go without its health and safety inspections.

The government is supposed to work for the American people, and neither cutting programs that people rely on nor shutting down the government serves that purpose. Thank you.

Mr. FALLON. Thank you. We are going to recess for votes, and the Committee will return 10 minutes after the close of the final vote. Thank you very much and we will be right back.

[Recess.]

Mr. FALLON. The Subcommittee will come to order. I now recognize myself for 5 minutes of questions.

Ms. Sheffield, in my district in North Texas, I have heard countless constituents, you know, they complain, I mean I feel it myself, about the cost of things. And like, for instance, I believe, roughly speaking, the average gasoline across the country was $2.39 when this Administration took office, and it is now, depending on where you are, national average is about $5. Well, actually, that was in June of last year. It is a little lower than that now. What examples like this would it say about the "success or lack thereof" of the Biden Administration's economic policies?

Ms. SHEFFIELD. I would say just looking at the numbers, but going beyond the numbers as well, just talking to people that the headline inflation is certainly not actually how families feel and how they are actually experiencing when you are talking about food inflation, fuel inflation. You know, my esteemed colleague, with all due respect, his graph that he has here when he is comparing the inflation to other countries, it excludes energy, food, and housing, which are pretty much what you need to survive. So, I do not—

Mr. FALLON. Would it be fair to say those three things are——

Ms. SHEFFIELD. Yes.

Mr. FALLON [continuing]. Main economic drivers?

Ms. SHEFFIELD. Absolutely, and especially for the people that are in your district, it is personal, it is their everyday life. And so, that is why Bidenomics is failing them.

Mr. FALLON. Mr. Antoni, what has been the impact of the expiration of the expanded child tax credit on poverty, and what has been the impact of inflation on poverty?

Mr. ANTONI. Thank you. In terms of inflation, I think it will probably be best to discuss that one first because inflation is actually the only thing that can increase the poverty threshold. And so, as inflation has outpaced earnings during the Biden Administration, it has caused more people to fall below that poverty threshold. That is literally just what the numbers tell us. There is nothing else that can increase that poverty threshold.

In terms of the expansion of the child tax credit, you would expect that once that went away that you would simply return poverty rates for children to the level that they were at previously, but that is not what we have seen. We have instead seen the rate go much higher. And again, the reason for that is because inflation has pushed that threshold so high that many people's nominal earnings have not kept pace with inflation and have therefore fallen below the threshold.

Mr. FALLON. And while we are visiting, what is the impact of supply chain distributions on inflation-disruptions, rather?

Mr. ANTONI. Mr. Chairman, in terms of supply chains, the disruptions there, well, let me put it this way. It is very similar to what we just said on poverty in that if supply chains really were the only driver behind inflation, if it had nothing to do with fiscal and monetary stimulus, then once those supply chain issues were resolved, not just inflation would come down, but prices would come down. Prices would simply return to where they were previously, and that is not what we have seen at all.

Actually, the last several reports from S&P Global, their Purchasing Manager Index that analyzes global supply chains, showed that there is no more pandemic-era impact in terms of supply chains. In other words, things are back to normal, and yet prices are not, and the reason for that is because the fiscal and monetary conditions today are not back to where they were——

Mr. FALLON. So, you are saying that there is an increased money supply, and the goods are out there. They remain steady, so when you have more money relative to the goods, the goods cost more, in very simplistic terms.

Mr. ANTONI. Exactly. Uh-huh.

Mr. FALLON. Yes. I mean, it is easy to wrap your mind around it. Now, is it true that real weekly earnings have exceeded infltion, the annual rate of inflation for 26 of the 31 months of the Biden Administration?

Mr. ANTONI. Yes, it is. You can see on page six of the testimony that I submitted. Only the first 2 months of the Biden Administration and now the most recent 3 months have seen positive annual real earnings compared to inflation, but in the 26 months in between, it was negative, which is a record.

Mr. FALLON. Thank you. Mr. Mulligan, you are an expert in economic growth. That is one of the purviews, of course, of this Committee, as well as regulatory reform, yet another purview of this Committee. Before the pandemic hit, the Trump Administration demonstrated some of the most pro-growth policies that we have seen in generations. How has the Biden Administration policies reversed the possibility of growth, and what do we need to do right now to get on the right track and get our economy moving again?

Mr. MULLIGAN. Really, all the policy levers have been pushed in the opposite direction of President Trump to the extent they could. President

Trump had a tax cut that needs some renewing, I guess, and that might not happen. A lot of the regulations have been totally reversed, not all of them, and both of these things go toward reducing productivity rather than productivity growing like you see in energy where we were pumping more and more and more. We are less productive. We are less able to do what we used to do.

Mr. FALLON. My time has expired. I yield to the Ranking Member for her 5 minutes of questions.

Ms. BUSH. Thank you, Mr. Chairman. St. Louis and I are here today because our economy needs to fully recover from the devastating effects of the pandemic. Housing is the bedrock of our Nation's economy. One of the biggest challenges facing St. Louis and communities across the country is a dire shortage of affordable housing. When landlords raise rents, my constituents face increased housing insecurity and the threat of eviction.

Renters in St. Louis and around the country are forced to contend with Wall Street investors who buy up homes in the area, jack up rents, and neglect building maintenance, all to extract greater profits. Private equity firms took advantage of unprecedented foreclosures during the 2008 recession, which forced millions of people from their homes. These corporations seized on historically low interest rates to purchase foreclosed homes. Local landlords and small business developers have been muscled out of the local housing market.

In 2022, the St. Louis Post-Dispatch estimated that out-of-state investors owned nearly 34,000 single-family homes in the region. Investors have doubled the percentage of homes they own in my district over the last 10 years. In one housing complex in my district called Ridgeview Apartments, the property has changed hands at least 4 times in the last 3 years. This wreaks havoc on residents and creates a dire lack of accountability. Ridgeview residents report there are so little communication that some people realize too late that they were sending their rent checks to the wrong place, and it is difficult to keep track of who their landlords are.

The St. Louis area is experiencing a housing crisis, and evictions are at the highest level in years and still on the rise. Wall Street speculators have turned places like Ridgeview from homes for families into assets on their balance sheets. Working families can no longer afford to buy or even rent many places that were previously affordable. Mr. Kogan, what are the advantages of homeownership for building household and generational wealth?

Mr. KOGAN. Thank you, Congresswoman. Homeownership is one of the best ways for families to build wealth and to pass on intergenerational wealth. And to the extent that we have seen policies in U.S. history, such as redlining, that have discriminated against people in the United States, this thing that is supposed to work for everyone has been limited to a certain cohort. And to the extent that the economy does not work for a whole host of Americans, then that is not working for Americans.

Homeownership is beneficial because it is forced savings that allows you to build equity and also pushes costs away from when you are stuck in a fixed-income later, and pushes it to when you are more able to afford it. And so, as home equity, as private—I am sorry—as private equities come and buy up a lot of the housing stock, this limits the ability of individuals to capitalize on this ability to take advantage of these mechanisms. So as the forced savings goes away, folks are not able to kind of to use that. Sorry. Thank you.

Ms. BUSH. No, you are fine, and I think you started to hit on this point, but Mr. Kogan, how would you say that private equity snapping up these housing makes it more difficult for the average American family to purchase a home? Like, you started there, but if you could go a little further with that.

Mr. KOGAN. Sure. So typically, a lot of people will be able to buy from an individual with a whole lot of buyers or a whole lot of sellers. There is kind of a broad ability. You can shop around. You can find someone who fits whatever you are looking for. And to the extent that more and more of the housing stock is being bought up by a few select companies, we are moving toward or moving closer and closer to a monopsony where a few sellers are able to set all the prices. And so through this, it is limiting kind of the ability for folks to shop for what they need and able to find what they can do.

Ms. BUSH. OK. Thank you. Mr. KOGAN. Thank you.

Ms. BUSH. The Biden-Harris Administration is working to address this problem. The Administration's Housing Supply Action Plan will reduce barriers for families to access housing by expanding financing for low-income and climate-ready housing and promoting the conversion of unused commercial space to residential space. Moreover, the American Rescue Plan, that not a single one of my Republican colleagues voted for, included the home program, which will add at least 20,000 units of affordable housing across the United States while supporting 23,000 households with rental assistance. congressional Democrats and the President have taken fundamental steps that support American families. Far too many people struggle to secure basic housing, and yet our colleagues across the aisle and their type of economics seek to cut taxes for the wealthy and cut services for those in need. It is absolutely shameful, but I yield back.

Mr. FALLON. Thank you. The Chair now recognizes Mr. Edwards of North Carolina.

Mr. EDWARDS. Thank you, Mr. Chair. Ms. Sheffield, in opening comments, I heard that inflation, since Joe Biden had been our President, had increased. I heard somebody testify 16.6 percent, I heard somebody testify 17.1 percent, and I also heard a testimony that the additional cost for many of the things that people have to buy now is being financed on their credit cards. What is the long- term effect of $1 trillion in credit card debt? Where are we headed?

Ms. SHEFFIELD. It is extremely corrosive to building intergenerational wealth to have, you know, especially rollover balances from month to month and having to pay these very high interest rates. So, it becomes this hole that you cannot dig out of, and that is really the whole that is the fruit of Bidenomics to pile on consumer debt onto families. In terms of housing, I think it is important because housing is, you know, quite often the largest budget chunk of the family budget. First of all, the redlining was created by FDR, a racist administration. The FDR New Deal program was the one that created redlining, so that is very, very important to just historically put on the record.

But when it comes to housing supply, if you talk about St. Louis and other cities, the vast majority where these urban pockets of construction of housing supplies are constricted, they are run by Democrat regulation. They are run by progressive policies that constrict the supply of housing. So, if you want to have more housing supply, you need to have zoning regulation that is more competitive. And unfortunately, these areas where the worst housing supply constrictions occur are in progressive areas. And so, I would say that that is my recommendation in terms of improving housing supply.

The other massive increase in inflation is energy. And so, we see just recently, within the last couple of weeks, the Biden Administration again saying we are going to constrict drilling in Alaska and other areas of the United States. Who wins in this scenario? It is OPEC that wins. It is Russia that wins. And so, it is so counterproductive for U.S. taxpayer dollars to go and fund to fight the Ukrainian war against Russia, meanwhile Joe Biden is here domestically constraining our own domestic oil prices and hitting families over and over.

Mr. EDWARDS. Thank you for that. So, with inflation hitting the American household, we heard a couple of different numbers there. I am going to round it off to $5,000 a year. What are folks doing without? How are their purchasing habits changing, because surely, most of us could agree that when we are looking at 17-percent inflation, most of the harm falls on working-class families and the poor because much of their disposable income is being eradicated by inflation, and I think that would be a concern to all of us in this room. So how are they coping? What are they doing without?

Ms. SHEFFIELD. Sure. I would say it is the poor as well as retirees as well where, you know, typically when you retire, it is when your highest peak net assets or net worth. But unfortunately, because of Bidenomics and what has happened with inflation, the net worth of many seniors living on fixed income is incredibly tight. And so, you are seeing grandparents having to forego vacations or forego helping with their grandchildren's education. You are seeing people actually just dropping out of the education situation altogether, especially young men just not even going to college because it is so expensive. And unfortunately, the Biden Administration's plan on student loans, it is so counterproductive, it does nothing to actually address the root cause of inflation in education. It simply takes the U.S. tax money and subsidizes the wasteful policies that are being held at the university instead of actually holding the university accountable for the rise of inflation for student tuition.

So, you are seeing people forgo education. You are seeing them having to intergenerational, you know, housing, more people within the same, you know, family, grandparents living together, which, you know, could be good or bad depending on the family dynamic, but yes, people are making do. But unfortunately, as I said earlier in my opening statement, I believe it is 52 or 54 percent of families, according to CNBC, reporting that they are dipping into their savings to pay for groceries and to pay for everyday expenses like rent. That is deeply unsustainable, and it is the fruit of Bidenomics.

Mr. EDWARDS. All right. Thank you. Mr. Chair, I yield.

Mr. FALLON. Thank you. The Chair now recognizes Ms. Brown from Ohio. Oh, she is not here? All right. Well, you know why, because Notre Dame is playing Ohio State, she is probably trying to get ready, and Notre Dame will thrash them, but that is an editor's comment.

Ms. BUSH. Oh, OK.

Mr. FALLON. OK. The Chair now recognizes Ms. Norton from D.C.

Ms. NORTON. I thank the Chair. Mr. Kogan, during the height of the COVID–19 pandemic, the world faced a bleak economic future. High unemployment, tangled supply chains, and inflation, all threatened the future of American families, but let us look at where we are now. Unemployment has stayed below 4 percent for 19 straight months. Grocery store shelves are full. Inflation is less than half its peak. So, Mr. Kogan, would you describe the Biden- Harris economy as fairly healthy?

Mr. KOGAN. Thank you, Congresswoman. Yes, I would say that we have had enormous progress in the past 2 1/2 years.

Ms. NORTON. Yes. Low unemployment, inflation improving, it is hard to top that. The Treasury Department has shown that the American Rescue Plan led to 4 million additional jobs and almost doubled GDP growth. These benefits have also served to address historical inequities and increase opportunities for all Americans. Mr. Kogan, can you expand more about how the American Rescue Plan has benefited the economy and American families, particularly those families that may traditionally be left out of economic upswings?

Mr. KOGAN. Absolutely. So, there are two kind of main parts of the American Rescue Plan. The first was to provide assistance right then, and the second thing was to try to make sure that we would have a strong job market coming out of the COVID recession. So, in the first part, it built on a lot of the bipartisan things in the Trump Administration. It sent out more money to families. It continued the expanded unemployment insurance at a lower rate as was necessary at that time. It expanded the Child Tax Credit and kind of made it a monthly benefit to make sure that working parents were able to—and also the most vulnerable parents—were able to better afford the cost of having children. So, that sort of stuff all helped families at the time.

And then by also pumping money into the economy, helping invest in the future, it created the strongest job market in U.S. history. Right now, the employment-to-population ratio adjusted for demographics is the strongest it has ever been, and that has redounded to the benefit of the American people. And we see that low wage earners are actually doing the best out of any cohort of folks.

Ms. NORTON. Well, let us turn to another one of the Biden-Harris Administration signature achievements, the Inflation Reduction Act. Mr. Kogan, this bill, which passed without a single Republican vote, has already resulted in 170,000 new jobs in clean energy and climate resilience with projections estimating that the IRA will catalyze more than 1.5 million additional new jobs over the next 10 years. So, Mr. Kogan, how will these new jobs created by the IRA improve the U.S. economy?

Mr. KOGAN. Thank you, Congresswoman. So, the point here is to make sure that not only could we have clean energy, we would also be able to be energy independent. And these jobs were intended to, for instance, rebuild if you had a broken-down coal mine that was no longer operable. It was intended to turn that into something that would be able to work in the future, right, so whether it is now a battery plant or something like that. So, these jobs are intended to exist going forward in terms of our energy security and to exist for the years to come.

Ms. NORTON. Mr. Kogan, my colleagues seem very concerned about the deficit. What effect will the IRA have on it?

Mr. KOGAN. Thank you, Congresswoman. So, CBO scored at a savings of about $300 billion. We believe that is an underestimate because it does not take into account the indirect effects of the tax enforcement. Of course, to the extent that some of that gets repealed, then some of the savings go away. Since then, we have found that some of the tax credits are going to work better than previously thought and therefore be a little bit more costly. The most recent estimate is that it might still save maybe $100 billion or some. I do not have the exact number off the top of my head, but that it still saves money.

Ms. NORTON. Democrats' American Rescue Plan and Inflation Reduction Act are the kind of investment that the United States has needed for decades. I continue to support the President and Bidenomics for investing in American communities that have faced decades of neglect, and I yield back.

Mr. FALLON. Thank you. The Chair now recognizes Mrs. Boebert from Colorado.

Mrs. BOEBERT. Thank you, Mr. Chairman, and thank you to our witnesses who are here. It has been very enlightening just hearing the wealth of information that you all are sharing and answering the questions.

My first question is directed to Mr. Kogan. In your testimony, you falsely claim that because of the trillions of dollars spent in the Biden Administration that America has the "strongest economy recovery in more than a generation." And I just want to know, are you aware that just yesterday, America exceeded $33 trillion in debt? This is the first time in history, $33 trillion in history. And are you also aware that inflation's impact is on groceries and that is at an all-time high?

Mr. KOGAN. Thank you for the question, Congresswoman. What I was saying was that real GDP, we are leading the pack in terms of real economic growth among the G7 nations. We are back to where CBO thought we would be, roughly, and then we have had the first V-shaped recovery of my entire life.

Mrs. BOEBERT. So, Mr. Kogan, at $33 trillion in debt, all of this is due to wasteful Washington spending by Biden, by Pelosi. They financed and borrowed and printed money that we do not have. We are spending more than we are bringing in, and yet your testimony places blame on House Republicans who are working diligently to be fiscally responsible.

We are in meetings daily right now trying to get our fiscal house in order so we do not go off of this fiscal cliff that we are all hanging on the edge of, but currently, we have 20 million Americans who cannot afford their electric bill. Americans have lost more than $2 trillion in retirement savings, and gas is nearly $4 a gallon, and, I mean, that is back up again under this Administration, and Americans are paying more for absolutely everything else.

People are struggling all throughout Colorado's 3d District. This is what I am hearing—people cannot afford to live, and this does not sound like the strongest economic recovery in more than a generation to me. So now, Mr. Kogan, you also state in your testimony that under this Administration "inflation has gone down," and this is a boldfaced lie. Americans are paying more for everything. Do you know how much American families will pay due to inflation, the inflation tax, in just over the next year?

Mr. KOGAN. Thank you, Congresswoman. Inflation in this case refers to the rate of inflation. That is how most folks talk about——

Mrs. BOEBERT. Yes, but that is not how they feel it. That is not how they are actually paying for the goods and the needs that they are trying to provide for their family—their food, their gas, their electric bills—all of these things that I have mentioned. The correct answer for how much American families will pay for this inflation tax over the next year is $8,581. That is per family. That is absolutely absurd, and in most cases, this is more than a monthly income for most families. And Joe Biden has claimed that for the past 4 decades, there has never been an economic failure, and the United States has never faced an inflation crisis as severe as we are facing under the Biden Administration. So now, do you know how much a gallon of gas is right now compared to 2020?

Mr. KOGAN. Right near me, my gas station right next to me is about $1.50 more. The reason it was so much lower during 2020——

Mrs. BOEBERT. Because President Trump had us energy independent, and we were producing American energy right here, good clean American energy. We were not relying on OPEC as much. We were relying on the

American Roughneck, so that is why it was lower. I will just answer that for you. But in 2020, retail gas prices averaged $2.17 per gallon, and now we are at $3.60, up to $4.32 per gallon. I mean, that is a 50-percent increase. That is absolutely dramatic and unaffordable to average Americans who are just struggling to get by. And what about a gallon of milk? I mean, that was $3.32 and now $4.09 for a gallon of milk. Eggs. Eggs were $1.46 a dozen, and now they are $3.44. That is a 42-percent increase. Families cannot afford this.

Now, my last question. You also state that gains have been particularly strong among lower-wage workers. Now, for the average American family, weekly paychecks have grown about $200, but those larger paychecks now buy about $100 less for those income earners. Do you know the annual impact inflation has on these American workers?

Mr. KOGAN. Congresswoman, real wages are up relative to prepandemic levels among nonsupervisory, and——

Mrs. BOEBERT. But that number is a fairy tale, is it not?

Mr. KOGAN. No.

Mrs. BOEBERT. If you are actually spending more for the same product that you were getting, but your paycheck looks bigger, but you are paying more for the goods that you were buying just a couple of years ago, the result is the equivalent of a $5,600 annual pay cut. So, it may look good on paper. I know engineers love that. I know bureaucrats love that. I know the folks in Washington, DC. in the bubble love the way things look on paper, but in the real world, that does not work. Bidenomics is failing American families, and so are these policies. And I hope that you would actually take a look into the real world rather than just on paper. Thank you, Mr. Chairman. I yield.

Mr. FALLON. Thank you. The Chair recognizes Ms. Stansbury from New Mexico.

Ms. STANSBURY. All right. Well, thank you, Mr. Chairman, and I am glad that the last comments wrapped up around the concept of what is happening with the economy in the real world, because the single largest threat to the economy in the real world right now is a government shutdown. And what is especially strange and ironic to me is that we are sitting here this afternoon after the Majority failed to even get a continuing resolution to the floor to keep the U.S. Government open, more or less passed a single appropriations bill to keep this government functioning.

So, if we want to talk about real-world impacts, if we want to talk about people being able to pay their bills, put a roof over their head, buy groceries, and all of the things that we are talking about here today, let us talk about funding the government and making sure that the American Government and our economy can stay afloat, because that is the real world, and that is our constitutional duty and responsibility. But it is also, you know, a strange hearing that we are having here this afternoon as we are on the eve of this shutdown and hearing a bunch of distorted and strange representations of the economy.

Now, I am going to admit I am not an economist. I am a sociologist by training, but I am a former OMBer, and I want to welcome my colleague who also served in the Budget Office in the White House. And I know when folks actually understand the economy and do not understand the economy, and I just want to talk about the facts for a minute.

You know, Mr. Kogan, I appreciated some of the charts that you included in your written testimony to the Committee. And I want to make sure that we share some of those today publicly because what we are talking about is the overall macroeconomy. When we say that the macroeconomy is actually doing well in the United States, in spite of this post-pandemic hangover, and we will talk about that and its impacts here in a moment, what we are talking about is the gross domestic product.

And what we see in, Mr. Kogan, in your testimony, you have provided this chart here, which is the real GDP of the United States. Is this correct? And——

Mr. KOGAN. Yes.

Ms. STANSBURY. What do we see right here? What is happening in the year 2023?

Mr. KOGAN. Thank you, Congresswoman. You can see that it is back at the trend. That is back where CBO thought it would be before the pandemic.

Ms. STANSBURY. And what you can also see on this chart is that by billions of dollars by annual rate that we are above where we have previously been, so the GDP for the United States is on the rise. Now, part of the reason why we are seeing the economy come roaring back is exactly because of the policies that this body passed last Congress and which President Biden helped to champion.

So first of all, I want to talk about the American Recovery Plan. Now, at the height of the pandemic, we had millions of Americans who were unemployed, people who did not know if they were going to lose their homes. They did not know if they are going to be able to buy groceries. They did not know if they were going to be able to go to the doctor, and we passed the American Recovery Plan to get through the pandemic. It was not intended to be a stimulus in and of itself at the onset. It was meant to keep millions of

Americans from falling through the crack and the most significant economic disruption that this country has seen since the Great Depression, and that is what it did. It kept millions of American people housed. It kept food on their table. It helped children get through the huge catastrophic impacts, parents. That is what the American Recovery Plan was about.

Now, subsequently, we have passed three significant bills that have been causing the GDP to do this. That is the CHIPS Act, which has helped to re-shore American manufacturing. It is the Inflation Reduction Act, which we have just been talking about. And it is the Bipartisan Infrastructure Law, which is going to rebuild our roads, our water systems, and all of the infrastructure that we know our communities need to have a thriving economy. And guess what? The data does not lie. The data show us that American manufacturing and investment in American manufacturing is coming back with astounding consequences, because here we are up here at the highest rate ever in American history.

Finally, if my colleagues want to talk about inflation, let us compare American inflation to post-pandemic inflation in other countries. And what you can see in this chart in the testimony that has been provided to everyone on this Committee is that American inflation, with respect to other developed countries across the world, is at the lowest rates, lower than Canada, lower than the U.K., and lower than most of the European community.

So, if our folks want to talk about facts, let us talk about facts in the real world. The American economy is strong. It is coming back, but families are struggling. They are struggling because of the pandemic. They are struggling because we still have the effects of supply chain disruptions, of soaring housing costs and soaring food costs, and we have got to address them. And I can tell you factually one thing that is not going to make it better, and that is shutting down this government. So, if my friends on the Majority want to actually help American families, then pass the budget, and I yield back.

Mr. FALLON. The Chair now recognizes Mr. Langworthy from New York.

Mr. LANGWORTHY. Thank you, Mr. Chairman, and I would like to thank all of our witnesses today for being here, and the media has been busy championing the Administration's message of Bidenomics' success. However, I spent just a ton of time traveling my district, New York's 23rd congressional District, the counties along the Pennsylvania line and the suburbs of Buffalo, speaking with my constituents and getting a real sense of their top concerns. And let me tell you, I did not meet one person that thought that Bidenomics was any step in the right direction for this country. But things that stood out loud and clear is that Americans are having a really difficult time affording groceries and gasoline and keeping the lights on in their home, and there is a lot of angst about the costs of gas and groceries. This is the reality of Bidenomics for many Americans.

Mr. Antoni, your extensive research on inflation has shed light onto the role of as a hidden tax on American households. I am aware of your findings indicating that this inflation tax frequently surpasses Federal income taxes. Can you elaborate on how this is possible?

Mr. ANTONI. Certainly. Thank you for the question. We have to understand that inflation, because it is a devaluation of the dollar for the sake of creating new dollars, when those new dollars come into existence, where did their value come from? A portion of the wealth of every other dollar that existed previously is siphoned away and goes into those new dollars. So as the government creates inflation, it is taking that wealth away from dollar holders. So that is how the government actually takes wealth away from you through the hidden tax of inflation, and all they need to do is do this at a fast enough rate that the amount of wealth being transferred is going to exceed the amount of wealth being transferred via the Federal income tax.

To be clear, this is not the first time that this has happened in our Nation's history. You know, this exact same phenomenon happened 40 years ago when we had very high inflation rates then as well.

Mr. LANGWORTHY. Thank you. and I am sure we have all heard the Biden Administration's promise that taxes would not increase for those earning less than $400,000 a year. Would you say that he has kept his promise?

Mr. ANTONI. No, not at all, especially when you consider the fact that inflation falls most heavily on those who make lower incomes. There are a lot of different reasons for that, one of which is that lower earners tend to have incomes which adjust slower to inflation, but also looking at the things that those people buy. You know, just one example here would be, let us say, someone in the middle class would buy fillet occasionally, but now they cannot afford to, so they just buy ground beef instead.

You are moving to a foodstuff which is already disproportionately purchased by people with lower income. So, what you have done now is not only is, if you want to call it an income effect from everyone having less money or less real money due to inflation so they can afford less. But now, there is also a substitution effect, if you want to call it that, where there is an increase in demand for things disproportionately bought by people with lower incomes. In other words, the prices of the things they buy go up even faster than the average.

Mr. LANGWORTHY. Makes a lot of sense. When we think about basic economics, we know that in times of high inflation, one's money does not go as far. One cannot buy the same amount of goods that one was able to purchase before, and often those most impacted are those with less flexibility in their budget, less of a backstop for their own personal economy.

As I mentioned earlier, during my discussions with my constituents in the district, it became abundantly clear their concerns are revolving every day about covering the essential costs of feeding their families and managing their energy bills and their transportation costs. These are everyday families who, not too long ago, they could afford a weekend getaway. They could, you know, take the kids on vacation in the summer, sign their kids up for sports teams. Today, these simple pleasures, these little luxuries, they have become unattainable as they grapple with the increasing burden of paying for the necessities in life.

Ms. Sheffield, what should Congress be thinking about when considering the downstream impacts that the recent massive spending packages have had on American households in their expenses?

Ms. SHEFFIELD. Well, given that we know that the Bidenomics bills, massive bills that were already passed, exacerbated inflation, my recommendation would be to contain your spending. Do not pass these massive multi trillion-dollar additional bills that would further exacerbate inflation, and, in fact, consider supporting—your colleague recently put forward a balanced budget amendment, Jodey Arrington. I highly recommend this because it certainly would contain not only the inflation, but it would also help the long-term trajectory of the congressional budget which is on, you know, the interest payments alone will be drowning out significant investments in the public good.

Mr. LANGWORTHY. Well, thank you very much for the testimony. I certainly have more questions, but we are out of time, and I yield back.

Mr. FALLON. Thank you. Members, with that, I would like to ask unanimous consent to submit these documents and statements into the record: "The Impact of Biden Economic Policies On Americans' 401(k) and Other Retirement Plans," by Stephen Moore and E.J. Antoni; "Payroll Tax Revenue Down $400 Billion to $900 Billion Due to Lower Wages, Less Growth," by Casey Mulligan; "The Cost of Biden's War on Oil and Gas: Nearly $100 Billion a Year in Lost Output," by Stephen Moore and Casey Mulligan; "Paying Americans Not to Work," by Casey Mulligan and E.J. Antoni, and without objection, so ordered.

Mr. FALLON. The Chair now recognizes Ranking Member Bush for her closing statement.

Ms. BUSH. Thank you, Mr. Chairman. Despite my colleagues' claims, the U.S. economy is actually growing, and this growth directly contrasts with failed Republican economy policies, policies that include the massive tax giveaway that former President Trump signed into law 2018, which prompted the most severe economic contraction in the United States since 1946 and cost the United States $1.9 billion.

Republicans' economic proposals do not work and are currently driving us toward a government shutdown that will hurt families and devastate our economy. Rather than having yet another hearing to bolster Republican talking points, we should be focused on funding the government. In less than 2 weeks, millions of families in need will lose access to vital programs such as SNAP, TANF, WIC, and the administration of Social Security, Medicare, and Medicaid will grind to a halt because our Federal workforce will be unable to serve our communities.

Just a couple of hours ago, House Republican leaders postponed the vote, voting on a rule to bring a stopgap bill to the floor. We also know that a shutdown would have a devastating impact on the economy. The partial shutdown from 2018–2019 reduced economic output in the United States by $11 billion over 2 quarters, $3 billion of which the economy never regained. The difference is clear and of massive consequences to our communities. Economic recovery should be the highest priority of the Biden Administration, and we are thankful. With that, I yield back.

Mr. FALLON. Thank you. You know, we have staffs that help us with our comments because we are spread out a little thin, but I took some notes during this hearing and I wanted to share them with you. So, you hear Members from each party make claims and then they cite statistics and studies, and if you had lived on another planet or another galaxy and you came to this hearing, you would be scratching your head going I do not know who to believe. So, let us just talk about some indisputable facts. No. 1, inflation is now at a 40-year high. Nobody can dispute that. No. 2, interest rates are now at a 22-year high. That is also indisputable. Real weekly earnings have exceeded annual inflation for 5 of the 31 months, 84 percent of the time during this Administration. And if you want to talk about generational wealth, generational wealth is built on a foundation of three things to start: No. 1, graduate high school; No. 2, have a full-time job; and No. 3, do not have children until you are married. If you do those three tenets, regardless of race, religion, creed, region that you live in, it is very difficult to live below the poverty line. I am sure CNN or MSNBC will find somebody that did all those three things and is below the poverty line, but is absolutely the exception and not the rule.

Then, we talk about the only Federal spending program that progressive Members ever want to talk about cutting is defense. That is the only one. Now, they ignore the fact that we live in a very small world, a very dangerous world, and a very interconnected world. And while they are all too comfortable, in fact, perfectly comfortable with cutting defense, they are also willing to give Ukraine a blank check for Ukrainian defense, which I find a little bit hypocritical or at least inconsistent. And then when you look at say 2022's deficit, which is the debt for that particular year, it was $1.38 trillion. So, if we did not spend $1 on defense, we would still have over a half a trillion dollars in deficit spending. Defense is not the issue. In fact, defense has been the slowest growing major Federal spending category since 2000, and even that 2000-year base, that base year, was following 10 years of post-cold war cuts. So, the U.S. military as a share of GDP remains the lowest level since World War II.

So, more spending is not the solution to inflation because if all of those spending programs worked as well as my Democratic colleagues have claimed, well, why did we stop at $3 trillion or $4 trillions of spending? Why didn't we spend $40 trillion if it is so good? And then let us talk about, because the American people or my friend from the other galaxy that attended this hearing, need to see contrasts. So, my colleague and Ranking Member mentioned about student loans and said that student loan forgiveness she fully supports. Well, I completely disagree because it is not student loan forgiveness. It is student loan transfer.

First, that program would cost, general consensus, cost about $400 billion. And it would benefit, ironically, the highest earners will reap about two-thirds of that benefit of the giveaway. And then you have to think about, what about the folks that had never went to college? What about the folks that went to college and did not take out a loan? What about the folks that went to college, took out the loan, and then paid it back? Is that fair to them, and the answer to that question is, of course, no. It is patently unfair. It is patently un-American, in fact.

The outstanding Federal loan debt is about $1.7 trillion. There are 255 million adult Americans. Forty-five million have student loan debt, so that would make it to 210 million adult Americans would have to bear the burden for, not this forgiveness, but this transfer. And the median borrower, they did a study in 1992 and they just recently did another study and they found the same thing, that about four percent of their monthly income is spent on student loans. They got plenty of money to pay off their loans, and it also sets a horrible precedent to folks that willingly went into an agreement to say I will borrow money and I promise to pay it back. And then what about future borrowers that say, hey, they give loan forgiveness? I will sign this thing, but I am probably going to get forgiveness in the future, or, again, more accurately transfer. It is simply unfair.

And so, we have to recognize the fact that we do have a $33 trillion debt. And I believe from CBO, that if we continue to spend at the rate we are going now, that in 10 years, half of the Federal budget will go to loan repayment, will go to paying service on the debt. That means that there is going to be less money for defense, there will be less money for infrastructure, and there will be less money, ironically, for entitlements.

So, I remember this very hyperbolic commercial that some org nization put out where you had an actor playing Paul Ryan, and he was pushing grandma off the cliff. Well, it seems to me that folks that did not want to address this runaway spending, which would be my Democratic colleagues or at least most of them, are proverbially, hyperbolically are they pushing grandma off the cliff because it is going to be a heck of a lot less money for entitlements if we do not get our fiscal house in order.

I want to thank the witnesses for coming today. Thank you for your testimony and your knowledge and sharing your points of view.

And with that and without objection, all Members will have 5 legislative days within which to submit materials and to submit additional written questions for the witnesses, which will be forwarded to the witnesses for their response.

Mr. FALLON. If there was no further business and without objection, the Subcommittee stands adjourned. Thank you.

[Whereupon, at 4:36 p.m. the Subcommittee was adjourned.]

Chapter 6

Fueling Unaffordability: How the Biden Administration's Policies Catalyzed Global Energy Scarcity and Compounded Inflation*

Committee on Oversight and Accountability

Wednesday, March 29, 2023
Washington, D.C.

The Subcommittee met, pursuant to notice, at 2:48 p.m., in room 2154, Rayburn House Office Building, Hon. Pat Fallon [Chairman of the Subcommittee] presiding.

Present: Representatives Fallon, Donalds, Boebert, Edwards, Langworthy, Bush, Brown, and Stansbury.

Mr. FALLON. This hearing on the Subcommittee on Economic Growth, Energy Policy and Regulatory Affairs will come to order. I want to welcome everyone for coming.

Without objection, the Chair may declare a recess at any time. I recognize myself for the purpose of making an opening statement.

In the 118th Congress, the Subcommittee on Economic Growth, Energy Policy and Regulatory Affairs has taken its mission seriously to conduct oversight over the Federal Government. This Subcommittee has already held two hearings examining the Biden Administration's misuse of government power. We have explored how this Administration continues to erode our country's energy security by depleting the Strategic Petroleum Reserve. And

* This is an edited, reformatted and augmented version of Hearing Before the Subcommittee on Economic Growth, Energy Policy, and Regulatory Affairs of the Committee on Oversight and Accountability, House of Representatives, Serial No. 118–18, dated March 29, 2023.

In: Inflation: Background, Causes and Current Policies
Editor: Julie Taylor Lowe
ISBN: 979-8-89530-696-3

we have also looked into the Administration's abuse of the administrative state, burdening the Second Amendment rights of law-abiding gun owners. Today, we are going to turn to the Biden Administration's policies on inflation and energy prices.

Every American is suffering from inflation. I think we can all agree on that, and the rising energy prices, but Americans with low and fixed incomes are being the hardest hit. This focus stands in stark contrast to the last Congress where the Democrats' work in this hearing room focused on, believe it or not, investigating flea and tick collars and an NFL football team. In fact, we had two hearings on that because somebody had a bee in their bonnet about Daniel Snyder. So, I am proud to lead the third Committee hearing and look forward to focusing more on important matters to the American people.

And, as I stated today, we are examining the inflation's effect on energy prices, and inflation—you know, the primary driver for inflation is going to be government spending. And if you inject trillions of dollars into the money supply with a finite amount of goods and services, those things are going to end up costing more. And what inflation is, at the end of the day, is an invisible, or not an invisible, very visible tax on us all, on everything that we need and everything that we buy.

Unfortunately, under the Biden Administration, the price of utilities and goods and services have jumped from month to month. You know, it is burdening household budgets and increasing economic uncertainty. The average American household's purchasing power has decreased by almost $5,000. And when President Trump left office, inflation sat at 1.4 percent, and under Joe Biden, inflation shot up to 9.1 percent last summer, which was a 40-year high. So, when inflation was at its highest levels, the Energy Index alone rose about 42 percent. So, it is no surprise that energy price volatility is directly tied to the rapid retirement of fossil fuel power plants, lags in domestic natural gas pipeline construction, and the over reliance on expensive green energy alternatives without any plan for a smooth transition from traditional energy sources.

Now, I think a lot of my Democratic colleagues are going to say the Putin price hike, it is all Vladimir Putin's fault that gas costs more. Well, let us look at some empirical data. On January 20, when Joe Biden took office, the average price of gasoline in this country was $2.39 and at its high was at $5.01. But, before Vladimir Putin got into those tanks and headed toward Kyiv, the price of gasoline was $3.61, and today it is $3.53, so it is actually ironically slightly lower after the invasion. And, cut it the way you will, it is 48 percent higher when you buy a gallon of gas today than it was when Joe Biden took office.

So, this began when President Biden did take office and he canceled the Keystone XL pipeline right away, and they are dragging their feet and they slow walked drilling permits on Federal lands and waters. So, unfortunately, at the end of the day, Americans with low and fixed incomes are, you know, most harshly are feeling the immediate impact of the skyrocketing energy prices. And as a result of higher prices, larger portions of take-home income must go to daily necessities, forcing Americans to choose between feeding their families and fueling their cars, receiving healthcare, or even heating their homes.

So, what this hearing is going to do, is we are going to examine the relationship between the Biden Administration's policies, energy production, and supply as price drivers, and, ultimately, the share of overall inflation attributable to rising energy prices. So, I want to thank all the witnesses for coming today, thank you very much for your participation, and we look forward to hearing your testimony.

And with that, I now recognize Ranking Member Bush for the purpose of making her opening statement.

Ms. BUSH. Thank you, Chairman Fallon. St. Louis and I are here today to highlight the urgent need for new investments in renewable, reliable energy. Instead, Republicans are wasting our time on the preposterous and offensive oil industry wish list that House Republicans are bringing to the Floor for a vote this week as the Polluters Over People Act.

At our last energy hearing, we considered the global nature of inflation and the price hike caused by the pandemic, Russia's violent invasion of Ukraine, and supply chains shortages. We also discussed how the United States has been harmed by a precarious reliance on unsafe and unstable energy sources such as coal, oil and gas. For me, and many of my colleagues, it is clearer than ever that our best path to energy security is to rapidly diminish our reliance on fossil fuels. Until we do, Black, Brown, and indigenous communities will continue to bear the heaviest burden of this energy crisis and our reliance on fossil fuels.

At the same time, to achieve energy security and independence, we need far more public investments in energy efficiency and renewable energy. Energy security means regular, everyday people can keep their lights on at night, and kids, especially Black and Brown kids, can play outside without getting asthma. It does not mean securing the profit margins of coal barons. In the Polluters Over People Act, House Republicans have put forward an alarmingly harmful energy policy that will serve as a giveaway to oil tycoons and eviscerate the voices of affected communities like mine. This bill is so extremist and unscientific that it could only have been written by the industry that will profit the most, Big Oil.

The bill will repeal some of the most effective provisions of President Biden's Inflation Reduction Act, including provisions to eliminate fees on methane emissions, and zero out programs to reduce home utility bills. The bill will make oil and gas leasing unbelievably cheap and allow companies to trample over communities in the blind pursuit of profit. Imagine throwing money at companies whose actions are driving the climate crisis, and then asking them to monitor themselves and calling it policy. The inhumanity is heartbreaking.

Almost as alarming as the provisions of this bill and the false premise of this hearing, many of the bill's provisions are the same as they were six years ago. Industry couldn't think of anything more favorable, and Republicans have made few updates to their energy policy in six years. I suppose if their work builds off of industry marketing documents, we would be better off if they weren't doing anything at all. But still, I would love the opportunity to work with my Republican colleagues to invest in energy security and lower prices for families. Sadly, they are more interested in economic security for corporations that security for people. congressional Democrats have a different idea. We intend to do what the government was set up to do: spend public dollars supporting people and not corporations. We will invest in community-based organizations and green jobs. We will build renewable energy infrastructure to scale. We will fight and we will win a green new deal for everyone. Thank you, and I yield back.

Mr. FALLON. Thank you. I am pleased to introduce our three witnesses today. Oliver McPherson-Smith is Director for energy, trade and environmental policy at the American Consumer Institute for Citizen Research. His work and research focuses on energy and resource-wealthy economies. Mandy, and Mandy help me with your last name.

Ms. GUNASEKARA. Gunasekara.

Mr. FALLON. That is not that scary.

Ms. GUNASEKARA. It isn't.

Mr. FALLON. All right. Could you say it one more time?

Ms. GUNASEKARA. Gunasekara.

Mr. FALLON. Gunasekara.

Ms. GUNASEKARA. Yes, or just Mandy. Mandy is easy.

Mr. FALLON. Awesome. That is a cool last name. Mandy Gunasekara, my good friend, serves as the Director of Center for Energy and Conservation of the Independent Women's Forum. Ms. Gunasekara—Ms. G. previously served as the Chief of Staff of the United States Environmental Protection Agency and the Principal Deputy Assistant Administrator for the EPA's Office of Air and Radiation.

And we have Mark Paul, who is an assistant professor of economics at the Edward J. Bloustein School of Planning and Public Policy at Rutgers University and a member of Rutgers Climate Institute. And I believe you used to teach at UMass, is that correct, or were you——

Mr. PAUL. I received my Ph.D. from UMass.

Mr. FALLON. UMass. OK. Excellent. Well, I attended the University of Massachusetts Amherst for one year and then transferred to Notre Dame, but I still love my Minutemen and our Lacrosse program. I look forward to hearing from each of you on this important topic.

Pursuant to Committee Rule 9(g), the witnesses will please stand and raise their right hands.

Do you solemnly swear or affirm that the testimony that you are about to give is the truth, the whole truth and nothing but the truth, so help you God?

[A chorus of ayes.]

Mr. FALLON. Thank you. Please take your seats. Let the record show that the witnesses all answered in the affirmative, and we appreciate all of you being here today and look forward to your testimony. Again, I want to thank you.

Let me remind the witnesses that we have read your written statements, and they will appear in full in the hearing record. Please limit your oral statements to five minutes. As a reminder, please press the button on your microphone in front of you when you speak so the Members can hear you. And when you begin speaking, there is a light in front of you that will turn green. After four minutes it will turn yellow, and then when the red light comes on, that means wrap it up.

I recognize Dr. McPherson-Smith to please begin his opening statement.

Statement of Oliver McPherson-Smith, Director for Energy, Trade, and Environmental Policy, American Consumer Institute for Citizen Research

Mr. MCPHERSON-SMITH. Thank you, Chairman Fallon, Ranking Member Bush, and other Members of the Subcommittee for inviting me here today.

The Nation's continued economic recovery from the coronavirus pandemic has provided a welcome return to family and commercial life for millions of Americans. However, this recovery has neither been seamless nor balanced. The crude oil market provides an indicative case study. U.S. crude oil production peaked shortly before the pandemic in November 2019, at a monthly average of around 13 million barrels per day. Now, while production has gradually recovered from its pandemic low of around 9.7 million barrels per day in May 2020, it nonetheless has remained below the pre-pandemic peak. However, the Nation's lagging oil production only tells half the story.

Consumers and businesses typically purchase refined petroleum products, not crude oil. America's capacity to refine its own petroleum products has undergone an even starker decline. This lower supply of crude oil and diminished capacity to refine it unfortunately coincided with an increase in demand attributable to the repeal of pandemic restrictions and the resumption of commercial, leisure, and industrial transportation. This mismatch between supply and demand is evident in the persistently higher gasoline prices of the past two years.

Oil production is determined by a variety of technical, economic, and political factors at the local, national, and international levels. Nonetheless, Federal policy has a tangible effect on shaping production. Since January 2021, the Federal executive branch of government has sought to inhibit and disincentivize the domestic production and refining of fossil fuels. These efforts include and are not limited to the cancellation of the Keystone XL pipeline, an ultimately unsuccessful moratorium on oil and gas leases on public land; the outlawing of oil and gas development within 2.8 million acres of the National Petroleum Reserve in Alaska; and the continued absence of an offshore oil and gas leasing schedule following the expiry of the 2017 to 2022 schedule.

Additionally, a range of proposed or impending policies at the Federal level serve to disincentivize investment in future productive capacity within much of the American energy industry. From the Securities and Exchange Commission's proposed environmental, social, and governance, or ESG, disclosure, to the Inflation Reduction Act's impending methane tax on oil and gas producers, these policies reduce investment in the short term and risk raising consumer prices in the long term.

Had the Biden Administration simply mirrored the Trump Administration's oil production growth rate, daily oil production would have reached almost 15 million barrels by December 2022. This represents a hypothetical shortfall of almost 3 million barrels each day by December 2022, a significantly larger amount than the average OPEC members' production of 2.23 million barrels per day in that same month.

In aggregate, this hypothetical scenario would have facilitated the additional production of more than 850 million barrels of oil since January 2021. This sits in stark contrast to the Biden Administration's recent sale of 180 million barrels from the SPR. The absence of this oil left the American economy and American families vulnerable to international oil market fluctuations, such as that associated with Russia's renewed and unjustified invasion of Ukraine.

The academic literature on the pass-through of energy prices into overall inflation is varied and vast. Energy is used by virtually every business in the United States. Consequently, elevated energy costs appear not only as individual components within the measurements of inflation but also within consumer prices of goods and services via higher business costs of lighting, heating, and transportation.

Finally, I would like to draw your attention to a potential remedy to the enduring consumer challenge of energy inflation, which is a Federal all-of-the-above energy policy. Facilitating greater energy production from all sources, whether they be fossil fuel, renewable, nuclear, or otherwise, enables consumer and community choice competition among companies, competition among technologies, innovation, and lower prices. I thank you again for the opportunity to testify today and look forward to your questions.

Mr. FALLON. Thank you. Ms. Gunasekara, you are recognized for your statement.

Statement of Mandy Gunasekara, Director of Center for Energy and Conservation, Independent Women's Forum

Ms. GUNASEKARA. Thank you. Chairman Fallon, Ranking Member Bush, Members of the Subcommittee, thank you for the opportunity to participate in today's hearing.

Rising energy costs and inflation have created immense financial burdens on the American people. One in six Americans is behind on their electricity bills. The cost for an average household has gone up by around $10,000 over the past two years. Everyday goods, like groceries and gas, are exorbitantly expensive. Beyond high costs, Americans have had to endure supply chain disruptions, creating shortages on baby formula, over-the-counter cold medicine for children, women's hygiene products, and many more. This constant drip of daily hardship is suppressing opportunity, and the reality is weighing heavily on the American psyche.

A poll came out yesterday revealing that 78 percent of parents fear their children will be worse off than them. Now, these outcomes are not the result of some uncontrollable forces outside the reach of our national leaders. It is actually the result of bad policies being implemented and pushed by the Biden Administration, and among the worst is the ongoing war against American energy. Our lives and our economy run on energy. Eighty percent of this energy that we use comes from coal, oil, and natural gas.

Since January 2021, President Biden and Democrats in Congress have taken over 125 actions aimed at shutting out the use and development of the very energy resources we need more of, not less. Suppressing domestic supply and setting America on a path toward energy scarcity has exacerbated inflation and made costs skyrocket. These cost increases are extremely pervasive and impact Americans in very different ways. I would like to highlight a few.

Low-income Americans are the hardest hit by high energy prices. They are being forced to choose between heating their homes or putting food on the table. One recent survey found that in the face of high energy costs, 36 percent of low-income households will go without food for a day, 41 will go without medical care or dental care, 31 percent will not fill a prescription or take less to try and stretch the supply. These short-term consequences are unacceptable and truly heartbreaking, and in the long run, it can lead to more poverty and longer-term generational dependence.

For small businesses on Main Street, it is getting harder to keep afloat. They struggled through COVID only to be met with increased overhead in the form of higher electricity bills. Power disruptions caused by an increasingly unreliable grid brings productivity to an absolute halt in some instances. They have also been met with higher taxes, and they have had to deal with the woke investment trend of ESG, which inhibits access to credit or investors if they don't check the right boxes.

Also, middle-class moms, or as I like to call them, the CEOs of kitchen table economics, are forced to make tough decisions. Typically, they are not forced to choose between essentials like heating and eating, but they are forced to make tough decisions that impact the quality of life of which they have worked so hard to achieve. Moms are nervous about filling up their gas tanks and thinking about what they can cut from their planned dinner. Moms are worried that if their son or daughter makes the team that they have been working so hard to actually make, are they going to be able to afford the equipment or the uniform? They are foregoing trips to see family members, especially during holidays, where it has become so expensive, and they have canceled summer vacations. It is a sinking feeling for so many parents that have worked hard to live in a good, safe community, but have to cut back on how their children get to actively engage and enjoy that community because it is too great a financial burden to bear.

This is so frustrating because none of this is necessary. It is not required to improve the environment, it is not required to lower emissions, and it is not required to ensure we create a planet future generations can continue to enjoy. We know how to expand our energy productivity while protecting the environment. Just a few years ago, we were top energy exporters, and we continue to cut air pollution, cleanup water quality, and we lead the world in cutting greenhouse gas emissions. Best of all, our economy was experiencing massive growth.

There are numerous policy options available to fix the current situation. We need to be building a future of energy abundance. Congress can help by prioritizing solutions that strengthen our energy system with proven reliable technologies while encouraging continued innovation. We do not need to ban certain technologies or cancel U.S. coal, oil, or natural gas. With the right policies in place and a pragmatic mindset from our leaders, we can build strong energy systems that reliably deliver low-cost energy whenever it is needed.

Again, thank you for your time. It is an honor to be here, and I look forward to your questions.

Mr. FALLON. Thank you very much. The Chair recognizes Dr. Paul for his statement.

Statement of Mark Paul, Assistant Professor of Economics, Edward J. Bloustein School of Planning and Public Policy, Rutgers University

Mr. PAUL. Chairman Fallon, Ranking Member Bush, and Members of the Subcommittee, thank you for inviting me to testify today. My research agenda concerns the economic and policy pathways to achieve decarbonization in the United States. My testimony today is based on my scholarship, and the views I present with you are my own.

Climate change is the greatest crisis humanity has faced. It poses an existential threat to the well-being of the American people and to the strength and stability of the American economy. If we continue with business as usual, the planet will be on track to warm by three degrees Celsius above pre-industrial levels by the end of the century. The effects of this level of warming would be catastrophic, causing severe damage to the physical and economic security of the Nation.

At the same time, recent price spikes in energy, fueled by Russia's invasion of Ukraine, geopolitical instability, and corporate price gouging have indeed highlighted the need to transition to a clean energy economy to protect consumers and achieve our shared goals of economic prosperity and energy independence.

My testimony will focus on three points. First, the economic costs of inaction are substantially larger than the cost of rapidly and equitably decarbonizing the economy. Second, the evidence is clear that an investment-led decarbonization effort, as is being undertaken following the passage of the Inflation Reduction Act, will create millions of good jobs, strengthen the economy, and lower energy costs for American families. And third, decarbonizing the economy will bolster domestic energy security and reduce inflationary pressures associated with historically volatile fossil fuel prices, thus promoting economic and national security goals. Indeed, high energy prices are not the result of the energy transition, but are fueled by a combination of international conflict, corporate profiteering, and supply chain disruptions.

I begin with the costs of business as usual. Climate change already presents a clear and present danger to American lives and livelihoods. In 2017, for example, extreme weather events linked to climate change were responsible for over $300 billion in damages, wiping out more than half of the Nation's economic growth that year. In a world that warms to 3C or more, recent studies estimate that that could reduce GDP by 10 percent permanently. To avoid these effects, peer-reviewed research finds that limiting warming necessary to such levels would require no new fossil fuel extraction and a managed wind down of existing extraction.

Turning to my second point, decarbonization should be understood as an economic opportunity for the United States. Empirical studies find that just in GDP terms, decarbonization would bring trillions in benefits, including creating upwards of 25 million new American jobs in the next 15 years. What is more, this transition would help the average American family save between $1,000 and $2,500 a year on energy bills. Decarbonizing the economy is also crucial to bolster domestic energy security and help insulate the United States from international conflicts that have repeatedly led to energy instability. Putting the Nation on a path toward decarbonization must be understood as a path that prioritizes both national security and economic prosperity.

While the United States has long sought energy independence, increasing extraction of fossil fuels has not achieved these goals and simply cannot due to the international nature of fossil fuel commodity markets. The clean energy transition, on the other hand, will delink the U.S. economy from hostile authoritarian regimes and position the U.S. to support other nations in doing the same.

Finally, I would like to talk briefly about inflation. Energy played a key role in recent inflationary events. Most of the price increase in energy markets were first experienced across nations and, thus, not a unique phenomenon to the United States, and second, were largely attributable to the illegal Russian invasion in Ukraine.

Complementary research finds that a substantial portion of energy price increases faced by American consumers can be attributable to corporate profiteering, a key component of inflation today. Big Oil took advantage of the crisis to rake in record profits. These price increases disproportionately benefit low-income communities and communities of color, further adding to inflation, inequality, and macroeconomic instability. There is strong evidence that Biden's use of the SPR along with the passage of the Inflation Reduction Act has put downward pressure on energy prices, thus reducing inflationary pressures in the economy. The Treasury Department estimates that the SPR reduced the price of gas by $0.20 to $0.40 per gallon.

Thank you for the opportunity to speak with you today, and I look forward to your questions.

Mr. FALLON. I want to thank all the witnesses again for your testimony, and I think that we are all aware that inflation remains three times higher, you know, than the target rates here. So, I have a question for Dr.—and I apologize if I called you "mister" before—but Dr. McPherson-Smith. Has the United States reduced our carbon emissions or increased our carbon emissions over the last roughly 20 years?

Mr. MCPHERSON-SMITH. Consistently decreased.

Mr. FALLON. Is it in line with your research that it is about a 20 percent decrease over the last 20 years?

Mr. MCPHERSON-SMITH. Ballpark, yes.

Mr. FALLON. OK. And has China increased or decreased their carbon emissions over the last same period of time, 20 years or so?

Mr. MCPHERSON-SMITH. In an unparalleled fashion, increased.

Mr. FALLON. Increased. Over 100 percent, 200 percent maybe even.

Mr. MCPHERSON-SMITH. It is going up. I mean, it depends how far you want to go back, but year-on-year, we are looking ballpark figure, 10 percent.

Mr. FALLON. Why do you think our friends on the other side of the aisle don't ever talk about China's emissions or India's emissions and it is always the United States' emissions, even though we produce energy in the cleanest fashion in the world?

Mr. MCPHERSON-SMITH. Because virtue signaling doesn't win elections.

Mr. FALLON. And you know, we are all on the same planet. The United States isn't, you know, its own planet. We are just one of the countries. So, Mr. McPherson, Dr. McPherson-Smith, please explain how high energy prices lead to higher overall inflation.

Mr. MCPHERSON-SMITH. So, consumers use energy. They use it to gas up their car or they use it to power up their Tesla, but we also have to remember that businesses themselves use energy. So, unless you are living on a subsistence farm, for example, you are probably going to shop in a physical shop, or maybe you use Amazon, whatever. These companies transport their goods and services. They have to keep the lights on themselves, and so these costs flow through. It is known as flow-through within inflation.

Mr. FALLON. So, energy just touches everything, right? I mean, the cars, the fuel, the trucks, the stores, that people are driving to and from work. How did the impact of energy prices on inflation change from the Trump Administration to the Biden Administration?

Mr. MCPHERSON-SMITH. So we have seen inflation, energy inflation itself, up about 40 percent under the current Administration. That is from taking office in January 2021 up until about January of this year. That is down from the 60 percent we saw last summer.

Mr. FALLON. You think this—the difference was a result of deliberate policy choices?

Mr. MCPHERSON-SMITH. If it were an accident, it would be spectacular in size and scale.

Mr. FALLON. Ms. Gunasekara, what energy policies did the Biden Administration implement that catalyzed energy price inflation?

Ms. GUNASEKARA. Well, there is certainly a number. I think what really set the table was the canceling of the Keystone XL pipeline, but I think most offensively, it was shifting the role of the Federal agencies. Instead of looking at environmental problems, in particular, and fixing them by making them more efficient, using the might of the Federal Government, through its regulatory role, to squeeze certain industries out of existence or to squeeze their operations in a sense to where they become so expensive that it becomes difficult to extract and utilize the very resources that we need more of.

Mr. FALLON. And who is impacted by high energy prices and inflation the most?

Ms. GUNASEKARA. Well, certainly those that are the most vulnerable when it comes to economic standing in this country. The low- and fixed-income individuals are the ones that are impacted the worst. As I expressed, it truly forces them in a situation where they have to choose between heating their homes in the dead of winter or putting food on the table. And there are all sorts of other damaging decisions that they will ultimately make because of the impact of high energy prices.

Mr. FALLON. Yes, I mean, $5,000 is nothing to sneeze at as far as the purchasing power that is lost in real dollars. The Biden Administration has championed, I think it is clear, a radical climate change agenda at the expense of economic prosperity for all Americans and falsely advertised their efforts as a necessity for economic mobility. Do you believe that forcing low-income Americans to choose between gas in their tanks to get to work or putting food on the table for their families sounds like environmental justice to you?

Ms. GUNASEKARA. No. I think that it is distracting the actual impact, which is an economic injustice. And I have got a board member that works under the Center, who has looked extensively into this, and what she often says is that high energy prices impede upward mobility, especially for low- and fixed-income households. So, to suggest that some version of climate justice is to make lives more expensive while ignoring the real economic impact that that has on the most vulnerable members of our society, again, I think that is a distraction, and it is not indicative of thoughtful policy we should be focused on if we truly want to help people live better lives.

Mr. FALLON. Thank you very much, and you did that exactly on the five-minute time. I appreciate that. I now recognize Ranking Member Bush for five minutes of questions.

Ms. BUSH. Thank you, and thank you to our witnesses for being here. Despite House Republicans' claims to the contrary, we understand that the United States is currently the world's largest oil and natural gas producer. The U.S. is also an enormous consumer. These embarrassing facts drive energy insecurity in this country, and it is important to understand how dangerous our reliance on fossil fuels—how that affects regular people.

In St. Louis, in my community, we experience energy insecurity in a myriad of ways. For me, when I was a young single mom of two, I became aware of the vast disparity in energy security. My electricity and heating bills were at times $1,800 a month for just one of them, which was double my rent. These high bills made my family struggle. When we want to talk about understanding economic justice or environmental justice, let us talk to people who actually experience it and have which some of those folks are sitting up here.

A high utility bill meant I had to choose between paying off my electric bill or buying food for my babies. One winter, while my kids were still babies, when the utility bill was so high, the company shut off our heat and wouldn't make a payment plan, and we went the entire winter without heat, and because I connected my home to heaters, we almost burned the house down. I will never forget that cold, I will never forget that energy insecurity, but thank goodness my kids will never remember.

Last year, St. Louis experienced two 1-in-1,000-year flooding events within three days. Our community was devastated, and we are still rebuilding homes and infrastructure. The event was made far more likely and severe by the burning of fossil fuels that is driving this climate crisis. In St. Louis, we know a lot about energy insecurity. We have seen power outages and electric wires underwater, as we have seen in other places. We have gotten asthma from dirty energy, which I have. We have become unhoused due to high energy bills, which I have.

So, Dr. Paul, which is more affordable, let me ask you, solar energy, oil, or gas?

Mr. PAUL. According to recent data, renewables are substantially cheaper than new fossil fuels. So, to give you some numbers here, utility-scale solar is one-third cheaper than new natural gas here in the United States, and offshore wind is roughly 40 percent cheaper. To boot, solar, on average, utility-scale solar goes only one percent over budget. On average, wind goes four percent over budget. Fossil fuel projects, on the other hand, go on average 33 percent or more over budget. So, renewables are substantially cheaper.

Ms. BUSH. Thank you. So, what is more likely, Dr. Paul, to give my children asthma, a gas facility or a wind turbine?

Mr. PAUL. Unfortunately, there is strong evidence to suggest that fossil fuels are directly linked to asthma in the United States. Households, for instance, with gas stoves in their houses experience far higher rates of asthma for their children, double-digits higher. Wind turbines, on the other hand, are not associated with asthma or other public health concerns.

Ms. BUSH. Thank you. Dr. Paul, which is more likely to fluctuate, solar energy in a country where the sun rises every day or limited fossil fuel resources that are subject to global spikes from wars and pandemics?

Mr. PAUL. There is strong evidence to suggest that prices driven by a clean and renewable grid will be substantially more stable and will help delink the United States' economy from international conflicts, those that drive repeated price spikes for fossil fuels. So, both this most recent event with Russia, as well as the 1978–1979 crisis, which that inflationary crisis was also driven by political instability this time in the Middle East.

Ms. BUSH. Thank you. Finally, I want to talk about the scale of our need. To achieve energy security, we know we not only must never develop new fossil fuel infrastructure again, but we also must invest in public renewable energy. So, lastly, Dr. Paul, what scale of further public investments are needed to deliver energy security and stem the climate crisis?

Mr. PAUL. If we actually want to decarbonize the country as we have promised to do, by rejoining the Paris Climate Agreement, then we need to invest substantially more in deep decarbonization efforts. The Inflation Reduction Act is a key downpayment, but is just that, a downpayment. We need hundreds of billions of dollars more in public investments to direct the economy toward decarbonization and improve the health and affordability of our national economy.

Ms. BUSH. Thank you, and I yield back.

Mr. FALLON. Thank you. The Chair recognizes Congresswoman Boebert for her questions.

Mrs. BOEBERT. Thank you, Mr. Chairman. Today, we are here to conduct some oversight on the Biden Administration's policies that are regulating our communities into poverty. The Biden Administration's all-out war on domestic American energy has resulted in record high inflation, a crisis that has shifted the cost of Joe Biden's multitrillion dollar spending spree to the American taxpayers. While my colleagues on the other side of the aisle want to play the blame game, they seem to be pointing the finger at everyone but themselves.

It is really unfortunate to hear energy crisis stories, energy poverty stories where a mother has to choose between feeding her family or paying the electric bill. But, that is where more than 20 million Americans are right now because of Joe Biden's energy policies that he enforced on Americans, January 20, 2021, where we were energy secure, and he completely surrendered that energy security. This week, House Republicans are pushing back against the left's anti-American, anti-energy policies to pass H.R. 1 to put us back on track toward energy independence and, in turn, reduce inflationary pressures and lower costs for families.

Dr. Paul, in your recently released paper, 'An Economist's Case for Restrictive Supply Side Policies', you advocate for nationalizing the United States' oil and gas industry. Do you still agree with that statement?

Mr. PAUL. Yes. In that research paper, we highlight 10 policies that would facilitate and manage decarbonization.

Mrs. BOEBERT. So, let me get this straight, Dr. Paul. So, you support a communist-style takeover of our oil and gas industry because that is exactly what this is, nationalizing our oil and gas industry.

Mr. PAUL. The majority of countries around the globe that have substantial fossil fuel reserves have public ownership of those reserves so that they can manage it——

Mrs. BOEBERT. This is a communist-style takeover, and we have even heard from my colleagues on the other side of the aisle that they never want to invest in fossil fuels and the infrastructure of it here in America again, which is quite alarming.

Dr. McPherson, prices for heating American homes rose by more than 27 percent in the past year. And in my home state of Colorado, we had a very cold winter, which means these increased costs hit even harder for the people that live in my district, in Colorado's 3d District. Do you think that the Biden Administration's proposal to place a ban on gas stoves nationwide will reduce energy prices for people in my district?

Mr. MCPHERSON-SMITH. No, it is going to force them to, unfortunately, have to purchase a new stove if that were to come to pass. Mrs. BOEBERT. Yes, and we have seen this Administration make other extreme proposals for families concerned about energy costs, including Mayor Pete, who had the nerve to say that families concerned about high gas prices should just shell out $55,000 for an electric vehicle. So, we have some politician saying, you know, just go buy brand new electric appliances, others saying completely ditch your car and get an electric vehicle. Now, Dr. McPherson, do you think that simply buying new electric vehicles, as Mayor Pete recommended, is a realistic energy solution for American families

living month-to-month and already struggling to pay their bills?

Mr. MCPHERSON-SMITH. There are hidden inflationary effects within electric vehicles, which in the right place, in the right context, for the right people, are excellent. But we have to remember, to fill up an electric vehicle, at the moment, it takes about 30 minutes or so to fill up a tank, so to speak. You can get about 170 miles out of that. But if you have got kids, for example, you got a family, you have got somewhere to be, you have got to be at work, that half an hour is going to add up.

Now, if you are trying to transport freight, for example, across the United States, half an hour every time to fill up is going to add up. Now, that is either going to be reflected in workers' wages because they are going to demand more because that time and their time should be compensated, so that will be inflation, or workers won't be compensated for all that time that adds up. There are hidden inflationary effects that we need to think seriously about.

Mrs. BOEBERT. Thank you, Dr. McPherson. And we have seen states like California say that we want to ban electric vehicles by 2035, and then the next week saying, hey, please don't charge your electric vehicles because our grid cannot handle this. You know, with this, there is a lot of talk of decarbonization going on. I am pro-forest management, which would certainly help with reduce of carbon emissions that are emitted with the catastrophic wildfires. And I would encourage the witnesses to also just consider the fact that these solar panels require mining to be done in China-owned mines in the Congo for that cobalt where that child and slave labor is being used. Thank you, Mr. Chairman, I yield.

Mr. FALLON. The Chair recognizes Congresswoman Brown for five minutes.

Ms. BROWN. Thank you, Mr. Chairman. Now, I have to admit, I am a little confused as to why we are having the same hearing again. We held an almost identical hearing just three weeks ago. And at that hearing, we considered factors driving inflation and gas prices, among them a once-in-a-century pandemic and Russia's assault on Ukraine. Then, like now, we discussed the Biden's Administration's exceptional action to counter these twin crisis and bring solutions to the American people. At the hearing three weeks ago, we sadly heard the same misinformation about the Strategic Petroleum Reserve and the status of American energy independence from my friends on the other side. Now, I am happy to set the record straight once again.

The Biden Administration took bold and necessary action to secure America's energy needs in a time of international disruption. We had no rolling blackouts, our gas prices came down, and inflation is receding. This should be credited to the Administration, though my colleagues hold regular hearings to grasp at straws and make it appear otherwise. Not only did the Biden Administration and congressional Democrats mitigate impacts in the short term, but we set the country on a brighter path. Due to the Inflation Reduction Act, 99.6 percent of businesses in Ohio will be eligible for tax credit on solar power installation. That means money into pockets, all while addressing the climate emergency. The Inflation Reduction Act will also provide grants that allow the average new homeowner in Ohio to save 12 percent on their utility bills.

So, Dr. Paul, how have we addressed American energy needs and the climate crisis in recent legislation, like the American Rescue Plan and the Inflation Reduction Act?

Mr. PAUL. Thank you for those questions. I believe there are two things that the Biden Administration has done that have helped promote energy security and stability for households. One is helping put money in needy American households' pockets. By pursuing a economic agenda that prioritizes low-income workers across this Nation, we are helping lift wages so that the Biden Administration can ensure that people can afford their bills. Second, by pursuing a clean and renewable domestic energy sector, they are trying to make energy both more affordable and more reliable and actually reduce energy poverty.

The main challenge right now that we see associated between inflation and energy is the fact that fossil fuel firms are still profiting in record ways.

Ms. BROWN. Thank you for that. Now, Dr. Paul, how would Republican energy proposals, like expanding fossil fuel production, gutting environmental review regulations, and eliminating the Greenhouse Gas Reduction Fund, exacerbate the climate change in the near future?

Mr. PAUL. Unfortunately, Republican plans are intended to increase the extraction of fossil fuels. The IEA cites that if we are to meet our goals of limiting warming to 1.5 degrees Celsius, no new extraction can occur. Further, research published in the Journal of Science notes that if we are to meet our warming goals, we actually need to develop a plan for a managed wind down of already-existing extraction. So, there is simply no way we can meet our global warming goals and increase the extraction of fossil fuels. Further, since renewables are cheaper, we will be locking in expensive, dirty, polluting energy for current and future generations that will harm both the health and economic stability of the Nation.

Ms. BROWN. Thank you, again. So, I will close with this. Congressional Democrats and the Biden Administration continue to work tirelessly to address the energy needs of the American people, while responsibly addressing the climate emergency. It is my sincere hope that we can move toward bipartisan solutions better for the environment and our constituents. And with that, Mr. Chairman, I yield back the balance of my time.

Mr. FALLON. Thank you. The Chair recognizes Congressman Edwards for his five minutes.

Mr. EDWARDS. Thank you, Mr. Chair. Dr. McPherson, you referenced ESG scores in your opening comments. How could ESG metrics be making energy more expensive?

Mr. MCPHERSON-SMITH. Sure. So, now, there are a variety of different metrics out there, so we need to be somewhat specific. But, generally speaking, the SEC, by its own admission, is for the proposed disclosure, will have billions upon billions of dollars in compliance costs, first and foremost. So, there are additional costs to businesses across the board, which will trickle down to consumers. In addition to that, though, depending on how the ESG measure is structured, it would be very easy to rank lower companies that do produce greenhouse gas emissions. That would stymie investment, make it more expensive for them to borrow. Those higher borrowing costs for CapEx, or whatnot, would once again be passed through to consumers.

Mr. EDWARDS. And can you tell us how the Inflation Reduction Act provides billions to fund green energy initiatives, and are those initiatives currently bringing down the price of energy?

Mr. MCPHERSON-SMITH. So, the price of energy still remains far above what it was when President Biden took office by about 40 percent or so. If one were to argue that the IRA is reducing costs, we are yet to see it in a substantial way vis-a-vis when President Biden took office.

Mr. EDWARDS. And are there any hurdles that you see to sourcing the raw materials needed to implement the renewable energy initiatives outlined in the Inflation Reduction Act?

Mr. MCPHERSON-SMITH. The United States has a wealth of natural resources, and, in theory, we could mine these resources here at home.

However, due to onerous restrictions, the NEPA process, capricious removals of land from leasing, all things we have seen under the Biden Administration, unfortunately it just takes far too long. So, on average, it is believed that it can take between five and seven years to permit a mine here in the United States. In Canada and Australia, they can do it in three to five years.

We do not need to repeal all of our environmental regulations. We need to protect the environment, but we also need to learn from comparable countries like Canada, like Australia, who can do it just so much quicker and in a responsible way.

Mr. EDWARDS. And Dr. McPherson, President Biden has just proposed a $6.8 trillion budget. If fully implemented, how would that budget effect inflation?

Mr. MCPHERSON-SMITH. It is a simple question of supply and demand when it comes to energy. We know over the past few years, the past two years, to be specific, about 25 percent of the inflation that we have seen is either related to direct energy costs or that pass-through that affects businesses that then affects consumers. Now, if the Biden Administration were to implement that budget, but maintain its current energy policies, that will increase demand for energy across the board, wherever it is from, but stymie supply. That is going to push prices higher.

Mr. EDWARDS. Not good news for folks back in my district. Last question, Dr. McPherson, President Biden said in 2021 that inflation was just temporary. Did that end up being true?

Mr. MCPHERSON-SMITH. I mean, maybe it is a question of semantics because it is still here.

Mr. EDWARDS. All right. Thank you, Mr. Chair. I yield.

Mr. FALLON. The Chair recognizes the gentlelady from New Mexico, Ms. Stansbury.

Ms. STANSBURY. Thank you, Mr. Chairman, and I want to greet everyone who is here with us today, and thank you, our witnesses, for coming to testify today.

I want to just take a few moments to really talk about what drives global oil and gas prices and how that impacts domestic production. So, Dr. McPherson-Smith, I really appreciate you being here and sharing your thoughts on the macro situation with respect to oil and gas, but let me just ask you very briefly, are you familiar with the Permian Basin?

Mr. MCPHERSON-SMITH. Yes.

Ms. STANSBURY. Yes. So, the Permian Basin is the largest unconventional oil and gas basin in the United States, which is actually in New Mexico, which is my home state as well as Texas. And have you ever been there?

Mr. MCPHERSON-SMITH. I have not.

Ms. STANSBURY. And are you aware of the astronomical growth in drilling that has happened in the Permian Basin over the last decade-and-a-half?

Mr. MCPHERSON-SMITH. Yes.

Ms. STANSBURY. You are. So, are you aware of how many wells were actually in operation in the basin in 2010 when this huge increase in production began. Take a stab.

Mr. MCPHERSON-SMITH. I will trust you to inform me of that.

Ms. STANSBURY. No idea, right? So, 350 wells were in production in 2010. How many wells do you think are in production as of last year?

Mr. MCPHERSON-SMITH. Again, I trust you to inform us.

Ms. STANSBURY. Well, I appreciate that. I know you are here to be an expert witness for us. As of 2021, there were 4,524 wells in the Permian Basin. That is a 1,292-percent increase in the number of wells in the Permian Basin. And Dr. McPherson, do you know why there was such an astronomical increase in production in the Permian Basin?

Mr. MCPHERSON-SMITH. It sounds like a lot of jobs were created, and there was a high demand for work, a high demand for oil.

Ms. STANSBURY. So, you don't know. So, the reason why there was such an astronomical increase in production is because of development of technologies that allowed for horizontal drilling and for increased production in formations like the Permian, which is why domestic energy production during that decade went through the roof and why the United States became one of the largest oil and gas producers in the world. Now, I would expect our expert witnesses who are here to testify on oil and gas markets to understand what is actually driving global markets and production. Dr. McPherson-Smith, do you know how many million barrels a day are being produced by the Permian right now?

Mr. MCPHERSON-SMITH. Again, I trust you to inform us because there are 12 million barrels being produced nationally.

Ms. STANSBURY. Right. 5.6 million of them are coming out of the Permian itself. It is one of the largest-producing basins. That is an all-time high in production in the United States and it was hit in the end of last year, and, in fact, it is going to hit an all-time high again this year. In fact, in the 4th quarter of this year, it is anticipated that the Permian is going to be producing over 6 million barrels of oil a day. This will be the largest increase in domestic oil production in the history of the United States.

OK. So, let us talk about facts and what is actually happening with domestic production. Now, there was a little bit of a dip in that decade-and-a-half of increased production, and that happened in the spring of 2020. And Dr. Paul, can you tell us what happened in the spring of 2020?

Mr. PAUL. There was a global pandemic and an unprecedented recession.

Ms. STANSBURY. Exactly. There was a global pandemic. There were lockdowns. People were in their houses. They weren't driving their cars. And so, as a response to the market, our oil and gas companies reduced their production because oil prices dropped so low that spring that it was no longer profitable for them to be operating their drill rigs, OK? And they had over-capitalized in places like the Permian where they had literally sunk billions of dollars into individual wells because these are massive operations. These are global multinational companies, right? A single well could have $2 billion in capital actually in the ground due to the horizontal drilling infrastructure. But it wasn't profitable at the time for them to have increased production because of that over-capitalization and the price of oil.

Now, the price of oil, of course, did recover, as we know, and, in fact, it not only recovered, but it spiked last year, and it spiked last year because of another global incident. Dr. Paul, can you tell us why did it spike last spring?

Mr. PAUL. Largely due to the Ukraine war led by Russia.

Ms. STANSBURY. Right. So, we had another global shortage. One of our major international oil producers, which is Russia, invaded Ukraine. There was another shortage. They worked with OPEC+, and then they collaborated to constrain global oil production, and so we ended up in a situation with sky-high prices and domestic companies that were not producing at their capacity. Now, what they have begun to do is they have begun to produce again, and we expect to see huge production in the next year as we are tackling the climate crisis. Thank you, Mr. Chairman. I yield back.

Mr. FALLON. Thank you. The Chair recognizes the gentleman from New York, Mr. Langworthy.

Mr. LANGWORTHY. Thank you so much, Mr. Chairman, and thank you very much for the witnesses for joining us here today. In my home state of New York, our former Governor, Andrew Cuomo, our current Governor, Kathy Hochul, their administrations have halted our ability to safely extract natural gas. And, as you may or may not know, my district, New York's 23d District with New York's Southern Tier along the Pennsylvania line, has the

Marcellus Shale in it, you know, arguably the Saudi Arabia of natural gas that straddles the New York and Pennsylvania line. And while New York state policy has crushed my district's ability to create jobs and opportunity and lower natural gas costs, the Pennsylvanian economy has been transformed in some formerly depressed areas of that state. Meanwhile, we suffer, and I want to take some time to look at the Biden Administration.

Ms. Gunasekara, we have heard talk of the Biden Administration looking toward mass electrification of the energy grid. Now, just last December, Western New York was hit with some of the worst blizzards the U.S. has ever seen, the deadliest storm I have ever lived through, and I am from Buffalo. The storm left thousands without power and nearly 50 dead. In your opinion, does mass electrification of the energy grid pose any risk to the American people?

Ms. GUNASEKARA. Yes, absolutely. I think putting too many eggs in any one energy basket is a irresponsible approach to the importance of energy policy.

Mr. LANGWORTHY. Yes, as I have warned our Governor that her mass electrification plans, you know, could have very easily added one, if not two, zeros to our death toll in that horrible storm. You know, we need to take moments like that to reevaluate this path that we are on. Dr. McPherson Smith, would greater domestic production of natural gas reduce the price of energy across the Nation?

Mr. MCPHERSON-SMITH. Absolutely.

Mr. LANGWORTHY. Now, would the jobs created by domestic production of oil and natural gas benefit Americans and the economy as a whole?

Mr. MCPHERSON-SMITH. I believe so.

Mr. LANGWORTHY. And last, the Inflation Reduction Act, it provides billions to fund green energy initiatives, but are those initiatives actually bringing down the price of energy in your opinion?

Mr. MCPHERSON-SMITH. I mean, again, I believe it is perhaps too early to say. Again, inflation and energy inflation remains above what we encountered when President Biden first took office.

Mr. LANGWORTHY. I mean, my constituents, you know, have seen drastic increases in the cost of propane and home fuel oil, as well as, you know, their electric bills this year. It has been a very difficult winter for, you know, many, especially the lower-income or fixed-income seniors that live in my district. I am a supporter of an all-of-the-above energy approach. However, right now, I don't think that we are in the position to shut off, you know, fossil fuel exploration. You know, at this point, Dr. McPherson, you know, there have been a lot of things posed to you. If you would like to take any time to kind of elaborate on other points, I mean, I would welcome you to do so.

Mr. MCPHERSON-SMITH. Thank you. To pick up on the point you made about the importance of an all-of-the-above energy policy, it would be imprudent for us to rush too quickly into any solution. We know that energy policy needs to be nuanced. Energy policy cannot follow a one-size-fits-all approach for the diversity that we see across our country. I challenge anyone to point to a similarly developed and industrialized country that has such diversity climatically. If you think of, between Alaska and Hawaii, for example, they have different energy needs, and we need to tailor energy policy and support energy development to meet those individual needs.

Mr. LANGWORTHY. I think it is a sad moment in our country when our American President goes on bended knee to the Saudis and OPEC nations to beg for more oil when we have the opportunity to explore more energy right here at home, and H.R. 1 will get us on the right direction to do this. I mean, Americans don't want handouts from the government. They just want a fair shake, and they want the opportunity to make ends meet. And greater domestic production on all-of-the-above strategy, whether it is natural gas or oil or any of the other opportunities that we have to create fossil fuels here at home, will do just that. So, I thank you very much for your time and your testimony, and I yield back, Mr. Chairman.

Mr. FALLON. Thank you. I want to thank everybody again, and all the witnesses for their testimony today. In closing, I want to thank our panelists, again, you know, just very insightful.

With that and without objection, all Members will have five legislative days within which to submit materials and to submit additional written questions for the witnesses, which will be forwarded to the witnesses for their response.

Mr. FALLON. If there is no further business, without objection, the Subcommittee stands adjourned.

[Whereupon, at 3:49 p.m., the Subcommittee was adjourned.]

Index

P

R

S

T

U

V

W

Y